THE ORIGINAL HOME SCHOOLING SERIES

# School Education

# CHARLOTTE M. MASON

CHARLOTTE MASON
RESEARCH & SUPPLY

This Charlotte Mason Research & Supply edition
contains the complete text of Charlotte Mason's original work.

Originally published by Kegan Paul, Trench, Trubner
and Co. Ltd., London, England, 1925
Reprinted by J.M. Dent and Sons Ltd., London, England, 1954

Available only as part of a six-volume set from
Charlotte Mason Research & Supply
ISBN 1-889209-00-7

Introduction copyright ®1989 by Dean Andreola
Foreword copyright ®1989 by John Thorley
All rights reserved
Printed in the United States of America

SOMETIMES treasures of unique value are unearthed while rummaging in the past. Charlotte Mason was a distinguished British educator at the turn of the century, whose work had a wide and lasting influence. At that time many of the upper-class children were educated at home, and Mason's insights changed their lives. Her ideas were also brought to life in many schools (mostly private), which gave the children an unusual and rich start in their education and development.

Nearly a hundred years later, a changing society often leaves us disappointed with its tangled, worn-out, and narrow practices in education. We chart a "falling capital" in the product that matters most: the life education and character of our children. Is it not the moment to look at some of the roots? To start again?

At last, after hundreds have searched for these original texts, these seminal books are back in print. Harvard University has Charlotte Mason's books; now, at last, you can too!

These writings will give important priorities and guidelines to parents, teachers, and schools. I believe that once again we need to think of all of life, our culture and heritage, so that our children may be nurtured with the nutrients of life and not sawdust. Welcome back, my dear valued mentor, Charlotte Mason! Our children need you as never before.

**Susan Schaeffer Macaulay**
director of L'Abri Fellowship, Switzerland, and
author of *For the Children's Sake: Foundations of Education for Home and School* (Crossway Books)

THE ORIGINAL HOME SCHOOLING SERIES

# Introduction to the
## *Original Home Schooling Series*

It was amidst a maze of opinions and conflicting points of view on child education that we were introduced to the life and work of Charlotte Mason.

While working for a literature mission in England, my wife, Karen, and I were home schooling our children. Child raising and schooling at home developed into a stressful and draining process for the whole family. Even after reading much on the subject of child raising and education we still seemed to lack direction. We discussed our dilemma with a coworker. She shared a book with us by Susan Schaeffer Macaulay called *For the Children's Sake.* This book hit close to home in many areas that concerned us. It was an introduction to the works of Charlotte Mason, and this whetted our appetites to learn more about Miss Mason's teachings.

Working in publishing, we thought it would be a simple matter to track down some of these books, especially in England where they were originally published many years ago. However, it took us many months searching secondhand bookshops, libraries, and book search services to find out that her books are not available anymore. They have not been published in a complete six volume set for over eighty years. When we had given up hope of finding them, we were informed about the Charlotte Mason College at Ambleside in the Lake District near Keswick, England. Through the kindness and cooperation of the principal, Dr. John Thorley, the college's copies of these rare books were loaned to us from their archives for this special edition of Charlotte Mason's Home Schooling Series.

This series is unique among other child-raising books because of its broad subject matter and amount of detailed study. Mason's teachings stress that both home and school education should be a learning and growing process for the child, parent, and teacher alike. Reading her works, we discover a great deal about ourselves and realize that we must continue to understand and educate ourselves if we wish to have success in educating our children.

Charlotte Mason is a bright light in the art of illuminating a child's mind. Her ideas are practical; they identify problems and offer well-tested and creative solutions. She gives us sweeping visions of what education could and should be and grave warnings about the neglect and abuse of our responsibility and authority.

Although she wrote generations ago, Mason boldly challenges us today. Many parents seem lost in their own homes, and many teachers and children are floundering in our educational systems. These systems are still seeking to educate our children without any parental and biblical influence; they prepare our youth for examinations and not *life!*

Recent books and magazine articles have referred to Charlotte Mason with information obtained from secondary sources. Now, to a new generation, Charlotte Mason speaks for herself in this brilliant, original series.

May these books offer hope and life to parents, teachers, and children, as Charlotte Mason said, "For the Children's Sake!"

*Dean and Karen Andreola*

*For information on future publications, products, newsletters, and curriculum compatible with Miss Mason's principles, please visit our website at:*

*www.charlotte-mason.com*

# Foreword to the
## *Original Home Schooling Series*

Charlotte Mason founded her "House of Education" in Ambleside, in the heart of the English Lake District, in 1892. "It is far from London," she wrote at the time, "but in view of that fact there is much to be said in its favour. Students will be impressed with the great natural beauty around them, will find a country rich in flowers, mosses and ferns. They will learn to know and love the individuality of great natural features—mountain pass, valley, lake and waterfall." The "House of Education" is now the principal's house, "Springfield," and I am writing this foreword in the room that was Charlotte Mason's own living room. I look out of the window and can confirm all its attractions.

Charlotte Mason came to Ambleside when she was nearly fifty, and the college was to be the main focus of her life's work from then until her death in 1923. Hers was no simple success story. Her early childhood is obscure, and she seems never to have wished to elucidate it. She was probably brought up by her father, a Liverpool merchant who, it seems, went bankrupt and then died when Charlotte was still in her teens. Aided by friends of her family, Charlotte became a pupil teacher in Birkenhead and then attended a training college for teachers in London from 1860 to 1861. After qualifying, she taught in an infant school in Worthing, Sussex, until 1873. She then obtained a post on the staff of Bishop Otter Teacher Training College, Chichester, where she lectured in elementary school teaching method. The college was in the forefront of educational thinking in its dedication to the principle of education for all—including girls. W. E. Forster's Education Act of 1870, which provided for elementary schools to be set up across the country, was still fresh and needed trained teachers to implement the promises. The Bishop Otter College certainly influenced Charlotte Mason's thinking, but, for reasons that are difficult now to disentangle, in 1878 Charlotte felt dissatisfied with her work, left the college, and went to live with friends in Bradford in Yorkshire.

Apparently with financial help from these friends (she was certainly never rich), Charlotte began to write. In 1880 she published a series of books on the geography of England, which were well received. But it was her book *Home Education*, published in 1886, that sparked off the most interest. In it one can certainly see the influence of other educational thinkers of the nineteenth century, particularly the child-centered views of Pestalozzi and the artistic ideas of John Ruskin. What Charlotte Mason added was a practical, down-to-earth perspective that showed how one could actually set about and *do* it. Her style and her exposition were homely, both in the sense that she wrote in an easy, intelligible way, and in the sense that she stressed the influence and responsibility of the home. She also wrote from a firmly held evangelical perspective.

The book turned out to be a kind of educational "Dr. Spock" avidly bought by women anxious to ensure the best possible upbringing for their offspring. The need was real, especially among middle-class women of modest means. Education was a subject of much debate and discussion, which had led to the Education Act of 1870, though the reality of primary education all too often was but the palest reflection of Pestalozzi, Ruskin, or even W. E. Forster. Many concerned parents, perhaps more particularly concerned mothers, were looking for something better. Charlotte Mason's *Home Education* offered it. It explained how parents could—and should—provide their children with a broad, stimulating, even exciting education, far removed from the common diet of so many elementary schools of the day.

The book sold well and in influential circles. Very soon the Parents National Education Union (PNEU) was established, with the bishop of London as its first president. Miss Beale, a formidable protagonist in the fight for women's education, was an early member of the organization, as was Anne Clough, the founder of Newnham College, Cambridge. Branches were set up in many major towns and cities, and by 1890 the organization had its own monthly magazine, "The Parents Review," edited by Charlotte Mason herself. Charlotte had quickly become a leading authority on early childhood.

In 1891 Charlotte came to live in Ambleside. A friend of her student days, Selina Healey, had lived in Ambleside, and Charlotte had visited her and had gotten to know the Lake District well. She loved the area, particularly the quiet town of Ambleside. When she moved into Springfield, she was sure she had found the ideal place to train governesses for young children.

So, in January 1892, the House of Education was established. There were four students. Two years later, with thirteen students, the college moved into Scale how, a beautiful Georgian house across the main road from Springfield on a hill amid the trees with fine views of the town and of Loughrigg across the Rothay valley.

Charlotte saw children as thinking, feeling human beings, as spirits to be kindled and not as vessels to be filled. And she demonstrated how it could be done. She believed all children were entitled to a liberal education based upon good literature and the arts. These were in her own day radical thoughts and practices, certainly not just confined to Charlotte Mason, but few of her contemporaries had the sheer practicality that she displayed. The practicing school attached to the House of Education took in local children with no payment; Charlotte firmly believed that her liberal education ideas were applicable to all children regardless of class, status, or ability, and she put her ideas into practice, as she always did.

The college flourished, never larger than fifty students in Charlotte's own lifetime but with a reputation out of proportion to its size. By the 1920s the PNEU had established several schools as well as a correspondence school, run from Ambleside, which sent out lesson notes and advice on educational matters to parents and governesses.

Charlotte died on January 16, 1923; by then she was the object of deep veneration within the movement. She was buried in the churchyard at Ambleside, close to the graves of W. E. Forster and the Arnold family. Educationists flourished—and died—in Ambleside.

The college and the correspondence school continued on the same site until 1966, when the PNEU (now with the added title of "World Education Service") moved to new premises in London and absorbed the correspondence school. PNEU/WES has continued to provide full syllabuses and educational advice to PNEU affiliated schools in the UK and in many countries abroad where English-medium schools have been established. But much of its work is still with parents, mainly with those parents living abroad who need to educate their children at home. The principles established by Charlotte Mason over a hundred years ago are still the guiding principles of all the work of PNEU/WES. They have proved themselves through the many changes in syllabus content and educational demands of the twentieth century.

Meanwhile, the college has undergone its own development. Until 1960 it continued as an independent teacher training institution, but then transferred to the control of the then Westmorland Local Education Authority, and at the same time took over the Kelsick site on Stockghyll Lane, the town's former secondary school. In 1968 the college changed its validating university from Manchester to the newly founded University of Lancaster, some thirty-five miles from Ambleside. Local government reorganization in 1970 resulted in the absorption of Westmorland into the new county of Cumbria. On April 1, 1989, after fifteen years of fruitful partnership with Cumbria, the college became an independent corporation.

*John Thorley*
Principal
Charlotte Mason College

# Preface to the 'Home Education' Series

THE educational outlook is rather misty and depressing both at home and abroad. That science should be a staple of education, that the teaching of Latin, of modern languages, of mathematics, must be reformed, that nature and handicrafts should be pressed into service for the training of the eye and hand, that boys and girls must learn to write English and therefore must know something of history and literature; and, on the other hand, that education must be made more technical and utilitarian—these, and such as these, are the cries of expedience with which we take the field. But we have no unifying principle, no definite aim; in fact, no philosophy of education. As a stream can rise no higher than its source, so it is probable that no educational effort can rise above the whole scheme of thought which gives it birth; and perhaps this is the reason of all the 'fallings from us, vanishings,' failures, and disappointments which mark our educational records.

Those of us, who have spent many years in pursuing the benign and elusive vision of Education, perceive

that her approaches are regulated by a law, and that
this law has yet to be evoked. We can discern its
outlines, but no more. We know that it is pervasive ;
there is no part of a child's home-life or school-work
which the law does not penetrate. It is illuminating,
too, showing the value, or lack of value, of a thousand
systems and expedients. It is not only a light, but a
measure, providing a standard whereby all things,
small and great, belonging to educational work must
be tested. The law is liberal, taking in whatsoever
things are true, honest, and of good report, and
offering no limitation or hindrance save where excess
should injure. And the path indicated by the law is
continuous and progressive, with no transition stage
from the cradle to the grave, except that maturity takes
up the regular self-direction to which immaturity
has been trained. We shall doubtless find, when we
apprehend the law, that certain German thinkers—
Kant, Herbart, Lotze, Froebel — are justified ; that,
as they say, it is 'necessary' to believe in God; that,
therefore, the knowledge of God is the principal knowledge, and the chief end of education. By one more
character shall we be able to recognise this perfect law
of educational liberty when it shall be made evident.
It has been said that 'The best idea which we can
form of absolute truth is that it is able to meet every
condition by which it can be tested.' This we shall
expect of our law—that it shall meet every test of
experiment and every test of rational investigation.

Not having received the tables of our law, we

fall back upon Froebel or upon Herbart; or, if we belong to another School, upon Locke or Spencer; but we are not satisfied. A discontent is it a divine discontent? is upon us; and assuredly we should hail a workable, effectual philosophy of education as a deliverance from much perplexity. Before this great deliverance comes to us it is probable that many tentative efforts will be put forth, having more or less of the characters of a philosophy; notably, having a central idea, a body of thought with various members working in vital harmony.

Such a theory of education, which need not be careful to call itself a system of psychology, must be in harmony with the thought movements of the age; must regard education, not as a shut-off compartment, but as being as much a part of life as birth or growth, marriage or work; and it must leave the pupil attached to the world at many points of contact. It is true that educationalists are already eager to establish such contact in several directions, but their efforts rest upon an axiom here and an idea there, and there is no broad unifying basis of thought to support the whole.

Fools rush in where angels fear to tread; and the hope that there may be many tentative efforts towards a philosophy of education, and that all of them will bring us nearer to the *magnum opus*, encourages me to launch one such attempt. The central thought, or rather body of thought, upon which I found, is the somewhat obvious fact that the child is a *person* with all the possibilities and powers included in personality. Some of the members which develop from this nucleus have been exploited from time to time by educational thinkers, and exist vaguely in the general common sense, a notion here, another there. One thesis, which is, perhaps, new, that *Education is the Science of Relations*, appears to me to solve the question of curriculæ, as showing that the object of education is to put a child in living touch with as much as may be of the life of Nature and of thought. Add to this one or two keys to self-knowledge, and the educated youth·goes forth with some idea of self-management, with some pursuits, and many vital interests. My excuse for venturing to offer a solution, however tentative and passing, to the problem of education is twofold. For between thirty and forty years I have laboured without pause to establish a working and philosophic theory of education ; and in the next place, each article of the educational faith I offer has been arrived at by inductive processes ; and has, I think, been verified by a long and wide series of experiments. It is, however, with sincere diffidence that I venture to offer the results of this long labour ; because I know that in this field there are many labourers far more able and expert than I — the 'angels' who fear to tread, so precarious is the footing !

But, if only *pour encourager les autres*, I append a short synopsis of the educational theory advanced in the volumes of the 'Home Education Series.' The treatment is not methodic, but incidental ; here a little, there a little, as seemed to me most likely to meet the occasions of parents and teachers. I should add that in the course of a number of years the various essays have been prepared for the use of the Parents' Educational Union in the hope that that Society might witness for a more or less coherent body of educational thought.

"The consequence of truth is great ; therefore the judgment of it must not be negligent."

1. Children are born *persons*.

2. They are not born either good or bad, but with possibilities for good and evil.

3. The principles of authority on the one hand and obedience on the other, are natural, necessary and fundamental ; but—

4. These principles are limited by the respect due to the personality of children, which must not be encroached upon, whether by fear or love, suggestion or influence, or undue play upon any one natural desire.

5. Therefore we are limited to three educational instruments—the atmosphere of environment, the discipline of habit, and the presentation of living ideas.

6. By the saying, EDUCATION IS AN ATMO-SPHERE, it is not meant that a child should be isolated in what may be called a 'child environment,'

especially adapted and prepared; but that we should take into account the educational value of his natural home atmosphere, both as regards persons and things, and should let him live freely among his proper conditions. It stultifies a child to bring down his world to the 'child's' level.

7. By EDUCATION IS A DISCIPLINE, is meant the discipline of habits formed definitely and thoughtfully, whether habits of mind or body. Physiologists tell us of the adaptation of brain structure to habitual lines of thought—*i.e.*, to our habits.

8. In the saying that EDUCATION IS A LIFE, the need of intellectual and moral as well as of physical sustenance is implied. The mind feeds on ideas, and therefore children should have a generous curriculum.

9. But the mind is not a receptacle into which ideas must be dropped, each idea adding to an 'apperception mass' of its like, the theory upon which the Herbartian doctrine of interest rests.

10. On the contrary, a child's mind is no mere *sac* to hold ideas; but is rather, if the figure may be allowed, a spiritual *organism*, with an appetite for all knowledge. This is its proper diet, with which it is prepared to deal, and which it can digest and assimilate as the body does foodstuffs.

11. This difference is not a verbal quibble. The Herbartian doctrine lays the stress of education— the preparation of knowledge in enticing morsels, presented in due order—upon the teacher. Children

taught upon this principle are in danger of receiving much teaching with little knowledge; and the teacher's axiom is, 'What a child learns matters less than how he learns it.'

12. But, believing that the normal child has powers of mind that fit him to deal with all knowledge proper to him, we must give him a full and generous curriculum; taking care, only, that the knowledge offered to him is vital — that is, that facts are not presented without their informing ideas. Out of this conception comes the principle that,—

13. EDUCATION IS THE SCIENCE OF RELATIONS; that is, that a child has natural relations with a vast number of things and thoughts: so we must train him upon physical exercises, nature, handicrafts, science and art, and upon *many living* books; for we know that our business is, not to teach him all about anything, but to help him to make valid as many as may be of—

'Those first-born affinities
That fit our new existence to existing things.'

14. There are also two secrets of moral and intellectual self-management which should be offered to children; these we may call the Way of the Will and the Way of the Reason.

15. *The Way of the Will.*—Children should be taught—

(*a*) To distinguish between 'I want and 'I will.'

(*b*) That the way to will effectively is to turn our

thoughts from that which we desire but do not will.

(c) That the best way to turn our thoughts is to think of or do some quite different thing, entertaining or interesting.

(d) That, after a little rest in this way, the will returns to its work with new vigour.

(This adjunct of the will is familiar to us as *diversion*, whose office it is to ease us for a time from will effort, that we may 'will' again with added power. The use of suggestion—even self-suggestion—as an aid to the will, is to be deprecated, as tending to stultify and stereotype character. It would seem that spontaneity is a condition of development, and that human nature needs the discipline of failure as well as of success.)

16. *The Way of the Reason.* — We should teach children, too, not to 'lean' (too confidently) 'unto their own understanding,' because the function of reason is, to give logical demonstration (a) of mathematical truth; and (b) of an initial idea, accepted by the will. In the former case reason is, perhaps, an infallible guide, but in the second it is not always a safe one; for whether that initial idea be right or wrong, reason will confirm it by irrefragable proofs.

17. Therefore children should be taught, as they become mature enough to understand such teaching, that the chief responsibility which rests on them as persons is the acceptance or rejection of initial ideas.

To help them in this choice we should give them principles of conduct and a wide range of the knowledge fitted for them.

These three principles (15, 16 and 17) should save children from some of the loose thinking and heedless action which cause most of us to live at a lower level than we need.

18. We should allow no separation to grow up between the intellectual and 'spiritual' life of children; but should teach them that the divine Spirit has constant access to their spirits, and is their continual helper in all the interests, duties and joys of life.

———————

*The 'Home Education' Series is so called from the title of the first volume, and not as dealing, wholly or principally, with 'Home' as opposed to 'School' education.*

# Preface

THE intention of the following volume is to offer some suggestions towards a curriculum for boys and girls under twelve. A curriculum, however, is not an independent product, but is linked to much else by chains of cause and consequence; and the manner of curriculum I am anxious to indicate is the outcome of a scheme of educational thought, the adoption of which might, I believe, place educational work generally upon a sounder footing.

The fundamental principles of docility and authority have been considered in the first place because they *are* fundamental; but, for that very reason, they should be present but not in evidence : we do not expose the foundations of our house. Not only so, but these principles must be conditioned by respect for the personality of children; and, in order to give the children room for free development on the lines proper to them, it is well that parents and teachers should adopt an attitude of 'masterly inactivity.'

Having considered the relations of teachers and taught, I have touched upon those between education and current thought. Education should be in the flow, as it were, and not shut up in a water-tight compartment. Perhaps, reverence for personality as such, a sense of the solidarity of the race, and a profound consciousness of evolutionary progress, are among the elements of current thought which should help us towards an educational ideal.

In considering the training of children under the convenient divisions of physical, mental, moral, and religious, I have not thought it necessary to enlarge upon matters of common knowledge and general acceptance, but have dwelt upon aspects of training under each heading which are likely to be over-looked. Under the phrase, 'Education is a life,' I have tried to show how necessary it is to sustain the intellectual life upon ideas, and, as a corollary, that a school-book should be a medium for ideas, and not merely a receptacle for facts. That normal children have a natural desire for, and a right of admission to, all fitting knowledge, appears to me to be suggested by the phrase, 'Education is the science of relations.'

These considerations clear the ground towards that of a curriculum.

The sort of curriculum I have in view should educate children upon *Things* and *Books*. Current thought upon the subject of education by *Things* is so sound and practical, and so thoroughly carried into effect, that I have not thought it necessary to dwell much here upon this part of education. Our great

failure seems to me to be caused by the fact that
we do not form the *habit of reading books that are
worth while* in children while they are at school and
are under twelve years of age. The free use of
books implies correct spelling and easy and vigorous
composition without direct teaching of these subjects.

The Appendices show, I think, that such use of
books in education works out well in practice, and
is a great saving of time and labour to both teacher
and pupils, especially relieving both of the deadly
dull labour wasted on '*corrections*.'

The much-diluted, or over-condensed, teaching of
the oral lesson, or the lecture, gives place to the
well thought out, consecutive treatment of the right
book, a *living* book in which facts are presented as the
outcome of ideas.

Children taught in this way are remarkable for
their keenness after knowledge, and do well afterwards
in any examination for which they may have to
prepare; and, what is of much more consequence, are
prepared to take their full share of all that life offers
of intellectual and practical interests.

AMBLESIDE, *November* 1904.

*Will the reader kindly substitute ' teachers ' for
' parents ' when the former title suits the case ?*

# Contents

## CHAPTER I

### DOCILITY AND AUTHORITY IN THE HOME AND SCHOOL

## CHAPTER II

### DOCILITY AND AUTHORITY IN THE HOME AND THE SCHOOL

#### *Part II.—How Authority Behaves*

## CHAPTER III

### 'MASTERLY INACTIVITY'

# CONTENTS

## CHAPTER IV

### SOME OF THE RIGHTS OF CHILDREN AS PERSONS

## CHAPTER V

### PSYCHOLOGY IN RELATION TO CURRENT THOUGHT

## CHAPTER VI

### SOME EDUCATIONAL THEORIES EXAMINED

# CONTENTS

## CHAPTER VII

### AN ADEQUATE THEORY OF EDUCATION

## CHAPTER VIII

### CERTAIN RELATIONS PROPER TO A CHILD

## CHAPTER IX

### A GREAT EDUCATIONALIST

#### *A Review*

# CONTENTS

## CHAPTER X

### SOME UNCONSIDERED ASPECTS OF PHYSICAL TRAINING

## CHAPTER XI

### SOME UNCONSIDERED ASPECTS OF INTELLECTUAL TRAINING

## CHAPTER XII

### SOME UNCONSIDERED ASPECTS OF MORAL TRAINING

# CONTENTS

## CHAPTER XIII

### SOME UNCONSIDERED ASPECTS OF RELIGIOUS EDUCATION

## CHAPTER XIV

### A MASTER-THOUGHT

## CHAPTER XV

### SCHOOL-BOOKS AND HOW THEY MAKE FOR EDUCATION

# CONTENTS

## CHAPTER XVI

### HOW TO USE SCHOOL-BOOKS

## CHAPTER XVII

### EDUCATION THE SCIENCE OF RELATIONS: WE ARE EDUCATED BY OUR INTIMACIES: *THE PRELUDE* AND *PRÆTERITA*

## CHAPTER XVIII

### WE ARE EDUCATED BY OUR INTIMACIES

#### Part II.—Further Affinities

# CONTENTS

## CHAPTER XIX

### WE ARE EDUCATED BY OUR INTIMACIES

#### *Part III.—Vocation*

## CHAPTER XX

### SUGGESTIONS TOWARDS A CURRICULUM

#### (*For Children under Twelve*)

#### *Part I.*

## CHAPTER XXI

### SUGGESTIONS TOWARDS A CURRICULUM

#### (*For Children under Twelve*)

#### *Part II.—School-books*

# CONTENTS

## CHAPTER XXII

### SUGGESTIONS TOWARDS A CURRICULUM

#### *Part III.—The Love of Knowledge*

## APPENDICES

# School Education

---◆---

## CHAPTER I

### DOCILITY AND AUTHORITY IN THE HOME AND THE SCHOOL

**Better Relations between Children and their Elders.**—All of us who have accepted education as our *métier* are keenly alive to the signs of the times as they are to be read in the conduct and manners of children. Upon one thing, anyway, we may congratulate ourselves with unmixed satisfaction : the relations between children and parents, and indeed between children and their grown-up friends generally, are far more intimate, frank and friendly than such relations used to be. There does not seem to be any longer that great gulf fixed between child thought and grown-up thought, which the older among us once tried to cross with frantic but vain efforts. The heads of the house, when we were little, were autocratic as the Czars of all the Russias. We received everything at their hands, from bread and milk to mother's love, with more or less gratitude, but with invariable docility. If they had stubborn questionings as to whether was better for us, this or that, they kept them to themselves. For us, everything was decreed, and all decrees were final. There were rebellious children, perhaps, as one in a score, or one in a hundred, but then these were rebellious with the fine courage of Milton's Satan : they dared everything and set themselves up in bold opposition. These were the open rebels who would, sooner or later, come to a bad end ; so we were told and so we secretly believed. For the others, there was no middle course. They were brought under rule, and that rule was arbitrary and without appeal.

The Elder Generation of Parents, Autocratic. —This is how children were brought up some forty or fifty years ago, and even young parents of to-day have, in many cases, grown up under a *régime*, happy, loving and wise very likely, but, before all things, arbitrary. There were what the Scotch would call 'ill-guided' homes, where the children did what was right in their own eyes. These will always exist so long as there are weak and indolent parents, unconcerned about their responsibilities. But the exceptions went to prove the rule ; and the rule and tradition, in most middle-class homes, was that of well-ordered and governed childhood. Every biography, that issues from the press, of the men and women who made their mark during the first half of the century, is a case in point. John Stuart Mill, Ruskin, the Lawrences, Tennyson, almost everyone who has made for himself a distinguished name, grew up under a martinet rule. Only the other day we heard of an instance, the recollection of which had survived for seventy years. A boy of twelve or thirteen had been out shooting rabbits. He came home in the early darkness of a bitterly cold winter evening. His father

asked him by which gate he had entered the park.
'By (such a) gate.' 'Did you shut it?' 'I don't
recollect.' 'Go and see'; and the boy went, though
he was already tired out, and the gate in question
was more than a mile from the house. Such an
incident would scarcely happen to-day; the boy
would protest, plead his own benumbed fatigue, and
suggest that a man should be sent to shut the gate, if,
as did not appear from the story, it was important
that it should be shut at all. Yet this was a kind
father, whom his children both loved and honoured;
but arbitrary rule and unquestioning obedience were
the habits of the household. Nor is this notion of
domestic government quite obsolete yet. I heard
the other day of a Scotch father who confined his
daughter of eighteen to her room for a week on
account of some, by no means serious, breach of
discipline. The difference is, that where you find an
arbitrary parent now, he is a little out of touch with
the thought and culture of the day; while, a few
decades ago, parents were arbitrary of set principle
and in proportion as they were cultivated and
intelligent.

Arbitrary Rule not always a Failure.—It cannot
be said that this arbitrary rule was entirely a failure.
It turned out steadfast, capable, able, self-governed,
gentle-mannered men and women. In our less hope-
ful moments, we wonder as we watch the children of
our day whether they will prove as good stuff as their
grandfathers and their fathers. But we need not fear.
The evolution of educational thought is like the
incoming of the tide. The wave comes and the wave
goes and you hardly know whether you are watching
ebb or flow; but let an hour elapse and then judge.

**But truer Educational Thought results in Worthier Character.**—After all allowances for ebb and flow, for failure here and mistake there, truer educational thought must of necessity result in an output of more worthy character. For one thing, this very arbitrariness arose from limitations. Parents knew that they must govern. Righteous Abraham, who ruled his house, was their ensample; and it is far easier to govern from a height, as it were, than from the intimacy of close personal contact. But you cannot be quite frank and easy with beings who are obviously of a higher and of another order than yourself; at least, you cannot when you are a little boy. And here we have one cause of the inscrutable reticence of children. At the best of times they carry on the busy traffic of their own thoughts all to themselves. We can all recollect the pathetic misgivings of our childish days which a word would have removed, but which yet formed the secret history of years of our lives. Mrs Charles, in her autobiography, tells us how her childhood was haunted by a distressing dream. She dreamed that she had lost her mother and hunted for her in vain for hours in the rooms and endless corridors of a building unknown to her. Her distress was put down to fear of 'the dark,' and she never told her tender mother of this trouble of the night. Probably no degree of loving intimacy will throw the closed doors of the child's nature permanently ajar, because, we may believe, the burden of the mystery of all this unintelligible world falls early upon the conscious soul, and each of us must beat out his conception of life for himself. But it is much to a child to know that he may question, may talk of the thing that perplexes him, and that there is comprehension for his perplexities. Effusive sympathy is a mistake, and bores a child when it does not make him silly. But just to know that you can ask and tell is a great outlet, and means, to the parent, the power of direction, and to the child, free and natural development.

Doctrine of the Infallible Reason.—With the advance of one line of educational insight, we have, alas, to note the receding of another and a most important principle. Early in the century, authority was everything in the government of the home, and the docility of the children went without saying, that is, always excepting the few rebellious spirits. However little we may be aware of the fact, the direction of philosophic thought in England has had a great deal to do with the relations of parents and children in every home. Two centuries ago Locke promulgated the doctrine of the infallible reason. That doctrine accepted, individual reason becomes the ultimate authority, and every man is free to do that which is right in his own eyes. Provided, Locke would have added, that the reason be fully trained, and the mind instructed as to the merits of the particular case; but such proviso was readily lost sight of, and the broad principle remained. The old Puritanic faith and the elder traditions for the bringing up of children, as well as Locke's own religious feelings and dutiful instincts, were too strong for the new philosophy in England; but in France there was a soil prepared for the seed. Locke was eagerly read because his opinions jumped with the thought of the hour. His principles were put into practice, his conclusions worked out to the bitter end, and thoughtful writers consider that this religious and cultivated English gentleman cannot be exonerated from a share of the guilt of the atrocities of the French Revolution.

**Leads to the Dethronement of Authority.**— We in the twentieth century have lost some of the safeguards that held good in the seventeenth, and we have our own, perhaps greater, philosopher, who carries the teaching of Locke to the inevitable conclusions which the earlier thinker shirked. Mr Herbert Spencer proclaims, as they did in France, the apotheosis of Reason. He sees, as they saw in France, that the principle of the infallible reason is directly antagonistic to the idea of authority. He traces this last idea to its final source and justification. So long as men acknowledge a God, they of necessity acknowledge authority, supreme and deputed. But, says Mr Spencer, in effect, every man finds his own final authority in his own reason. This philosopher has the courage of his convictions; he perceives, as they did in France, that the enthronement of the human reason is the dethronement of Almighty God. He teaches, by processes of exhaustive reasoning, that—

> "We sit unowned upon our burial sod,
>   And know not whence we come nor whose we be."

From the dethronement of the divine, follows the dethronement of all human authority, whether it be of kings and their deputies over nations, or of parents over families. Every act of authority is, we are taught, an infringement of the rights of man or of child. Children are to be brought up from the first self-directed, doing that which is right in their own eyes, governed by the reason which is to be trained, by experience of right and wrong, in the choosing of the right course. Life has its penalties for those who transgress the laws of reason, and the child should be permitted to learn these laws through the intervention of these penalties. But 'thou shalt' and 'thou shalt not' are to be eliminated from the vocabulary of parents. So complete and detailed is Mr Spencer's scheme for the emancipation of children from rule, that he objects to the study of languages on the ground that the rules of grammar are a transgression of the principle of liberty.

Authority not Inherent, but Deputed.—Mr Spencer's work on education is so valuable a contribution to educational thought that many parents read it and embrace it, as a whole, without perceiving that it is a part, and a carefully worked out part, of a scheme of philosophy with which perhaps they are little in sympathy. They accept the philosopher's teaching when he bids them bring up children without authority in order to give them free room for self-development ; without perceiving, or perhaps knowing, that it is the labour of the author's life to eliminate the idea of authority from the universe, that he repudiates the authority of parents because it is a link in the chain which binds the universe to God. For it is indeed true that none of us has a right to exercise authority, in things great or small, except as we are, and acknowledge ourselves to be, deputed by the one supreme and ultimate Authority. When we take up this volume on education, small as it is, easy reading as it is, we must bear in mind that we have put ourselves under the lead of a philosopher who overlooks nothing, who regards the least important

things from the standpoint of their final issue, and
who would not have the little child do as he is bid
lest he should learn, as a man, to obey that authority,
other than himself, which we believe to be Divine.

'Quick as Thought.'—The influence of his
rationalistic philosophy is by no means confined to
those who read this author's great works, or even to
those who read his manual on education. 'Quick as
thought' is a common phrase, but it would be interesting to know how quick thought is, to have any
measure for the intensity, vitality, and velocity of an
idea, for the rate of its progress in the world. One
would like to know how soon an idea, conceived in
the study, becomes the common property of the man
in the street, who regards it as his own possession,
and knows nothing of its source. We have no such
measures; but there is hardly a home, of even the
lowest stage of culture, where this theory of education
has not been either consciously adopted or rejected,
though the particular parents in question may never
have heard of the philosopher. An idea, once
launched, is 'in the air,' so we say. As is said of the
Holy Spirit, we know not whence it comes, nor whither
it goes.

The Notion of the Finality of Human Reason
Intolerable.—But, because philosophic thought is so
subtle and permeating an influence, it is our part to
scrutinise every principle that presents itself. Once
we are able to safeguard ourselves in this way, we
are able to profit by the wisdom of works which yet
rest upon what we regard as radical errors. It seems
not improbable that the early years of this very century may thus see the advent of England's truly great
philosopher, who shall not be confined by the limita-

tions of rationalistic or of materialistic thought. Men have become weary of themselves. The notion of the finality of human reason has grown an intolerable limitation. Nothing less than the Infinite will satisfy the spirit of a man. We again recognise that we are made for God, and have no rest until we find Him ; and philosophic thought, at home and abroad, has, to some degree, left these channels high and dry, and is running in other courses, towards the Infinite and the Divine.

Authority and Docility, Fundamental Principles.—One of the first efforts of this reconstructive thought, which is building us once more a temple for our spirits, a house not made with hands, is to restore Authority to its ancient place as an ultimate fact, no more to be accounted for than is the principle of gravitation, and as binding and universal in the moral world as is that other principle in the natural. Fitting in to that of authority, as the ball fits the socket to make a working joint, is the other universal and elemental principle of Docility, and upon these two hang all possibilities of law and order, government and progress, among men. Mr Benjamin Kidd, in his *Social Evolution*, has done much for the recognition of these two fundamental principles. Why a football team should obey its captain, an army its commanding officer ; why a street crowd should stand in awe of two or three policemen ; why property should be respected, when it is the many who want and the few who have ; why, in a word, there should be rule and not anarchy in the world—these are the sorts of questions Mr Kidd sets himself to answer. He turns to Reason for her reply, and she has none to give. Her favourite argument is that the appeal to

self-interest is final; that we do, individually and
collectively, whatever is shown to be for our advantage. But when that company went down in the
'Royal George,' standing at 'Attention!' because that
was the word of command; when the Six Hundred
rode 'into the valley of death' because—

> " Theirs not to make reply,
> Theirs not to reason why,
> Theirs but to do and die,"

—the subtlest reasoning can find no other motive
than the single and simple one of authority acting
upon docility. These men had been told to do these
things, and, therefore, they did them. That is all.
And that they did well, we know ; our own heart is the
witness. We speak of such deeds as acts of heroism,
but it is well to notice that these splendid displays of
human nature at its best resolve themselves for the
most part into acts of obedience to the word of
authority. The abuse of authority gives us the slave
and the despot, but slavery and despotism could not
exist except that they are founded upon elemental
principles in human nature. We all have it in us to
serve or to rule as occasion demands. To dream of
liberty, in the sense of every man his own sole
governor, is as futile as to dream of a world in which
apples do not necessarily drop from the tree, but
may fly off at a tangent in any direction.

Work of Rationalistic Philosophers, Inevitable.—What is Authority? The question shows us
how inevitable in the evolution of thought has
been the work of the rationalistic philosophers.
It is to them we owe our deliverance from the
autocrat, whether on the throne or in the family.

Their work has been to assert and prove that every human soul is born free, that liberty is his inalienable right, and that an offence against the liberty of a human being is a capital offence. This also is true. Parents and teachers, because their subjects are so docile and so feeble, are tempted more than others to the arbitrary temper, to say— Do thus and thus because I bid you. Therefore they, more than others, owe a debt of gratitude to the rationalistic school for holding, as they do, a brief for human freedom, including the freedom of children in a family. It would seem to be thus that God educates the world. It is not only one good custom, but one infallible principle, which may 'corrupt a world.' Some such principle stands out luminous in the vision of a philosopher; he sees it is truth; it takes possession of him and he believes it to be the whole truth, and urges it to the point of *reductio ad absurdum*. Then the principle at the opposite pole of thought is similarly illuminated and glorified by a succeeding school of thought; and, later, it is discerned that it is not by either principle, but by both, that men live.

**Authority, vested in the Office.**—It is by these countercurrents, so to speak, of mind forces that we have been taught to rectify our notion of authority. Easily within living memory we were upon dangerous ground. We believed that authority was vested in persons, that arbitrary action became such persons, that slavish obedience was good for the others. This theory of government we derived from our religion; we believed in the 'divine right' of kings and of parents because we believed that the very will of God was an arbitrary will. But we have been taught

better; we know now that authority is vested in
the office and not in the person; that the moment it
is treated as a personal attribute it is forfeited. We
know that a person in authority is a person authorised ;
and that he who is authorised is *under* authority.
The person under authority holds and fulfils a trust ;
in so far as he asserts himself, governs upon the
impulse of his own will, he ceases to be authoritative
and authorised, and becomes arbitrary and autocratic.
It is autocracy and arbitrary rule which must be
enforced, at all points, by a penal code ; hence the
confusion of thought which exists as to the connection
between authority and punishment. The despot
rules by terror ; he punishes right and left to uphold
his unauthorised sway. The person who is vested
with authority, on the contrary, requires no rigours of
the law to bolster him up, because authority is behind
him ; and, before him, the corresponding principle of
docility.

# CHAPTER II

## DOCILITY AND AUTHORITY IN THE HOME AND THE SCHOOL

### PART II.—*HOW AUTHORITY BEHAVES*

**Mistakes made on Principle.**—Mr Augustus
Hare has, apparently, what somebody calls a *bad*
memory, *i.e.* one which keeps a faithful record of
every slight and offence that had been done to him
since the day he was born! For this reason *The
Story of My Life*[1] is not quite pleasant reading,
though it is full of interesting details. But all is fish
that comes to our net. We have seldom had a more
instructive record of childhood, even if we must
allow that the instruction comes to us on the lines
of what not to do. The fine character and beautiful
nature of Mrs Augustus Hare have been known to
the world since the *Memorials of a Quiet Life* were
published by this very son; and when we find how
this lady misinterpreted the part of mother to her
adopted and dearly beloved son, we know that we
are not reading of the mistakes of an unworthy or
even of a commonplace woman. Mrs Hare always
acted upon principle, and when she erred, the
principle was in fault. She confounded the two

---

[1] *The Story of My Life*, by Augustus Hare (George Allen).

principles of authority and autocracy. She believed
that there was some occult virtue in arbitrary action
on the part of a parent, and that a child must be the
better in proportion as he does as he is bidden—the
more outrageous the bidding the better the training.
Here is an example of what a loving mother may
force herself to do :—" Hitherto, I had never been
allowed anything but roast mutton and rice pudding
for dinner. Now all was changed. The most
delicious puddings were talked of—*dilated* on—until
I became, not greedy, but exceedingly curious about
them. At length *le grand moment* arrived. They
were put on the table just before me, and then, just
as I was going to eat some of them, they were
snatched away, and I was told to get up and carry
them off to some poor person in the village. I
remember that, though I did not really in the least
care about the dainties, I cared excessively about
Lea's wrath at the fate of her nice puddings, of which,
after all, I was most innocent." Here is another
arbitrary ruling :—" Even the pleasures of this home-
Sunday, however, were marred in the summer, when
my mother gave in to a suggestion of Aunt Esther
that I should be locked in the vestry of the church
between the services. Miserable, indeed, were the
three hours which—provided with a sandwich for
dinner—I had weekly to spend there ; and, though
I did not expect to see ghosts, the utter isolation of
Hurstmonceaux church, far away from all haunts of
men, gave my imprisonment an unusual eeriness.
Sometimes I used to clamber over the tomb of the
Lords Dacre, which rises like a screen against one
side of the vestry, and be sticken with vague terrors
by the two grim white figures lying upon it in the

silent desolation, in which the scamper of a rat across
the floor seemed to make a noise like a whirlwind.
. . . It was a sort of comfort to me, in the real
church-time, to repeat vigorously all the worst curses
in the Psalms, those in which David showed his most
appalling degree of malice, and apply them to Aunt
Esther & Co.   As all the Psalms were extolled as
beatific, and the Church of England used them
constantly for edification, their sentiments were all
right, I supposed."

And yet how wise this good mother is when she
trusts to her own instinct and insight rather than to
a fallacious principle:—"I find in giving any order
to a child, it is always better not to *look* to see if he
obeys, but to take it for granted that it will be done.
If one appears to doubt the obedience, there is
occasion given for the child to hesitate, 'Shall I do
it or no?'   If you seem not to question the possibility
of non-compliance, he feels a trust committed to him to
keep and fulfils it.   It is best never to repeat a command, never to answer the oft-asked question 'Why?'"

Authority distinguished from Autocracy.—
Mrs Hare, like many another ruler, would appear
to have erred, not from indolence, and certainly not
from harshness, but because she failed to define to
herself the nature of the authority she was bound to
exercise.   Autocracy is defined as independent or
self-derived power.   Authority, on the other hand,
we may qualify as not being self-derived and not
independent.   The centurion in the Gospels says:
"I also am a man set under authority, having under
me soldiers, and I say unto one, 'Go,' and he goeth;
to another, 'Come,' and he cometh; and to my
servant, 'Do this,' and he doeth it."

Here we have the powers and the limitations of authority. The centurion is set under authority, or, as we say, authorised, and, for that reason, he is able to say to one, 'go,' to another, 'come,' and to a third, 'do this,' in the calm certainty that all will be done as he says, because he holds his position for this very purpose—to secure that such and such things shall be accomplished. He himself is a servant with definite tasks, though they, are the tasks of authority. This, too, is the position that our Lord assumes; He says: "I came not to do mine own will, but the will of Him that sent me." That is His commission and the standing order of His life, and for this reason He spake as one having authority, knowing Himself to be commissioned and supported.

**Behaviour of Autocracy.**—Authority is not uneasy; captious, harsh and indulgent by turns. This is the action of autocracy, which is self-sustained as it is self-derived, and is impatient and resentful, on the watch for transgressions, and swift to take offence. Autocracy has ever a drastic penal code, whether in the kingdom, the school, or the family. It has, too, many commandments. 'Thou shalt' and 'thou shalt not,' are *chevaux de frise* about the would-be awful majesty of the autocrat. The tendency to assume self-derived power is common to us all, even the meekest of us, and calls for special watchfulness; the more so, because it shows itself fully as often in remitting duties and in granting indulgences as in inflicting punishments. It is flattering when a child comes up in the winning, coaxing way the monkeys know how to assume, and says, '*Please* let me stay at home this morning, only this once!' The next stage is, 'I don't want to go out,' and the next, 'I won't!' and the home or school ruler, who has no principle behind his own will, soon learns that a child can be autocratic too—autocratic and belligerent to an alarming extent.

**Behaviour of Authority.**—Authority is neither harsh nor indulgent. She is gentle and easy to be entreated in all matters immaterial, just because she is immovable in matters of real importance ; for these, there is always a fixed principle. It does not, for example, rest with parents and teachers to dally with questions affecting either the health or the duty of their children. They have no authority to allow children in indulgences—in too many sweetmeats, for example—or in habits which are prejudicial to health ; nor to let them off from any plain duty of obedience, courtesy, reverence, or work. Authority is alert ; she knows all that is going on and is aware of tendencies. She fulfils the apostolic precept—" He that ruleth (let him do it), with diligence." But she is strong enough to fulfil that other precept also, " He that showeth mercy (let him do it), with cheerfulness " ; timely clemency, timely yielding, is a great secret of strong government. It sometimes happens that children, and not their parents, have right on their side : a claim may be made or an injunction resisted, and the children are in opposition to parent or teacher. It is well for the latter to get the habit of swiftly and imperceptibly reviewing the situation ; possibly, the children may be in the right, and the parent may gather up his wits in time to yield the point graciously and send the little rebels away in a glow of love and loyalty.

**Qualities proper to a Ruler.**—Nobody understood this better than Queen Elizabeth, who contrived to make a curious division of her personality and be, at the same time, a model ruler and, as a woman, full of the weaknesses of her sex. It has been well said that she knew when to yield and how to yield. Her adroitness in getting over many a dangerous crisis has been much praised by historians; but, possibly, this saving grace was not adroitness so much as the tact born of qualities proper to all who are set in authority —the meekness of one who has been given an appointed work, the readiness to take counsel with herself and with others, the perception that she herself was not the be-all and the end-all of her functions as a queen, but that she existed for her people, and the quick and tender open-minded sympathy which enabled her to see their side of every question as well as her own—indeed, in pre-ference to her own. These are the qualities proper to every ruler of a household, a school, or a kingdom. With these, parents will be able to order and control a fiery young brood full of energy and vitality, as Elizabeth was, to manage the kingdom when the minds of men were in a ferment of new thought, and life was intoxicating in the delightfulness of the possibilities it offered.

**Mechanical and Reasonable Obedience.**—It is a little difficult to draw the line between mechanical and reasonable obedience. 'I teach my children obedience by the time they are one year old,' the writer heard a very successful mother remark; and, indeed, that is the age at which to begin to give children the ease and comfort of the habit of obeying lawful authority. We know Mr Huxley's story of the retired private who was carrying home his Sunday's dinner from the bakehouse. A sergeant passed by who recognised the man's soldierly gait, and was bent on a practical joke. 'Attention!' he cried, and the man stood at attention while his mutton and potatoes rolled in the gutter. Now, this kind of obedience is a mere question of nerves and muscles, a habit of the brain tissue with which the moral consciousness has nothing to do. It is a little the fashion to undervalue any but reasonable obedience, as if we were creatures altogether of mind and spirit, or creatures whose bodies answer as readily to the ruling of the spirit as does the ship to the helm. But, alas for our weakness! this description fits us only in proportion as our bodies have been trained to the discipline of unthinking mechanical obedience. We all know the child who is fully willing to do the right thing so far as mind is concerned, but with whom bodily *vis inertiæ* is strong enough to resist a very torrent of good intentions and good resolutions; and if we wish children to be able, when they grow up, to keep under their bodies and bring them into subjection, we must do this *for* them in their earlier years.

**Response of Docility to Authority, a Natural Function.**—So far as the daily routine of small obediences goes, we help them thus to fulfil a natural function—the response of docility to authority. It may be said that a child who has acquired the habit of involuntary obedience has proportionately lost power as a free moral agent; but, as the acts of obedience in question are very commonly connected with some physical effort, as, 'Make haste back,' 'Sit straight,' 'Button your boots quickly,'—they belong to the same educational province as gymnastic exercises, the object of which is the masterly use of the body as a machine capable of many operations.

Now, to work a machine such as a typewriter or a bicycle, one must, before all things, have practice; one must have got into the way of working it involuntarily, without giving any thought to the matter: and to give a child this power over himself—first in response to the will of another, later, in response to his own, is to make a man of him.

**The Habit of Prompt Obedience.**—It is an old story that the failures in life are not the people who lack good intentions; they are those whose physical nature has not acquired the habit of prompt and involuntary obedience. The man who can make himself do what he wills has the world before him, and it rests with parents to give their children this self-compelling power as a mere matter of habit. But is it not better and higher, it may be asked, to train children to act always in response to the divine mandate as it makes itself heard through the voice of conscience? The answer is, that in doing this we must not leave the other undone. There are few earnest parents who do not bring the power of conscience to bear on their children, and there are emergencies enough in the lives of young and old when we have to make a spiritual decision upon spiritual grounds—when it rests with us to choose the good and refuse the evil, consciously and voluntarily, because it is God's will that we should.

**The Effort of Decision.**—But it has been well said by a celebrated preacher that the effort of decision is the greatest effort of life. We find it so ourselves; shall we take this line of action or the other, shall we choose this or the other quality of carpet, send our boy to this or the other school? We all know that such questions are difficult to settle, and the wear and tear of nervous tissue the decision costs is evidenced often enough by the nervous headache it leaves behind. For this reason it is, we may reverently believe, that we are so marvellously and mercifully made that most of our decisions arrive, so to speak, of themselves: that is, ninety-nine out of a hundred things we do, are done, well or ill, as mere matters of habit. With this wonderful provision in our tissues for recording repeated actions and reproducing them upon given stimuli—a means provided for easing the burden of life, and for helping us to realise the gay happiness which appears to be the divine intention for us so far as we become like little children — it is startling and shocking that there are many children of thoughtful parents whose lives are spent in day-long efforts of decision upon matters which it is their parents' business to settle for them. Maud is nervous, excitable, has an over-active brain, is too highly organised, grows pale, acquires nervous tricks. The doctor is consulted, and, not knowing much about the economy of the home, decides that it is a case of over-pressure. Maud must do no lessons for six months; change of air is advised, and milk diet. Somehow the prescription does not answer, the child's condition does not improve; but the parents are slow to perceive that it is not the soothing routine of lessons which is exhausting the little girl, but the fact that she goes through the labour of decision twenty times a day, and not only that, but the added fatigue of a contest to get her own way. Every point in the day's routine is discussed, nothing comes with the comforting ease of a matter of course; the child always prefers to do something else, and commonly does it. No wonder the poor little girl is worn out.

**Authority avoids Cause of Offence.**—On the other hand, children are before all things reasonable beings, and to some children of acute and powerful intelligence, an arbitrary and apparently unreasonable command is cruelly irritating. It is not advisable to answer children categorically when they want to know the why for every command, but wise parents steer a middle course. They are careful to form habits upon which the routine of life runs easily, and, when the exceptional event requires a new regulation, they may make casual mention of their reasons for having so and so done ; or, if this is not convenient and the case is a trying one, they give the children the reason for all obedience—"for this is right." In a word, authority avoids, so far as may be, giving cause of offence.

**Authority is Alert.**—Another hint as to the fit use of authority may be gleaned from the methods employed in a well-governed state. The importance of *prevention* is fully recognised : police, army, navy, are largely preventive forces ; and the home authority, too, does well to place its forces on the Alert Service. It is well to prepare for trying efforts : 'We shall have time to finish this chapter before the clock strikes seven'; or, 'we shall be able to get in one more round before bedtime.' Nobody knows better than the wise mother the importance of giving a child time to collect himself for a decisive moment. This time should be spent in finishing some delightful occupation ; every minute of idleness at these critical junctures goes to the setting up of the *vis inertiæ*, most difficult to overcome because the child's will power is in abeyance. A little forethought is necessary to arrange that occupations do come to an end at the right moment ; that bedtime does not arrive in the middle of a chapter, or at the most exciting moment of a game. In such an event authority, which looks before and after, *might* see its way to allow five minutes' grace, but would not feel itself empowered to allow a child to dawdle about indefinitely before saying good-night.

**Who gave thee this Authority?**—We need not add that authority is just and faithful in all matters of promise-keeping; it is also considerate, and that is why a good mother is the best home-ruler; she is in touch with the children, knows their unspoken schemes and half-formed desires, and where she cannot yield, she diverts; she does not crush with a sledge-hammer, an instrument of rule with which a child is somehow never very sympathetic.

We all know how important this, of changing children's thoughts, diverting, is in the formation of habit. Let us not despise the day of small things nor grow weary in well-doing; if we have trained our children from their earliest years to prompt mechanical obedience, well and good; we reap our reward. If we have not, we must be content to lead by slow degrees, by ever-watchful efforts, by authority never in abeyance and never aggressive, to 'the joy of self-control,' the delight of proud chivalric obedience which will hail a command as an opportunity for service. It is a happy thing that the 'difficult' children who are the readiest to resist a direct command are often the quickest to respond to the stimulus of an idea. The presentation of quickening ideas is itself a delicate art, which I have, however, considered elsewhere.

I am not proposing a one-sided arrangement, all the authority on the one part and all the docility on the other; for never was there a child who did not wield authority, if only over dolls or tin soldiers. And we of the ruling class, so far as the nursery and school-room go, are we not fatally docile in yielding obedience to anyone who will take the trouble to tell us we had better do this or that? We need not be jealous for the independence of children : that will take care of itself.

To conclude: authority is not only a gift, but a grace; and,

> "As every rainbow hue is light,
> So every grace is love."

Authority is that aspect of love which parents present to their children ; parents know it is love, because to them it means continual self-denial, self-repression, self-sacrifice : children recognise it as love, because to them it means quiet rest and gaiety of heart. Perhaps the best aid to the maintenance of authority in the home is for those in authority to ask themselves daily that question which was presumptuously put to our Lord—" Who gave Thee this authority ? "

# CHAPTER III

## 'MASTERLY INACTIVITY'

**Increased Sense of Responsibility.**—It would be an interesting task for a literary expert to trace the stages of ethical thought marked by the uses, within living memory, of the word *responsibility*. People, and even children, were highly responsible in the fifties and sixties, but then it was for their own character, conduct, and demeanour. It is not at all certain that we hold ourselves responsible in this matter to the same degree. We are inclined to accept ourselves as inevitable, to make kindly allowance for our own little ways and peccadilloes, and are, perhaps, wanting in that wholesome sense of humour, 'the giftie' which should "gie us

"To see oursels as ithers see us."

**A Sign of Moral Progress.**—If we take ourselves more easily, however, we take other people more seriously. The sense of responsibility still rests upon us with a weight 'heavy as frost'; we have only shifted it to the other shoulder. The more serious of us are quite worn with the sense of what we owe to those about us, near and far off. Men carry the weight more easily than women, because, for most of them, each day brings work that must be done, and they have less time than women to think anxiously about their relations with, and duties to, others. By the way, it is rather a note of the time that the translators of the Revised Version have given us— 'Be not *anxious* for your life,' instead of the older rendering. But, if women feel the wear of responsibility for others more constantly, let but a burning question arise—the condition of East London, Home Rule, massacres in Armenia—and men feel it more intensely and passionately. This sharpened sense is not a malady of the age, but a sign of the times.

To those of us who believe we are all at school and have our lessons set as we are fit to take them in, this general sense of responsibility for others is an encouraging sign that we are being taught from above, and are, on the whole, getting on.

Parental Responsibility.—If we all feel ourselves responsible for the distressed, the suffering, the sick, the feeble in body or mind, the deficient, the ignorant, and—would that we all felt this particular burden more—for the heathen, there is one kind of responsibility which is felt by thoughtful people with almost undue acuteness. Parental responsibility is, no doubt, the educational note of the day. People feel that they *can* bring up their children to be something more than themselves, that they *ought* to do so, and that they *must*; and it is to this keen sense of higher parental duty that the Parents' Union owes its successful activity.

Anxiety the Note of a Transition Stage.—Every new power, whether mechanical or spiritual, requires adjustment before it can be used to the full. In the scientific world there is always a long pause between the first dawn of a great discovery—as the Röntgen rays, for example—and the moment when it is applied to the affairs of everyday life with full effect and without the displacement of other powers whose functions are just as important and as necessary. We should regard with suspicion any attempt to make the Röntgen rays supply the place of stethoscope, thermometer, and all other clinical apparatus. Just so is it in the moral sphere. Our keener sense of responsibility arises from a new development of altruistic feeling—we have greater power of loving and wider scope for our love; we are more leavened by the Spirit of Christ, even when we do not recognise the source of our fuller life. But to perceive that there is much which we ought to do and not to know exactly what it is, nor how to do it, does not add to the pleasure of life or to ease in living. We become worried, restless, anxious ; and in the transition stage between the development of this new power and the adjustment which comes with time and experience, the fuller life, which is certainly ours, fails to make us either happier or more useful.

A Fussy and Restless Habit.—It is by way of an effort towards this adjustment of power that I wish to bring before parents and teachers the subject of 'masterly inactivity.' We ought to do so much for our children, and are able to do so much for them, that we begin to think everything rests with us and that we should never intermit for a moment our conscious action on the young minds and hearts about us. Our endeavours become fussy and restless. We are too much with our children, 'late and soon.' We try to dominate them too much, even when we fail to govern, and we are unable to perceive that wise and purposeful letting alone is the best part of education. But this form of error arises from a defect of our qualities. We may take heart. We *have* the qualities, and all that is wanted is adjustment; to this we must give our time and attention.

'Masterly Inactivity.'—A blessed thing in our mental constitution is, that once we receive an idea, it will work itself out, in thought and act, without much after-effort on our part; and, if we admit the idea of 'masterly inactivity' as a factor in education, we shall find ourselves framing our dealings with children from this standpoint, without much conscious effort. But we must get clearly into our heads what we mean by masterly inactivity. Carlyle's happy phrase has nothing in common with the *laisser allez* attitude that comes of thinking 'what's the good?' and still further is it removed from the sheer indolence of mind that lets things go their way rather than take the trouble to lead them to any issue. It indicates a fine healthy moral pose which it is worth while for us to analyse. Perhaps the idea is nearly that conveyed in Wordsworth's even more happy phrase, 'wise passiveness.' It indicates the power to act, the desire to act, and the insight and self-restraint which forbid action. But there is, from our point of view at any rate, a further idea conveyed in 'masterly inactivity.' The mastery is not over ourselves only; there is also a sense of authority, which our children should be as much aware of when it is inactive as when they are doing our bidding. The sense of authority is the *sine quâ non* of the parental relationship, and I am not sure that without that our activities or our inactivity will produce any great results. This element of strength is the backbone of our position. 'We could an' if we would,' and the children know it. They are free under authority, which is liberty; to be free without authority is license.

**The Element of Good Humour.**—The next element in the attitude of masterly inactivity is good humour—frank, cordial, natural, good humour. This is quite a different thing from overmuch complacency, and a general giving-in to all the children's whims. The one is the outcome of strength, the other of weakness, and children are very quick to see the difference. 'Oh, mother, may we go blackberrying this afternoon, instead of lessons?' The masterly 'yes' and the abject 'yes' are quite different notes. The first makes the holiday doubly a delight; the second produces a restless desire to gain some other easy victory.

**Self-confidence.**—The next element is confidence. Parents should trust themselves more. Everything is not done by restless endeavour. The mere blessed fact of the parental relationship and of that authority which belongs to it, by right and by nature, acts upon the children as do sunshine and shower on a seed in good soil. But the fussy parent, the anxious parent, the parent who explains overmuch, who commands overmuch, who excuses overmuch, who restrains overmuch, who interferes overmuch, even the parent who is with the children overmuch, does away with the dignity and simplicity of that relationship which, like all the best and most delicate things in life, suffer by being asserted or defended.

**The fine, easy way of Fathers.**—Fathers are, sometimes, more happy than mothers in assuming that fine easy way with their children which belongs of right to their relationship, but this is only because the father is occupied with many things, and the mother is apt to be too much engrossed with her children. It is a little humiliating to the best of us to see a careless, rather a selfish mother, whose children are her born slaves and run to do her bidding with delight. The moral is, not that all mothers should be careless and selfish, but that they should give their children the ease of a good deal of letting alone, and should not oppress the young people with their own anxious care. The small person of ten who wishes to know if her attainments are up to the average for her age, or he who discusses his bad habits with you and the best way of curing them, is displeasing, because one feels instinctively that the child is occupied with cares which belong to the parent only. The burden of their children's training must be borne by the parents alone. But let them bear it with easy grace and an erect carriage, as the Spanish peasant bears her water-jar.

Confidence in the Children.—Not only confidence in themselves, but confidence in their children, is an element of the masterly inactivity, which I venture to propose to parents as a 'blue teapot' for them 'to live up to.' Believe in the relation of parent and child, and trust the children to believe in it and fulfil it on their part. They will do so if they are not worried.

Omniscience of Parents and Teachers.—Parents and teachers must, of course, be omniscient; their children expect this of them, and a mother or father who can be hoodwinked is a person easy to reckon with in the mind of even the best child. For children are always playing a game—half of chance, half of skill; they are trying how far they can go, how much of the management of their own lives they can get for the taking, and how much they must leave in the hands of the stronger powers. Therefore the mother who is not *up to* children is at their mercy, and need expect no quarter. But she must see without watching, know without telling, be on the alert always, yet never obviously, fussily, so. This open-eyed attitude must be sphinx-like in its repose. The children must know themselves to be let alone, whether to do their own duty or to seek their own pleasure. The constraining power should be present, but passive, so that the child may not feel himself hemmed in without choice. That free-will of man, which has for ages exercised faithful souls who would prefer to be compelled into all righteousness and obedience, is after all a pattern for parents. The child who is good because he must be so, loses in power of initiative more than he gains in seemly behaviour. Every time a child feels that he chooses to obey of his own accord, his power of initiative is strengthened. The bearing-rein may not be used. When it occurs to a child to reflect on his behaviour, he should have that sense of liberty which makes his good behaviour appear to him a matter of his own preference and choice.

'Fate' and 'Free-will.'—This is the freedom which a child enjoys who has the confidence of his parents as to his comings and goings and childish doings, and who is all the time aware of their authority. He is brought up in the school proper for a being whose life is conditioned by 'fate' and 'free-will.' He has liberty, that is, with a sense of *must* behind it to relieve him of that unrest which comes with the constant effort of decision. He is free to do as he ought, but knows quite well in his secret heart that he is not free to do that which he ought not. The child who, on the contrary, grows up with no strong sense of authority behind all his actions, but who receives many exhortations to be good and obedient and what not, is aware that he may choose either good or evil, he may obey or not obey, he may tell the truth or tell a lie; and, even when he chooses aright, he does so at the cost of a great deal of nervous wear and tear. His parents have removed from him the support of their authority in the difficult choice of right-doing, and he is left alone to make that most trying of all efforts, the effort of decision. Is the distinction between being free to choose the right at one's own option, and not free to do the wrong, too subtle to be grasped, too elusive to be practical? It may be so, but it is precisely the distinction which we are aware of in our own lives so far as we keep ourselves consciously under the divine governance. We are free to go in the ways of right living, and have the happy sense of liberty of choice, but the ways of transgressors are hard. We are aware of a restraining hand in the present, and of sure and certain retribution in the future. Just this delicate poise is to be aimed at for the child. He must be treated with full confidence, and must feel that right-doing is his own free choice, which his parents trust him to make; but he must also be very well aware of the deterrent force in the background, watchful to hinder him when he would do wrong.

**The Component Parts of Masterly Inactivity.** —We have seen that authority, good humour, confidence, both self-confidence and confidence in the children, are all contained in masterly inactivity, but these are not all the parts of that whole. A sound mind in a sound body is another factor. If the sound body is unattainable, anyway, get the sound mind. Let not the nervous, anxious, worried mother think that this easy, happy relation with her children is for her. She may be the best mother in the world, but the thing that her children will get from her in these vexed moods is a touch of her nervousness—most catching of complaints. She will find them fractious, rebellious, unmanageable, and will be slow to realise that it is her fault; not the fault of her act but of her state.

**Serenity of a Madonna.**—It is not for nothing that the old painters, however diverse their ideas in other matters, all fixed upon one quality as proper to the pattern Mother. The Madonna, no matter out of whose canvas she looks at you, is always serene. This is a great truth, and we should do well to hang our walls with the Madonnas of all the early Masters if the lesson, taught through the eye, would reach with calming influence to the heart. Is this a hard saying for mothers in these anxious and troubled days? It may be hard, but it is not unsympathetic. If mothers could learn to do for themselves what they do for their children when these are overdone, we should have happier households. Let the mother go out to play! If she would only have courage to let everything go when life becomes too tense, and just take a day, or half a day, out in the fields, or with a favourite book, or in a picture gallery looking long and well at just two or three pictures, or in bed, *without the children*, life would go on far more happily for both children and parents. The mother would be able to hold herself in 'wise passiveness,' and would not fret her children by continual interference, even of hand or eye—she would let them be.

Leisure.—Another element is leisure. Sometimes events hurry us, and sometimes—is it not true?—we like the little excitement of a rush. The children like it, too, at first. Father's birthday is coming, and Nellie must recite a poem for him ; the little *fête* has only been thought of a week in advance, and Nellie is seized at all sorts of odd moments to have some lines of the recitation crammed into her. At first she is pleased and important, and goes joyously to the task ; but by-and-by it irks her; she is cross and naughty, is reproached for want of love for father, sheds tears over her verses, and, though finally the little perform- ance may be got through very well, Nellie has suffered physically and morally in doing what, if it had been thought of a month beforehand, would have been altogether wholesome and delightful. Still worse for the children is it when mother or teacher has a 'busy' day. Friends are coming, or the family wardrobe for the summer must be seen to, or drawers and cupboards must be turned out, or an examination is at hand. Anyway, it is one of those fussy, busy days which we women rather delight in. We do more than we can ourselves, our nerves are 'on end,' what with the fatigue and what with the little excitement, and everybody in the house or the school is un- comfortable. Again, the children take advantage, so we say ; the real fact being that they have caught their mother's mood and are fretful and tiresome. Nerve storms in the nursery are the probable result of the mother's little ebullition of nervous energy.

Leisure for themselves and a sense of leisure in those about them is as necessary to children's well being, as it is to the strong and benign parental attitude of which I am speaking.

Faith.—Other ingredients go to the making of the delectable compound we call 'masterly inactivity,' but space will allow me to speak of only one more. That highest form of confidence, known to us as faith, is necessary to full repose of mind and manner. When we recognise that God does not make over the bringing up of children absolutely even to their parents, but that He works Himself, in ways which it must be our care not to hinder, in the training of every child, then we shall learn passiveness, humble and wise. We shall give children space to develop on the lines of their own characters in all right ways, and shall know how to intervene effectually to prevent those errors which, also, are proper to their individual characters.

Let us next consider a few of the various phases of children's lives in which parents and teachers would do well to preserve an attitude of ' masterly inactivity.'

# CHAPTER IV

**Children should be Free in their Play.**—We have considered the wisdom and duty of 'a wise passiveness,' 'a masterly inactivity,' in the bringing up of children. It remains to glance in detail at the various points in a child's life, where this principle should govern us. And, first, as regards children's *play*. There is a little danger in these days of much educational effort that children's play should be crowded out, or, what is from our present point of view the same thing, should be prescribed for and arranged until there is no more freedom of choice about play than that about work. We do not say a word against the educational value of games. We know that many things are learned in the playing-fields; that the qualities which we associate with the name of Englishman are largely the product of the laws of the games; and there is a pretty steady effort being made to bring these same forces to bear upon girls, that they, too, may grow up with the law-abiding principle, the moral stamina, and the resourcefulness, which are more or less the outcome of the education carried on in the playing-fields.

**Organised Games are not Play.**—But organised

games are not *play* in the sense we have in view. Boys and girls must have time to invent episodes, carry on adventures, live heroic lives, lay sieges and carry forts, even if the fortress be an old armchair; and in these affairs the elders must neither meddle nor make. They must be content to know that they do not understand, and, what is more, that they carry with them a chill breath of reality which sweeps away illusions. Think what it must mean to a general in command of his forces to be told by some intruder into the play-world to tie his shoe-strings! There is an idea afloat that children require to be taught to play—to play at being little fishes and lambs and butterflies. No doubt they enjoy these games which are made for them, but there is a serious danger. In this matter the child who goes too much on crutches never learns to walk; he who is most played with by his elders has little power of inventing plays for himself; and so he misses that education which comes to him when allowed to go his own way and act,

> " As if his whole vocation
> Were endless imitation."

**Personal Initiative in Work.**—In their *work*, too, we are too apt to interfere with children. We all know the delight with which any scope for personal initiative is hailed, the pleasure children take in doing anything which they may do their own way; anything, in fact, which allows room for skill of hand, play of fancy, or development of thought. With our present theories of education it seems that we cannot give much scope for personal initiative. There is so much task-work to be done, so many things that must be, not learned, but learned *about*, that it is only now and then a child gets the chance to produce himself in his work. But let us use such opportunities as come in our way. A very interesting and instructive educational experiment on these lines has lately been tried at the School Field, Hackney, where Mr Sargent got together some eighty boys and girls under the conditions of an ordinary elementary school, except that the school was supported, not by the Education Department nor by the rates, but by the founder. The results seem to have been purely delightful; the children developed an amazing capacity for drawing, perhaps because so soon as they were familiar with the outlines of the flower and foliage of a given plant, for example, they were encouraged to form designs with these elements. The really beautiful floral designs produced by these girls and boys, after quite a short art training, would surprise parents whose children have been taught drawing for years with no evident result. These School Field children developed themselves a great deal on their school magazine also, for which they wrote tales and poems, and essays, not prescribed work, but self-chosen. The children's thought was stimulated, and they felt they had it in them to say much about a doll's ball, Peter, the school cat, or whatever other subject struck their fancy. 'They felt their feet,' as the nurses say of children when they begin to walk ; and our non-success in education is a good deal due to the fact that we carry children through their school work and do not let them feel their feet.

Children must Stand or Fall by their own Efforts.—In another way, more within our present control, we do not let children alone enough in their work. We prod them continually and do not let them stand or fall by their own efforts. One of the features, and one of the disastrous features, of modern society, is that, in our laziness, we depend upon prodders and encourage a vast system of prodding. We are prodded to our social duties, to our charitable duties, and to our religious duties. If we pay a subscription to a charity, we expect the secretary to prod us when it becomes due. If we attend a meeting, do we often do so of our own spontaneous will, or because somebody asks us to go and reminds us half a dozen times of the day and the hour? Perhaps it is a result of the hurry of the age that there is a curious division of labour, and society falls into those who prod and those who are prodded. Not that anybody prods in all directions, nor that anybody else offers himself entirely as a pincushion. It is more true, perhaps, to say that we all prod, and that we are all prodded. Now, an occasional prick is stimulating and wholesome, but the *vis inertiæ* of human nature is such that we would rather lean up against a wall of spikes than not lean at all. What we must guard against in the training of children is the danger of their getting into the habit of being prodded to every duty and every effort. Our whole system of school policy is largely a system of prods. Marks, prizes, exhibitions, are all prods; and a system of prodding is apt to obscure the meaning of *must* and *ought* for the boy or girl who gets into the habit of mental and moral lolling up against his prods.

Boys and Girls are generally Dutiful.—It would be better for boys and girls to suffer the consequences of not doing their work, now and then, than to do it because they are so urged and prodded on all hands that they have no volition in the matter. The more we are prodded the lazier we get, and the less capable of the effort of will which should carry us to, and nearly carry us through, our tasks. Boys and girls are, on the whole, good, and desirous to do their duty. If we expect the tale of bricks to be delivered at the due moment without urging or entreating, rewarding or punishing, in nine cases out of ten we shall get what we look for. Where many of us err is in leaning too much to our own understanding and our own efforts, and not trusting sufficiently to the dutiful impulse which will carry children through the work they are expected to do.

**Children should Choose their own Friends.—** With regard to the choice of friends and companions, again, we should train children so that we should be able to honour them with a generous confidence ; and if we give them such confidence we shall find that they justify it. If Fred has made a companion of Harry Jones, and Harry is not a nice boy, Fred will find the fact out as soon as his mother if he is let alone, and will probably come for advice and help as to the best way of getting out of an intimacy which does not really please him. But if Harry is boycotted by the home authorities and made the object of various prohibitions and exclusions, why Fred, if he be a generous boy, will feel in honour bound to take his comrade's part, and an intimacy which might have been easily dropped becomes cemented. Ethel will not see the reason why she, as the daughter of a professional man, may not make a friend of Maud, who sits beside her at school and is the daughter of a tradesman. But these minor matters must be left to circumstances, and the mother who brings forward questions of class, appearance, etc., as affecting her children's choice of friends, does her best to create that obtuseness as to vital points of character which is the cause of most shipwrecked lives. In this matter, as in all others, the parent's inactivity must be masterly ; that is, the young people should read approval or disapproval very easily, and should be able to trace one or the other to general principles of character and conduct, though nothing be said or done or even looked in disparagement of the ally of the hour.

**Should be free to Spend their own Pocket-Money.**—In the spending of pocket-money is another opportunity for initiative on the children's part and for self-restraint on that of the parents. No doubt the father who doles out the weekly pocket-money and has never given his children any large thoughts about money—as to how the smallest income is divisible into the share that we give, and the share that we keep, and the share that we save for some object worth possessing, to be had, perhaps, after weeks or months of saving ; as to the futility of buying that we may eat, an indulgence that we should rarely allow ourselves, and never except for the pleasure of sharing with others ; as to how it is worth while to think twice before making a purchase, with the lesson before us of *Rosamund and the Purple Jar* —such a father cannot expect his children to think of money in any light but as a means to self-indulgence. But talks like these should have no obvious and immediate bearing on the weekly pocket-money; that should be spent as the children like, they having been instructed as to how they should like to spend it. By degrees pocket-money should include the cost of gloves, handkerchiefs, etc., until, finally, the girl who is well on in her teens should be fit to be trusted with her own allowance for dress and personal expenses. The parents who do not trust their young people in this matter, after having trained them, are hardly qualifying them to take their place in a world in which the wise, just, and generous spending of money is a great test of character.

**Should form their own Opinions.**—We have only room to mention one more point in which all of us, who have the care of young people, would do well to practise a wise 'letting alone.' There are burning questions in the air, seething opinions in men's minds : as to religion, politics, science, literature, art, as regards every kind of social effort, we are all disposed to hold strenuous opinions. The person who has not kept himself in touch with the movement of the thought of the world in all these matters has little cause to pride himself. It is our duty to form opinions carefully, and to hold them tenaciously in so far as the original grounds of our conclusions remain unshaken. But what we have no right to do, is to pass these opinions on to our children. We all know that nothing is easier than to make vehement partisans of young people, in any cause heartily adopted by their elders. But a reaction comes, and the swinging of the pendulum is apt to carry them to a point of thought painfully remote from our own. The mother of the Newmans was a devoted Evangelical, and in their early years passed her opinions over to her sons, ready-made; believing, perhaps, that the line of thought they received from her was what they had come to by their own thinking. But when they are released from the domination of their mother's opinions, one seeks anchorage in the Church of Rome, and another will have no restriction as to his freedom of thought and will, and chooses to shape for himself his own creed or negation of a creed. Perhaps this pious mother would have been saved some anguish if she had given her children the living principles of the Christian faith, which are not matters of opinion, and allowed them to accept her particular practice in their youth without requiring them to take their stand on Evangelical opinions as offering practically the one way of salvation.

In politics, again, let children be fired with patriotism and instructed in the duties of citizenship, but, if they can be kept out of the party strife of an election, well for them. Children are far more likely to embrace the views of their parents, when they are ripe to form opinions, if these have not been forced upon them in early youth when their lack of knowledge and experience makes it impossible for them to form opinions at first hand. Only by ' masterly inactivity,' ' wise passiveness,' able ' letting alone,' can a child be trained—

" To reverence his conscience as his king."

Spontaneity.—We all admire spontaneity, but this grace, even in children, is not an indigenous wild-flower. In so far as it is a grace, it is the result of training, — of pleasant talks upon the general principles of conduct, and wise ' letting alone ' as to the practice of these principles. To parents, who have in their hands the making of family customs, it belongs especially to beware—

" Lest one good custom should corrupt the world."

# CHAPTER V

**Educational Thought in the Eighteenth Century.**—If the end of the eighteenth and the end of
the nineteenth centuries have one feature in common
more than another, it is, that in both education comes
to the front as among the chief ends of man. The
eighteenth-century people had the best of it. They
had clear oracles in their Locke and their Rousseau.
They knew what they wanted to do, and they did it
with charming enthusiasm. The period teems with
memoirs; and it is very pleasant to read about the
philosophically and consistently brought up children of
the more thoughtful families. They had convictions,
and they had the courage of their convictions. We
are less happy. A few decades ago we too were in a
furore of joyous excitement about education. Educational 'movements,' schools, colleges, lectures, higher
education for women, 'public' day schools for girls,
examination tests which should give assurance on
every point, were multiplied all over the country and
all over the world. It was a forward movement
which has brought us incalculable gains; and not
the least of these gains is the fact that to-day we

are dissatisfied and depressed, and inclined to wonder
whether we are not on the wrong tack.   If educational
work of the best kind had not been going on amongst
us for the last two or three decades, we should not
have arrived at this 'divine discontent.'   All the same,
it is pretty evident that the time has come when we
must change our front.   Now, elementary schools,
now, girls' high schools, now, public schools, now,
women's colleges, are pronounced to be, on the whole,
'a failure.'   They do a great deal, it is said, but is
what they do worth doing?   Is it, in fact, education?
The bolder sceptics go so far as to attack our two
ancient universities ; but they, very likely, will weather
the storm because of the very inertness, the 'masterly
inactivity,' let us call it, which their opponents abuse ;
the universities do a great deal of 'letting-alone.'

General Dissatisfaction with Education.—Our
pretty general dissatisfaction with education, as it is,
is a wholesome symptom, and probably means that
sounder theory and happier practice are on their way
to us.   One thing we begin to see clearly, that the
stream can rise no higher than its source, that sound
theory must underlie successful work.   We begin to
suspect that we took up schemes and methods of
education a little hastily, without considering what
philosophy or, let us say, psychology, underlies those
schemes and methods ; now, we see that our results
cannot be in advance of our principles.   To-day the
*psychologist* is abroad, as, twenty or thirty years ago,
the *schoolmaster* was abroad.

Psychologies are many.—But, alas, psychologies
are many, and educational denominations are bitterly
opposed to one another.   We must feel our way to
some test by which we can discern a working psycho-

logy for our own age ; for, like all science, psychology is progressive. What worked even fifty years ago will not work to-day, and what fulfils our needs to-day will not serve fifty years hence ; there is no last word to be said upon education ; it evolves with the evolution of the race. At the same time, that there should be at least half a dozen systems in the field, no one of them entirely satisfactory even to the persons who adopt it, shows that we, who practise education, should at any rate attempt to know what are the requirements of a sound system of psychology.

Conditions of an Adequate System.—That system which shall be of use to practical people in giving purpose, unity and continuity to education, must satisfy the following demands : — *It must be adequate*, covering the whole nature of man and his relations with all that is other than himself. *It must be necessary*, that is, no other equally adequate psychology should present itself; and *it must touch at all points the living thought of the age ;* that is, it must not be a by-issue to be discussed by specialists at their leisure, but the intelligent man in the street should feel its movement to be in step with the two or three great ideas by which the world is just now being educated.

Sacredness of the Person.—Among the thoughts which the mysterious Zeitgeist is employing to bring us up, I think we may put first *the sacredness of the person.* Every person is interesting to us to-day. The interviewer does more than satisfy vulgar curiosity ; what he has to tell is equally welcome to us all, whether he interviews the London 'step-girl,' the costermonger, the man of the book-barrow, 'Arry and Arriet out for a holiday, an ambassador, an author, an artist, a royal personage ; every detail that will help us to realise the personality of one or other is more than welcome.   So, too, of what is called the ' Kailyard' literature ; it rests on a sound basis. Literary merit it may or may not have, but it tells us what we want to know—everyday details about the people, any people, of any county, or of any country. Slang dictionaries, collections of folk-lore, big biographies which tell us minutely how a man dines and breakfasts, walks and sleeps, all is grist to our mill. We set an enormous and, I think, an increasing value upon *persons,* simply, *per se* ; and any system of psychology which is to appeal to us must bring the *person* to the fore. ` He may be influenced by this and that ; but he, himself, the indefinable person, of whom we are sensible while he is yet in arms, and of whom we never finally lose sight, however he be marred by vice and misery, must play for himself the game of life, and shape for himself those influences of environment, education, and what not, that do their part to make him what he is.    A system of psychology which gives us man in this sort of relation to educational forces should become common property at once, because this is what every mother of a family and teacher of a school, every sort of director of men and women, knows about.

The Evolution of the Individual.—Next we demand of education that it should *make for the evolution of the individual* ; should not only put the person in the first place, but should have for its sole aim the making the very most of that person, intellectually, morally, physically.   We do not desire any dead accretions of mere knowledge, or externals of mere accomplishment.   We desire an education that shall be assimilated ; shall become part and parcel of the person ; and the psychology which shall show us how to educate our children in this vital way will meet our demands. The doctrine of evolution has brought about a greater *bouleversement* in philosophy than perhaps we are aware of, and we shall find by-and-by that 'education' means nothing less than the evolution of the human being at all points ; and that the acquisition of mere learning is not necessarily education at all.

The Solidarity of the Race.—One other idea that appears to be at work in the world for the elevation of mankind is that of *the solidarity of the race.* The American poet, Walt Whitman, expresses one side of this intuition when he tells us how *he* conquers with every triumphant general, bleeds with every wounded soldier, shares the spring morning and the open road and the pride of the horses with every jolly waggoner—in fact, lives in all other lives that touch him anywhere, even in imagination. This is something more than the brotherhood of man ; that belongs to the present ; but our sense of the oneness of humanity reaches into the remotest past, making us regard with tender reverence every relic of the antiquity of our own people or of any other ; and, with a sort of jubilant hope, every prognostic of science or philanthropy which appears to us to be the promise of the centuries to come. Is it too much to expect that psychology shall take cognisance of this great educational force as well as of the two others I have indicated ? I do not say that these three are the only, so to speak, *motor* ideas of our age ; but I think they are the three of which we are all most aware, and I think, too, that any system of psychology which takes no cognisance of either, or of all of them, does not afford that basis for our educational theory and practice of which we are in search.

**The Best Thought is Common Thought.**—Let us consider now some three or four of the psychologies which have the most widespread influence to-day. But we do not presume to do this as critics, rather as inheritors of other men's labour, who take stock of our possessions in order that we may use them to the most advantage. For the best thought of any age is common thought ; the men who write it down do but give expression to what is working in the minds of the rest. But we must bear in mind that truth behaves like a country gate allowed to 'swing to' after a push. Now it swings a long way to this side and now a long way to that, and at last after shorter and shorter oscillations the latch settles. The reformer, the investigator, works towards one aspect of truth, which is the whole truth to him, and which he advances out of line with the rest. The next reformer works at a tangent, apparently in opposition, but he is bringing up another front of truth. Then there is work for us, the people of average mind. We consider all sides, balance what has been done, and find truth, perhaps in the mean, perhaps as a side issue which did not make itself plain to original thinkers of either school. But we do not scorn the bridge that has borne us.

**Locke's 'States of Consciousness.'**—We need not go further back than Locke, who represents the traditional educational notions in the homes of the upper middle classes. People who bring up their children by 'common sense,' according to 'the way of our family,' do so more often than they know because their great-great-grandfathers read Locke. He did not concern himself with the *mind*, or *soul*, of man, but with '*states of consciousness.*' Ideas, images, were for him to be got only through the senses; and a man could know nothing but what he got hold of through his own senses and assimilated by his own understanding. As for choice and selection in these ideas and images, Locke gives a comprehensive counsel—'What it becomes a gentleman to know' is the proper subject-matter for education. The mind (*i.e.* the man?) appears to have little colour or character of its own, but has certain powers and activities for the employment of the ideas it receives; and to account for these, Locke invented the pestilent fallacy which has, perhaps, been more injurious than any other to the cause of education—the fallacy of the 'faculties of the mind.'

**Does not provide for the Evolution of the Person.**—Now let us bring Locke up to the standard which we have erected, remembering always that our power to raise a higher standard is due to him and such as he. There is no unity of an inspiring idea, no natural progress and continuity, no ennobling aim, in an education which stops at the knowledge a gentleman should acquire and the accomplishments a gentleman should possess. The *person* hardly appears except in the way of the semi-mechanical activities of his so-called faculties; he is practically the resultant of the images conveyed through his senses. The *evolution*, the expansion of the individual in the directions proper to him, has no place here; every man is shut tight, as it were, in his own skin, but is taught to behave himself becomingly within that limit. That intellectual commerce of ideas whereby the dead yet speak their living thoughts in the work they have left us, and by which as by links of an endless chain all men are bound to each and all men influence each, has no place in a philosophy which teaches that a man can know only through his own understanding working upon the images he receives through his senses. In so far as we wish to attain to the possibilities of the hour we must take farewell of Locke, though we do so with gratitude, and even with affection.

Modern    Physiological - Psychology. — The modern school, which regards psychology strictly as a 'natural science,' works more or less on the basis of Locke, plus an illuminating knowledge of biology. Here, as with Locke, the 'mind' is apprehended only as 'states of consciousness'; the senses are the sole avenues of knowledge, which reaches the brain in the form of ideas or images. But I shall represent this 'rational psychology' best by citing a few sentences from Professor James (Harvard University), whose wise and temperate treatment of the subject commands the respect and attention of even those who differ from him. He opens with a limiting definition of psychology as the '*description and explanation of states of consciousness as such.*' He treats psychology as a 'natural science.' After bringing forward facts familiar to most of us, showing the intimate connection between acts of thought and the cerebral hemisphere, he says: " Taking all such facts together, the simple and radical conception dawns upon the mind that mental action may be uniformly and absolutely a function of brain action varying as the latter varies, and being to the brain action as effect to cause. This conception is the working hypothesis which underlies all the physiological-psychology of recent years." This is not far removed from the announcement of the Frenchman that the brain secretes thought as the liver secretes bile, both processes being purely material and mechanical, and doing away with any requirement for the profoundest thinking beyond that of a well-nourished brain.

**Unjustifiable Materialism.** — No wonder the author finds himself compelled to admit that to some readers "such an assumption will seem like the most unjustifiable *à priori* materialism." The discussion of 'the self' might be supposed to present insuperable difficulties, but they are disposed of, and, says our author, "The logical conclusion seems to be that the *states of consciousness are all that psychology needs to do her work with. Metaphysics or theology may prove the soul to exist, but for psychology the hypothesis of such a substantial principle of unity is superfluous.*" That is to say, the important personage which I call *I, myself,* need be no more than perpetually shifting states of consciousness effected by the brain ; and the sameness or identity of person, which seems at first sight the one bit of solid ground in a shifting morass, rests upon no more than the fact that the brain may be conscious of the same objects to-day that it was conscious of years ago.

**Psychology, 'A Phrase of Diffidence.'** — But, after proving with great clearness and power through a considerable volume[1] that all the phenomena of intelligent life *may* have their sole source in the physical brain, Professor James concludes—"When, then, we talk of psychology as a natural science we must not assume that that means a sort of psychology that

[1] *Outlines of Psychology.*

stands at last on solid ground.  It means just the re-
verse ; it means a psychology particularly fragile and
into which the waters of metaphysical criticism leak
at every joint, a psychology all of whose elementary
assumptions and data must be reconsidered in wider
connections and translated into other terms    It is, in
short, a phrase of diffidence and not of arrogance, and
it is indeed strange to hear people talk triumphantly
of the 'New Psychology' and write 'Histories of
Psychology' when into the real elements and forces,
which the word covers, not the first glimpse of clear
insight exists.  A string of raw facts, a little gossip
and wrangle about opinions, a little classification and
generalisation on the mere descriptive level . . . .
but not a single law . . . . not a single proposition
from which any consequence can causally be deduced."
This is soothing, and we close Professor James's book
with satisfaction ; but the pity of it is that all the ' new '
psychologists are not so modest as the Professor,—
some of them are, may we venture to say so, not a little
arrogant : what is more, the student who goes carefully
through this text-book of psychology is only too
likely to consider that the author has proved his case
—that psychology is a 'natural science,' 'and it is,'
like Peter Bell's primrose, 'nothing more '—up to the
hilt, and he is not likely to go through a process of
reconversion at the last page.

We become Devitalised.—It is dreary to suppose
that one may not be anybody after all, but only a
momentary state of consciousness.  Hope goes out of
life, for there is nothing pleasant to look forward to.
If something agreeable should happen next year, there
is no *I, myself*, to enjoy it ; only the ' state of consciousness' of some moment to come.  Faith goes where

all is fortuitous ; when other people and ourselves are, so to speak, the circumstances of the moment. Where there are no persons, there is no possibility of that divine afflatus which we call enthusiasm ; for that recognition of another on a higher plane which we mean when we say ' I believe in so and so,' for that recognition of the divine Being which we call Faith. We become devitalised ; life is flat and grey ; we throw desperate, if dull, energy into the task of the hour because we shall so, any way, get rid of that hour ; we are glad to be amused, but still more glad of the stimulus of feverish work ; but the work, like ourselves, is devitalised, without living idea, without consecrating aim. Our manner becomes impassive, our speech caustic, our countenance dreary and impenetrable. This is the change that is passing over large numbers of the teaching profession, men and women of keen intelligence, who might well have been inspired by high ideals, quickened by noble enthusiasms, had they not imbibed an educational faith which meets all aspirations with a *Cui bono ?* We give what we have, and only what we have. What have these to pass on to the children under their care?

**This System Inadequate, Unnecessary, Inharmonious.**—But we need not sit down under this blighting system of thought. It is *inadequate*, as the best of their own prophets—Mr James, for example —freely allow; there is more in man than this philosophy has ever dreamt of. It is *unnecessary*, for, as we shall presently see, more than one other psychology accounts with greater, though never with complete, success for the phenomena which a human being presents. It is *inharmonious* with the *movement of the age*. It effaces that personality which the age tends to exalt and magnify, and to regard with tender interest, under even sordid conditions. The principle of *solidarity* is lost, and those of social and family life loosened ; for what binding tie can there be between beings whose entity *may* be no more than a state of consciousness ?

**Evolution is Checked.**—Again, the *evolution* of the individual is checked at the point of mechanical perfection. Good mathematicians, clear-headed scientists, may be turned out ; but what place is there for the higher forces of humanity, aspiration, speculation, devotion ? We have reason to keep watch at the place of the letting out of waters, that is, the psychology upon which our educational thought and action rest. There is delightful certitude in the results of anthropometrical research. You may predicate with certainty given facts about a child from the way in which he stretches out his arm. Good *pathological* work is being done, and many a child's hidden weakness is revealed and consequently brought under curative treatment by the tests which it is now possible to apply. The danger is that we should take a part for the whole and allow this 'new psychology' to usurp the whole field of education.

# CHAPTER VI

## SOME EDUCATIONAL THEORIES EXAMINED

**Theories of Pestalozzi and Froebel.**—It is refreshing to turn to that school of German educational thought which has produced the two great apostles, Pestalozzi and Froebel. What we may call the enthusiasm of childhood, joyous teaching, loving and lovable teachers and happy school hours for the little people, are among the general gains from this source. To look a gift horse in the mouth is unworthy, and it would seem pure captiousness to detect any source of weakness in a system of psychology to which our indebtedness is so great. But no stream can rise higher than its source, and it is questionable whether the conception of children as cherished plants in a cultured garden has not in it an element of weakness. Are the children too carefully tended? Is Nature too sedulously assisted? Is the environment too perfectly tempered? Is it conceivable that the rough-and-tumble of a nursery should lend itself more to the dignity and self-dependence of the *person* and to the evolution of individual character, than that delightful place, a child-garden? I suppose we have all noticed that children show more keen intelligence and more independent thought in home-play and

home-talk than one expects of the angelic little
beings one sees at school. I daresay the reader will
know Fra Angelico's picture of 'The Last Judgment,' one of the scenes in which gives us a circle of
little monks (become as little children) dancing
round, hand-in-hand, with gracious angels on their
way to Paradise. The little monks are obviously
very happy and very good; but somehow one misses
the force of personality; they do not look as if they
were capable of striking out a line for themselves;
and this may be a danger in the Kindergarten.

**Lack the Element of Personality.**—'Make
children happy and they will be good,' is absolutely
true, but does it develop that strenuousness, the first
condition of virtue, which comes of the contrary
axiom—'Be good and you will be happy'? Kindergarten teachers are doing beautiful work; but many
of them are hampered by the original metaphor of
the *plant*, which is exactly lacking in that element of
personality, the cherishing and developing of which
is a sacred and important part of education. The
philosophic German mind beheld in man a part or
the *Cosmos*, which, like the rest, needed only to be
placed in fit conditions to develop according to its
nature.

**The Struggle for Existence, a Part of Life.**—
The weak point in the argument is that man would
appear to fall under the laws of two universes, the
material and the spiritual; and that to energise and
resist and repel is the law of his being. It will be
said that this need not apply to the child; that the
struggle for existence may well begin after a happy
childhood has been secured; but probably any sort of
transition violates the principles of unity and continuity

which should rule education. No doubt all thoughtful
Kindergarten teachers recognise in what direction
the limitations—all men have their limitations—of
their Founder lay, and their practices are levelled up
to modern thought. The general substitution of free
brush-drawing, in which the children have some
initiative, for the cramped pencil drawing in chequers
of the old Kindergarten, is an illustration of the
modern spirit; but it is well for us all to remember
our origins and our tendencies, that we may recognise
and avoid our dangers.

**Herbartian Psychology.**—I have only space to
glance at one more 'psychology,' that which is,
curiously enough, dividing the American mind with
the school which regards psychology as a 'natural
science,' and at which English teachers are beginning
to snatch as a drowning man snatches at a straw.
This is the psychology of Herbart, another German
philosopher of the beginning of the last century,
contemporary with both Pestalozzi and Froebel
during the best years of his life. His theory of man
is wide as the poles apart from either of those we have
already considered ; and there is no denying that it
affords a tempting working basis for education. It is
only when we come to examine the Herbartian
psychology in connection with the two or three great
thoughts upon which, as we have seen, the world is
being educated, that it is found wanting. Herbart
begins to account for man minus what I have called
the *person*.[1] He allows a soul, but he says, "The
soul has no capacity nor faculty whatever either to
receive or to produce anything. It has originally

[1] 'Person' is used in the common-sense, every-day acceptance of
the word.

neither ideas nor feelings nor desires. It knows nothing of itself and nothing of other things. Further, within it lie no forms of intuition or thought, no laws of willing and acting, nor any sort of predisposition, however remote, to all this."[1] There remain two possibilities for the soul : an effective *vis inertiæ*, and what Herbart describes as the power of reacting on an idea ; that is to say, the soul itself is no longer quite as it was after it has thus reacted.

**The Person, an Effect and not a Cause.**—The problem is simplified anyway. All our complex notions of intellect, will, feeling and so on, disappear. The soul is thrown open to ideas—a fair field and no favour ; and ideas, each of them a living entity, according to the familiar Platonic notion, crowd and jostle one another for admission, and for the best places, and for the most important and valuable coalitions, once they have entered. They lie below the 'threshold' watching a chance to slip in. They hurry to join their friends and allies upon admission, they 'vault' and they 'taper,' they form themselves into powerful 'appreception masses' which occupy a more or less permanent place in the soul ; and the soul—what does it do ? It is not evident otherwise than as it affords a stage for this drama of ideas ; and the self, the soul or the *person*, however we choose to call him, is an effect and not a cause, a result, and not an original fact.

A philosopher who emphasises the potency of ideas does good work in the cause of education. We get glimpses of a perfect theory—how our function shall be, to supply the child always with fit ideas,

[1] *Lehrbuch zur Psychologie*, Part III., sects. 152, 153 (see *Herbartian Psychology*, by J. Adams).

and with the best ideas ; how we shall take care so to select and arrange these ideas that they shall naturally fly to one another and make strong 'apperception masses' once they have got beyond the 'threshold' in the child's soul.

**A Tempting Vista.**—A fascinating vista is open before us ; education has all things made plain and easy for her use; she has nothing to do but to select her ideas and turn out a man to her mind. Here is a tempting scheme of unity and continuity ! One might occupy all the classes in a school for a whole month upon all the ideas that combine in one 'apperception mass' with the idea 'book.' We might have object-lessons on the colours, shapes, and sizes of books ; more advanced object-lessons on paper-making and book-binding ; practical lessons in book-sewing and book-binding ; lessons, according to the class, on the contents of books, from A B C and little Bo-Peep to philosophy and poetry. A month ! why, a whole school education might be arranged in groups of ideas which should combine into one vast 'apperception mass,' all clustering about 'book.' The sort of thing was done publicly some time ago, in London, *apple* being the idea round which the 'apperception mass' gathered.

**Eliminates Personality.** — If one is to find the principles of unity and continuity in the *ideas* presented to the soul, this is all good and well. But if, as we believe, these principles must emanate from the soul, or person, himself, this tempting unity may result in the collection of a mass of heterogeneous and unassimilated information.

**Turns out Duplicates.**—Again, given two souls supplied with precisely the same ideas, in precisely the same order, and with no other ideas whatsoever, and we get duplicates of the same person, a possibility which would demolish once and for ever that great conception, the *solidarity of the race.* Once more, what does the Herbartian theory of man minister to our interest in personality, our sense of the *sacredness of the person?* The person is *non est*, or is the mere sport of the ideas which take possession of him. He has not so much as a special fitness for one class of ideas rather than for another; all is casual; and, as for the *evolution of the individual,* it is not he, but this or that mass of ideas which possesses him, that expands. The man appears to be no more than a sort of vessel of transport to carry ideas into their proper sphere of action. Herbartian psychology is rich in suggestion, but we cannot take it up as it stands without losing the educational value of the two or three leading principles which are, as we say, 'in the air' for the teaching of mankind.

**Each System fails to meet our Tests.**—I have now examined briefly the three or four psychologies which hold, more or less, the field of educational thought. We see that each *advances* truth, but that neither expresses the whole truth even so far as to afford a working basis for educators. So people either work on by rule of thumb, or they borrow a fragment here and a fragment there as the case appears to demand; like children with a hard sum whose answer they know, and who try now division, now multiplication, now subtraction, to make it come right. No doubt there are also many able psychologists who may not have written books, but who work out the problems of education, not with a view to the answer, but according to a code of inherent principles which they have discerned for themselves.

**A Psychology that meets the Demands upon it.**—What have we to bring forward in the way of a working psychology which shall meet the demands I have indicated?   We do not claim to be philosophers; we are modest and practical people looking out for a secure basis for education.   It is just possible that bringing unbiassed minds and a few guiding principles to the task, we have, not joined the parts of the puzzle, but perceived dimly how an outline here and an outline there indicate, not so many separate psychologies, but shadowings forth of a coherent, living, educational principle destined to assume more and more clearness and fulness until it is revealed to us at last as the *educational gospel*, the discovery of which may be the destined reward and triumph of our age.   Let me try to set forth, though with diffidence, what we have done, knowing that no man and no society can say of educational truth, ' This is mine and that is thine,' for all is common, and none of us can know how much he gives and how much he takes.

**Educational Truth a Common Possession.**— For years we have worked definitely and consistently upon a psychology which appears to me fairly adequate, necessary, and in touch with the thought of our age.[1]   Children brought up on this theory of education, wherever we come across them, have certain qualities in common.   They are curiously vitalised ; not bored, not all alive in the playing-field and dull and inert in the schoolroom—even when it is that place, proverbial for dulness, a home school-

---

[1] The references here and after are to the distinctive thought and work of the Parents' National Educational Union.

room taught by a governess. There is unity in their lives; they are not two persons, one with their play-fellows and quite other with their teachers and elders; but frank, fresh, showing keen interest in whatever comes in their way. Then, too, there is continuity in their education. Little children are always eager to know; but the desire for knowledge seldom survives two or three years of school-life. But these children begin on lines that go on from the first baby lessons, through boyhood, girlhood, womanhood, motherhood; there is no transition stage, but simple, natural, living progress. The claims I venture to make for these children must rest, not only on the evidence of the few, but on the principles upon which we work.

We take Children as Persons.—In the first place, we take children seriously as *persons* like ourselves, only more so ; the first question that comes before us is—What do we understand by a person? We believe the thinking, invisible soul and acting, visible body to be one in so intimate a union that—

"Nor soul helps flesh more now than flesh helps soul."

If the doctrine of the Resurrection had not been revealed to us, it would be a necessity, in however unimagined a form, to our conception of a person. The countenance of our friend with the thousand delicate changes which express every *nuance* of feeling ; the refinement, purpose, perception, power, revealed in his hand, the dear familiar carriage, these are all inseparable from our conception of the person. Whatever is advanced by the physiologist and the rational psychologist as to the functions of that most marvellous brain cortex, the seat of consciousness, as furnishing us with images and impulses, of the motor

nerves as originating action, of the brain as the seat
of habit; of the possibility of educating a child in
all becoming habits of act, in all sweet habits of
thought, by taking measures to secure that these
habits become, as it were, a memory of the brain to
be awakened by due stimuli,—all these things we
believe and receive; and we believe further that the
possibility of a rational education rests upon this
physiological basis, only fully discovered to us within
the present generation.

The Person Wills, and Thinks, and Feels.—But
then, we believe the assumption that all this delicate
mechanism is automatic to be gratuitous and inadequate; it is to be assumed that the *person* should possess
such vehicle of expression and medium of relation to
the outer world. For the rest, we believe that the
*person* wills and thinks and feels; is always present,
though not always aware of himself; is without parts
or faculties; whatever he does, *he* does, all of him,
whether he take a walk or write a book. It is so
much the habit to think of the person as a dual being,
flesh and spirit, when he is, in truth, one, that it is
necessary to clear our minds on this subject. The
person is one and not several, and he is no more
compact of ideas on the one hand than he is of
nervous and muscular tissues on the other. That he
requires nutriment of two kinds is no proof that he
is two individuals. Pleasant and well-cooked food
makes man of a cheerful countenance, and wine
gladdens the heart of man, and we all know the
spiritual refreshment of a needed meal. On the other
hand, we all know the lack-lustre eye and pallid
countenance of the well-fed who receive none of that
other nutriment which we call ideas; quick and

living thought is as necessary for the full and happy development of the body as it is for that of the soul.

**An Adequate Doctrine.**—Holding this view, we believe that our educational doctrine is *adequate*, because, while following the progress of biological psychology with avidity, and making use of every gain that presents itself, and while following with equal care the advance of philosophic thought, we recognise that each of these sees the chameleon in a different light, that the person includes both and is more than both ; and, if our educational creed is by no means conclusive, we think it is not narrow, because we have come across no problem of life or mind the solution of which is shut out from us by any dogma of ours. We cannot say that our doctrine is *necessary*, but we do say that some educational theory which shall include the whole nature of man and the results of scientific research, in the same or a greater degree, is necessary. We find ourselves, too, in touch with those three great ideas which seem to me to be the schoolmasters of the world at the present moment. The *person* of the child is sacred to us ; we do not swamp his individuality in his intelligence, in his conscience, or even in his soul ; perhaps one should add to-day, or even in his physical development. The person is all these and more. We safeguard the initiative of the child and we realise that, in educational work, we must take a back seat ; the teacher, even when the teacher is the parent, is not to be too much to the front. There is no more facile way of swamping character and individuality than by that idol of the 'fifties'— *personal influence.*

**Education the Science of Relations.**—We consider that *education is the science of relations*, or,

more fully, that education considers what relations
are proper to a human being, and in what ways these
several relations can best be established; that a
human being comes into the world with capacity for
many relations; and that we, for our part, have two
chief concerns—first, to put him in the way of forming
these relations by presenting the right idea at the
right time, and by forming the right habit upon the
right idea; and, secondly, by not getting in the way
and so preventing the establishment of the very
relations we seek to form.

**Teaching must not be Obtrusive.**—Half the
teaching one hears and sees is more or less obtrusive.
The oral lesson and the lecture, with their accompany-
ing notes, give very little scope for the establishment
of relations with great minds and various minds.
The child who learns his science from a text-book,
though he go to Nature for illustrations, and he who
gets his information from object-lessons, has no
chance of forming relations with things as they are,
because his kindly obtrusive teacher makes him
believe that to know *about* things is the same thing
as knowing them personally; though every child
knows that to know about Prince Edward is by no
means the same thing as knowing the boy-prince.
We study in many ways the art of standing aside.
People sometimes write that the books set in
our school constitute much of its usefulness; they
do not always see that the choice of books, which
implies the play of various able minds directly
on the mind of the child, is a great part of that
education which consists in the establishment of
relations.

**The Art of Standing Aside.**—I have even known

of teachers who have thought well to compose the songs and poems which their children use. Think of it! not even our poets are allowed to interpose between the poor child and the probably mediocre mind of the teacher. The art of standing aside to let a child develop the relations proper to him is the fine art of education, when the educator perceives the two things he *must* do and how to do these two things. The evolution of the individual is a natural sequence of the opening up of relations.

How we labour towards *the solidarity of the race* I hope to show more fully, later. But, for example, we do not endeavour to give children outlines of ancient history, but to put them in living touch with a thinker who lived in those ancient days. We are not content that they should learn the history of their own country alone; some living idea of contemporaneous European history, anyway, we try to get in; that the history we teach may be the more living, we work in, *pari passu*, some of the literature of the period and some of the best historical novels and poems that treat of the period; and so on with other subjects.

There is nothing new in all this; what we venture to claim is that our work is unified and vitalised by a comprehensive theory of education and a sound basis of psychology.

# CHAPTER VII

## AN ADEQUATE THEORY OF EDUCATION

**A Human Being.**—I have laid before the reader, as a working hypothesis,—that man is homogeneous, a spiritual being invested with a body—capable of responding to spiritual impulses, the organ by which he expresses himself, the vehicle by which he receives impressions, and the medium by which he establishes relations with what we call the material world ;— that will, conscience, affection, reason, are not the various parts of a composite whole, but are different modes of action of the person.

*His Capacities.*—That he is capable of many relations and consequently of many modes of action ; that, given the due relations, his power of expansion in these relations appears to be, not illimitable, but, so far as we know, as yet unlimited.

*His Limitations.*—But that, deprived of any or all of the relations proper to him, a human being has no power of self-development in these directions ; though he would appear not to lose any of his capacity for these relations.

*His Education.*—Again, that any relation once initiated leaves, so to speak, an organic memory of itself in the nervous tissue of the brain ; that in this physical registration of an experience or a thought, or of the memory of an experience or a thought, lies the possibility of habit ; that some nine-tenths of our life run upon lines of habit; and that, therefore, in order to educate, we must know something of both the psychological and physiological history of a habit, how to initiate it and how to develop it ; and, finally, that a human being under education has two functions —the formation of habits and the assimilation of ideas.

The Behaviour of Ideas. — Physiologists and 'rational psychologists' have made the basis of habit pretty plain to us. All who run may read. The nature, functions, and behaviour of ideas, and how ideas have power in their impact upon the cerebral hemisphere to make some sort of sensible impression —all this is matter as to which we are able only to make 'guesses at truth.' But this need not dismay us, for such other ultimate facts as sleep and life and death are equally unexplained. In every department of science we are brought up before facts which we have to assume as the bases of our so-called science. Where a working hypothesis is necessary, all we can do is to assume those bases that seem to us the most adequate and the most fruitful. Let us say with Plato that an idea is an entity, a live thing of the mind.

No one can Beget an Idea by Himself.— Apparently no one has power to beget an idea by himself; it appears to be the progeny of two minds. So-and-so 'put it in my head,' we say, and that is the history of all ideas—the most simple and the most profound. But, once begotten, the idea seems to survive indefinitely. It is painted in a picture, written in a book, carved into a chair, or only spoken to someone who speaks it again, who speaks it again, who speaks it again, so that it goes on being spoken, for how long? Who knows! Nothing so strikes the student of history as the persistent way in which ideas recur, except the way in which they elude observation until occasion calls them forth. Our natural progeny may indeed die and be buried; but of this spiritual progeny of ideas, who may forecast the history or foretell the end?

**Certain Persons attract Certain Ideas.**—Perhaps we may be allowed this further hypothesis—that, as an idea comes of the contact of two minds, the idea of another is no more than a *notion* to us until it has undergone a process of generation within us; and for that reason different ideas appeal to different minds—not at all because the ideas themselves have an independent desire to club into 'apperception masses,' but because certain persons have in themselves, by inheritance, may we assume, that which is proper to attract certain ideas. To illustrate invisible things by visible, let us suppose that the relation is something like that between the pollen and the ovule it is to fertilise. The ways of carrying the pollen are various, not to say promiscuous, but there is nothing haphazard in the result. The right pollen goes to the right ovule and the plant bears seed after its kind; even so, the person brings forth ideas after his kind.

**The Idea that 'Strikes' us.**—The *crux* of the situation is: how can an emanation so purely spiritual as an idea make an impression upon even the most delicate material substance? We do not know. We have some little demonstration that it is so in the fact of the score of reflex actions by which we visibly respond to an idea that 'strikes' us. The eye brightens, the pulse quickens, the colour rises, the whole person becomes vitalised, capable, strenuous, no longer weighed down by this clog of flesh. Every habit we have formed has had its initial idea, and every idea we receive is able to initiate a habit of thought and of action. Every human being has the power of communicating notions to other human beings ; and, after he is dead, this power survives him in the work he has done and the words he has said. How illimitable is life ! That the divine Spirit has like intimate power of corresponding with the human spirit, needs not to be urged, once we recognise ourselves as spiritual beings at all.

**Expansion and Activity of the Person.**—Nor does this teeming population of ideas arise to us without order and without purpose beyond the scope of our busy efforts and intentions. It would seem as if a new human being came into the world with unlimited capacity for manifold relations, with a tendency to certain relations in preference to certain others, but with no degree of adaptation to these relations. To secure that adaptation and the expansion and activity of the person, along the lines of the relations most proper to him, is the work of education; to be accomplished by the two factors of ideas and habits. Every relation must be initiated by its own 'captain'[1] idea, sustained upon fitting ideas ; and wrought into the material substance of the *person* by its proper habits. This is the field before us.

**Story of Kaspar Hauser.**—To make my meaning plainer, let me run over the story of Kaspar Hauser,

[1] Cf. Coleridge's *Method.*

that 'child of Nuremberg,' upon whom an unique experiment was said to have been tried, criminal in its character, and therefore not to be repeated. The story is as well accredited as most of our data, but we will assume its truth in so far only as the experience of this boy tallies with what we know of the experience of an infant; or, as regards the use of his senses, with the experience of an adult person who has for the first time attained to, sight, let us say. On 28th May 1828, the attention of a cobbler in Nuremberg was excited by a strange figure leaning, as if unable to support itself, against a wall and uttering a moaning sound. The figure was that of a young man of about seventeen, who, when the cobbler approached, moaned some incoherent sounds. He had fair hair and blue eyes, and the lower part of his face projected a little like a monkey's. Everyone who watched him came to the same conclusion, that his mind was that of a child of two or three, while his body was nearly grown up; and yet he was not half-witted, because he immediately began to pick up words and phrases, had a wonderful memory, and never forgot a face he had once seen or the name which belonged to it. At first, he was placed in the guard-house for safety, and the children of the gaoler taught him to walk and to talk as they did their own baby-sister. He was not afraid of anything. After six or seven weeks the towns-people decided to adopt him as the 'child of Nurem-berg.' He was placed under the charge of Professor Daumer, whose interest led him to undertake the difficult task of developing his mind so that it might fit his body. Later, Dr Daumer gleaned a short account of his previous life from Hauser by careful questioning. It was to this effect. 'He neither knows who he is nor where he came from. He always lived in a hole where he sat on straw on the ground. He never heard a sound nor saw any vivid light. He awoke and he slept and awoke again. When he awoke he found a loaf of bread and a pitcher of water beside him. Sometimes the water tasted nasty, and then he fell asleep again. He never saw the face of the man who came to him. At last the man taught him to stand and to walk, and finally carried him out of his hole.' For several months after he came to Nuremberg he refused to eat anything but bread and water, and was, in fact, made quite ill by the smell of meat, beer, wine or milk. For the first four months of his stay with Daumer, his senses of sight, taste, hearing and smell were very acute. He could see much further than most people by day, without, however, losing his power of seeing in the dark. At the same time he could not distinguish between a thing and a picture of that thing, and could not for a long time judge distances at all, for he saw everything flat. He thought a ball rolled because it wished to do so, and could not see why animals should not behave, at table for instance, like human beings. His sense of smell was very keen, painfully so, in fact, for he was made quite ill by the smell of the dye in his clothes, the smell of paper, etc. On the other hand, he could distinguish the leaves of trees by their smell. In about three months Dr Daumer was able to teach him other things besides the use of his senses. He was encouraged to write letters and essays, to use his hands in every way, to dig in the garden, etc. For the next eleven months he lived a happy, simple life with his friend and tutor, who mentions, however, that the intense acuteness of his senses was gradually passing away, but that he had still the charming, obedient, child-like nature which had won all hearts.

**What Nature does for a Child.**—Here we have an instance (more or less credible), and the only instance on record, of what Nature, absolutely unaided and unhindered, has done for a child. Kaspar Hauser came out of his long retirement, unusually intelligent, with his senses intensely acute, and sweet and docile in disposition. This is an object-lesson which cannot lawfully be repeated, and we may not take a single instance as proving any position. But certainly this illuminating story—coupled with the fact that Kaspar Hauser, on his emergence, was in some respects in the condition of an infant in arms—that is, he knew nothing of round, or flat, or far, or near, or hot, or cold, he had no experience; and in some respects in that of a child of two years old with quick intelligence, keen perceptive powers, capital memory, and child-like sweetness — Kaspar Hauser's story and our common experience go to prove that the labour we spend on developing the 'faculties,' or in cultivating the senses, is largely thrown away. Nature has no need of our endeavours in these directions. Under the most adverse conceivable conditions she can work wonders if let alone. What she cannot away with is our misdirected efforts, which hinder and impede her beneficent work. Nature left to herself hands over every child to its parents and other educators in this condition of acute perceptive powers, keen intelligence, and moral teachableness and sweetness. This solitary instance goes to show that she is even capable of maintaining a human being in this child-like condition until he reaches the verge of manhood.

**The Child has every Power that will serve Him.**

—What, then, have we to do for the child? Plainly we have not to develop the *person*; he is there already, with, possibly, every power that will serve him in his passage through life. Some day we shall be told that the very word education is a misnomer belonging to the stage of thought when the drawing forth of 'faculties' was supposed to be a teacher's business. We shall have some fit new word meaning, perhaps, 'applied wisdom,' for wisdom is *the science of relations*, and the thing we have to do for a young human being is to put him in touch, so far as we can, with all the relations proper to him.

**Fulness of Living depends on the Establishment of Relations.**—We begin to see light, both as to the lines upon which we should form habits and as to that much-vexed question—the subjects of instruction proper for children. We are no longer divided between the claims of the classical and the modern side. We no longer ask ourselves whether it is better to learn a few subjects 'thoroughly,' so we say, or to get a 'smattering' of many. These questions are beside the mark. In considering the relationships which we may initiate for a child, I will begin with what we shall probably be inclined to call the lowest rung of the ladder. We may believe that a person—I have a 'baby person' in view—is put into this most delightful world for the express purpose of forming ties of intimacy, joy, association, and knowledge with the living and moving things that are therein, with what St Francis would have called his brother the mountain and his brother the ant and his brothers in the starry heavens. Fulness of living, joy in life, depend, far more than we know, upon the establishment of these relations. What do we do? We consider the matter carefully; we say the boy will make a jumble of it if he is taught more than one or two sciences. We ask our friends—'What sciences will tell best in examinations?' and, 'Which are most easily learned?' We discover which are the best text-books in the smallest compass. The boy learns up his text, listens to lectures, makes diagrams, watches demonstrations. Behold! he has learned a science and is able to produce facts and figures, for a time any way, in connection with some one class of natural phenomena; but of tender intimacy with Nature herself he has acquired none. Let me sketch what seems to me the better way for the child.

**The Power of Recognition.**—His parents know that the first step in intimacy is recognition; and they will measure his education, not solely by his progress in the 'three R's,' but by the number of living and growing things he knows by look, name, and habitat. A child of six will note with eager interest the order of time in which the trees put on their leaves; will tell you whether to look in hedge, or meadow, or copse, for eyebright, wood-sorrel, ground-ivy; will not think that flowers were made to be plucked, for—

> "'Tis (his) faith that every flower
> Enjoys the air it breathes"—

but will take his friends to see where the milk-wort grows, or the bog-bean, or the sweet-gale. The birds of the air are no longer casual; he soon knows when and where to expect the redstart and the meadow pipit. The water-skater and the dragon-fly are interesting and admired acquaintances. His eyes have sparkled at the beauty of crystals, and, though he may not have been able to find them *in situ*, he knows the look of the crystals of lime and quartz, and the lovely pink of felspar, and many more.

Æsthetic Appreciation.—Æsthetic appreciation follows close upon recognition, for does he not try from very early days to catch the flower in its beauty of colour and grace of gesture with his own paint-brush ? The wise mother is careful to open her child's eyes to another kind of appreciation. She makes him look from a distance at a wild cherry-tree, or at a willow with its soft catkins, and she shows him that the picture on a Japanese screen has caught the very look of the thing, though when he comes to compare a single catkin or a single cherry blossom with those on the screen, there is no portraiture ; and so he begins to learn at a very early age that to paint that which we see and that which we know to be there, are two different things, and that the former art is the more gratifying.

First-hand Knowledge.—By-and-by he passes from acquaintance, the pleasant recognition of friendly faces, to knowledge, the sort of knowledge we call science. He begins to notice that there are resem-blances between wild-rose and apple blossom, between buttercup and wood-anemone, between the large rhododendron blossom and the tiny heath floret. A suggestion will make him find out accurately what these resemblances are, and he gets the new and delightful idea of families of plants. His little bit of knowledge is real science, because he gets it at first-hand ; in his small way he is another Linnæus.

Appreciative Knowledge and Exact Know-ledge.—All the time he is storing up associations of delight which will come back for his refreshment when he is an old man. With this sort of appreciative knowledge of things to begin with, the superstructure of exact knowledge, living science, no mere affair of text-books and examinations, is easily raised, because a natural desire is implanted. We might say the same of art, so far, any way, as the appreciation of art goes. The child who has been taught to see, appreciates pictures with discrimination.

**How a Child sets up a New Relation.**—This is how a child goes to work to set up a new relation : a little girl of seven was handling an oar for the first time and remarked—'What a lot of crab-water there is to-day!' Then the next day—'There's not near so much crab-water to-day.' She was asked—'How do you know when it's crab-water?' 'Oh! it's so tough and you can't get your oar through, and it knocks you off your seat!' The child was all wrong, of course, but she was getting a scrap of real science and would soon get on the right track. How much better this than to learn out of a text-book, 'the particles which constitute water have no cohesion, and may be readily separated by a solid substance.'

When we consider that the setting up of relations, moral and intellectual, is our chief concern in life, and that the function of education is to put the child in the way of relations proper to him, and to offer the inspiring idea which commonly initiates a relation, we perceive that a little incident like the above may be of more importance than the passing of an examination.

# CHAPTER VIII

## CERTAIN RELATIONS PROPER TO A CHILD

GEOLOGY, mineralogy, physical geography, botany, natural history, biology, astronomy—the whole circle of the sciences is, as it were, set with gates ajar in order that a child may go forth furnished, not with scientific knowledge, but with, what Huxley calls, common information, so that he may feel for objects on the earth and in the heavens the sort of proprietary interest which the son of an old house has in its heirlooms.

We are more exacting than the Jesuits. They are content to have a child till he is seven; but we want him till he is twelve or fourteen, if we may not have him longer. You may do what you like with him afterwards. Given this period for the establishing of relations, we may undertake to prepare for the world a man, vital and vigorous, full of living interests, available and serviceable. I think we may warrant him even to pass examinations, because he will know how to put living interest into the dullest tasks.

Dynamic Relations.—But we have not yet done with his relations with mother earth. There are, what I may call, *dynamic* relations to be established. He must stand and walk and run and jump with ease and grace. He must skate and swim and ride and drive, dance and row and sail a boat. He should be able to make free with his mother earth and to do whatever the principle of gravitation will allow. This is an elemental relationship for the lack of which nothing compensates.

**Power over Material.** — Another elemental relationship, which every child should be taught and encouraged to set up, is that of power over material. Every child makes sand castles, mud-pies, paper boats, and he or she should go on to work in clay, wood, brass, iron, leather, dress-stuffs, food-stuffs, furnishing-stuffs. He should be able to *make* with his hands and should take delight in making.

**Intimacy with Animals.**—A fourth relation is to the dumb creation; a relation of intelligent comprehension as well as of kindness. Why should not each of us be on friendly terms with the 'inmates of his house and garden'? Every child longs for intimacy with the creatures about him; and—

> "He prayeth best, who loveth best
> All things both great and small;
> For the dear God who loveth us,
> He made and loveth all."

**The Great Human Relationships.**—Perhaps the main part of a child's education should be concerned with the great human relationships, relationships of love and service, of authority and obedience, of reverence and pity and neighbourly kindness; relationships to kin and friend and neighbour, to 'cause' and country and kind, to the past and the present. History, literature, archæology, art, languages, whether ancient or modern, travel and tales of travel; all of these are in one way or other the record or the expression of persons; and we who are persons are interested in all persons, for we are all one flesh, and we are all of one spirit, and whatever any of us does or suffers is interesting to the rest. If we will approach them with living thought, living books, if we will only awaken in them the sense of personal relation, there are thousands of boys and girls to-day capable of becoming apostles, saviours, great orient-alists who will draw the East and the West together, great archæologists who will make the past alive for us and make us aware in our souls of men who lived thousands of years ago.

**The Awakening Idea.**—It rests with us to give the awakening idea and then to form the habit of thought and of life. Here is an example of what a youth could do. " Young Rawlinson had " (I quote from the *Academy*) "from the outset of his career, a taste for the history and antiquities of Persia, a leaning which he himself attributed to his conversa-tions with Sir John Malcolm on his first passage to India; and when with the Shah's army he chanced to be quartered at Kirmanshah, in Persian Kurdistan. Close to this stands the Rock of Behistun, bearing on its face a trilingual inscription which we now know to be due to Darius Hystaspes, the restorer of Cyrus' Empire. The cuneiform or wedge-shaped letters in which it is written had long baffled all attempts to decipher them. Rawlinson contrived, at the risk of life and limb, to climb the almost inaccessible face of the rock and to copy the easiest of the three versions of the inscription. A prolonged study of it enabled him to pronounce it to be in the Persian language, and, two years later, he succeeded in discovering the system by which the Persian words were reproduced in cuneiform characters." What is the result? "We can now produce the chronicles of empires, more highly-organised than was ever any Greek state, going back to dates millennia before that which our fathers used to assign to the earliest appearance of man upon the earth. The changes of thought consequent upon these discoveries are incalculable;" and all are more or less due to Rawlinson's climb up the face of the Behistun Rock, which again was due to the awakening of an idea by his conversation with Sir John Malcolm.

**Human Intelligence limited to Human Interests.**—We are not all Henry Rawlinsons, but there seems good reason to believe that *the limit to human intelligence arises largely from the limit to human interests*, that is, from the failure to establish personal relations on a wide scale with the persons who make up humanity,—relations of love, duty, responsibility, and, above all, of interest, *living* interest, with the near and the far-off, in time and in place. We hammer away for a dozen years at one or two languages, ancient or modern, and rarely know them very well at the end of that time, but directly they become to us the languages of persons whom we are aching to get at and can only do so through the medium of their own tongues, there seems no reason why many of us should not be like the late Sir Richard Burton, able to talk in almost any known tongue.

**The Full Human Life.**—I think we should have a great educational revolution once we ceased to regard ourselves as assortments of so-called faculties and realised ourselves as persons whose great business it is to ge int touch with other persons of all sorts and conditions, of all countries and climes, of all times, past and present. History would become entrancing, literature, a magic mirror for the discovery of other minds, the study of sociology, a duty and a delight. We should tend to become responsive and wise, humble and reverent, recognising the duties and the joys of the full human life. We cannot, of course, overtake such a programme of work, but we can keep it in view ; and, I suppose, every life is moulded upon its ideal. We talk of lost ideals, but perhaps they are not lost, only changed ; when our ideal for ourselves and for our children becomes limited to prosperity and comfort, we get these, very likely, for ourselves and for them, but we get no more.

**Duty not within the Scope of Present-day Psychology.**—The psychology of the hour has had a curious effect upon the sense of duty. Persons who are no more than a ' state of consciousness ' cannot be expected to take up moral responsibilities, except such as appeal to them at the moment. Duty, in the sense of relations imposed by authority and *due* to our fellows, does not fall within the scope of present-day psychology. It would be interesting to know how many children of about ten years of age can say the Ten Commandments, and those most clear interpretations of them which children are taught to call ' my duty towards God and my duty towards my neighbour ' ; or, if they are not members of the Church of England, whatever explanation their own Church offers of the law containing the whole duty of man. With the Ten Commandments as a basis, children used to get a fairly thorough ethical teaching from the Bible. They knew St Paul's mandates :— ' Love the brethren,' ' Fear God,' ' Honour the King,'

'Honour all men,' 'Study to be quiet.' They knew that thoughts of hatred and contempt were of the nature of murder. They knew what King Solomon said of the virtuous woman, of the sluggard, of the fool. Their knowledge was not confined to precepts; from history, sacred and profane, they were able to illustrate every text. We in England have not the wealth of moral teaching carved in wood and stone— so that the unlettered may read and learn—which some neighbouring countries rejoice in, but our teaching, until the present generation, has been systematic and thorough.

**Casual Ethical Teaching.**—I appeal to common experience as to whether this is now the case. We eschew for our children (and we often eschew wisely) all stories with a moral; their books must be amusing, and we ask little more; next after that, they must be literary, and then, perhaps, a little instructive. But we do not look for a moral impulse fitly given. It is not that we give no ethical teaching, but our teaching is casual. If we happen on a story of heroism or self-denial, we are glad to point the moral. But children rarely get now a distinct ethical system resting on the broad basis of the brotherhood of man. It is something for a child only to recite—'My duty towards my neighbour is to love him as myself,' and 'to do unto all men as I would that they should do unto me.' A great many fine things are said to-day about the brotherhood of man and the solidarity of the race, but I think we shall look in vain in modern writings for a sentence which goes to the root of the matter as does this authoritative code of duty.

**The Moral Relation of Person to Person.**—If we receive it, that the whole of education consists in the establishment of relations, then, the relations with our fellow-beings must be of the first importance; and all associations formed upon any basis except that of 'my duty towards my neighbour,'—as upon sympathy in art or literature, for example,—are apt to degenerate into sentimental bonds; and the power of original thought appears curiously to depart with that of moral insight. If you ask, 'But how are we to get a scheme of ethical teaching for our children?' I really do not know, if we choose to forego the Ten Commandments and the old-fashioned teaching of exposition and example founded upon them.   There are a thousand supplementary ways of giving such teaching; but these are apt to be casual and little binding if they do not rest upon the solid foundation of *duty* imposed upon us by God, and *due* to each other, whether we will or no. This moral relation of person to person underlies all other relations.   We owe it to the past to use its gains worthily and to advance from the point at which it left off.   We owe it to the future to prepare a generation better than ourselves.   We owe it to the present to *live*, to live with all expansion of heart and soul, all reaching out of our personality towards those relations appointed for us.

**The sense of what is due from us does not come by Nature.**—We owe knowledge to the ignorant, comfort to the distressed, healing to the sick, reverence, courtesy and kindness to all men, especially to those with whom we are connected by ties of family or neighbourhood; and the sense of these dues does not come by nature.   We all know the vapid young man and the vapid young woman who care for none of these things; but do we always ask ourselves—why? and whether there are not many children to-day growing up in good homes as untrained in their moral relations as are these young people whom we despise and blame, perhaps more than they deserve, for have they not been neglected children?

**Relations of Oneself with Oneself.**—Another preparation for his relations in life which we owe to a young person is, that he should be made familiar with such a working system of psychology or philosophy, whichever one likes to call it, as shall help him to conduct his relations with himself and with other people. The world is not ripe, perhaps, for a *bonâ fide* science of life, but we are unhappily more modest than the ancients, who made good use of what they had, and turned out a Marcus Aurelius, an Epictetus, a Socrates. Neither did they think that their youth were furnished for life without instruction in philosophy. Modern scientists have added a great deal to the sum of available knowledge which should bear on the conduct of those relations of oneself with oneself which are implied in the terms, self-management, self-control, self-respect, self-love, self-help, self-abnegation, and so on. This knowledge is the more important because our power to conduct our relations with other people depends upon our power of conducting our relations with ourselves. Every man carries in his own person the key to human nature, and, in proportion as we are able to use this key, we shall be tolerant, gentle, helpful, wise and reverent. The person who has 'given up expecting anything' of servants or of dependents, of employés, or of working people, proclaims his ignorance of those springs of conduct common to us all.

I think we may really take a little credit to ourselves as a Society[1] for an advance in this direction. Most people associated with us know something of the treatment of sensations, the direction of the will, the treatment of temper, the psychology of attention, the desires and affections which are the springs of conduct, and other practical matters concerned with the management of one's life. We hear of people who use that fine old nursery plan expressed in 'change your thoughts' with method and success in the case of cross, or even delirious, or morbid patients. We (of the Parents' Union) feel as if we had a tool in our hands and knew how to set to work. The principle, anyhow, we perceive to be right, and, if we blunder in its application, we try again, whether for ourselves or for our children. We know that 'one custom overcometh another,' and that one idea supplants another. We do not give up a child to be selfish, or greedy, or lazy. These are cases for treatment ; and a child who has been cured by his mother of some such blemish will not be slow to believe when he grows up in the possibility of reform for others, and in the use of simple, practical means.

Intimacy with Persons of all Classes.— Sociology is a long word, but it implies a practical relation with other people which children should begin to get, and it is a kind of knowledge they are very ready for. The carpenter, the gardener, the baker, the candlestick maker, are all delightful persons ; and it is surprising how much a child at the seaside will get to know about boats and sails and fishermen's lives that will pass by his unobservant elders. Most working men are on their honour with

[1] The Parents' National Educational Union.

children, and every craftsman is a valuable acquaintance to a child. Later, when his working neighbours
come before him in the shape of 'causes' and
'questions,' he will see the men and their crafts
behind the veil of words ; and in his ' Book of Trades,'
a *Who's Who* for the million, he will look out for the
heading *Recreation*, for shoemaker, tailor, factory-
hand, as well as for the distinguished author and the
member of Parliament. There is nothing like early
intimacy for helping one to know people. That is
why what the tub-orator calls 'the bloated aristocrat'
knows how to get on with everybody; he has been
intimate with all sorts and conditions of men since
his babyhood.

**Fitness as Citizens.**—The value of self-managed
clubs and committees, debating societies, etc., for
young people, is becoming more and more fully
recognised. Organising capacity, business habits,
and some power of public speaking, should be a part
of our fitness as citizens. To secure the power of
speaking, I think it would be well if the habit of
narration were more encouraged, in place of written
composition. On the whole, it is more useful to be
able to speak than to write, and the man or woman
who is able to do the former can generally do the
latter.

**Relations with each other as Human Beings.**
—But the subject of our relations with each other
as human beings is inexhaustible, and I can do no
more than indicate a point here and there, and state
again my conviction that a system of education
should have for its aim, not the mastery of certain
'subjects,' but the establishment of these relations
in as many directions as circumstances will allow.

**Relation to Almighty God.**—I have set before the reader the proposition that a human being comes into the world, not to develop his faculties nor to acquire knowledge, nor even to earn his living, but to establish certain relations; which relations are to him the means of immeasurable expansion and fulness of living. We have touched upon two groups of these relations—his relations to the universe of matter and to the world of men. To complete his education, I think there is but one more relation to be considered—his relation to Almighty God. How many children are to-day taught to say at their mother's knee, to learn from day to day and from hour to hour, in all its fulness of meaning—' My duty towards God is to believe in Him, to fear Him, and to love Him with all my heart, with all my mind, with all my soul, and with all my strength; to worship Him, to give Him thanks, to put my whole trust in Him, to call upon Him, to honour His holy name and His word, and to serve Him truly all the days of my life'? Whether children are taught their duty towards God in these or other words matters little; but few of us will venture to say that, in this short summary, more is demanded than it is our bounden duty and service to yield. But I fear that many children grow up untaught in these matters. The idea of *duty* is not wrought into the very texture of their souls; and *duty* to Him who is invisible, which should be the very foundation of life, is least taught of all. I do not say that children are allowed to grow up without religious sentiments and religious emotions, and that they do not say quaint and surprising things, showing that they have an insight of their own into the higher life.

**Sentiment is not Duty.**—But duty and sentiment are two things. Sentiment is optional; and young people grow up to think that they *may* believe in God, *may* fear God, *may* love God in a measure—but that they *must* do these things, that there is no choice at all about the love and service of God, that it is their duty, that which they *owe*, to love Him 'with all their heart, with all their mind, with all their soul, with all their strength,' these things are seldom taught and understood as they should be. Even where our sentiment is warm, our religious notions are lax; and children, the children of good, religious parents, grow up without that intimate, ever-open, ever-cordial, ever-corresponding relation with Almighty God, which is the very fulfilment of life; which, whoso hath, hath eternal life; which, whoso hath not, is, like Coleridge's 'lovely Lady Geraldine,' ice-cold and dead at heart, however much he may labour for the free course of all other relations.

> " I want,—am made for,—and must have a God,
> Ere I can be aught, do aught ;—no mere Name
> Want,—but the True Thing, with what proves its truth,—
> To wit, a relation from that Thing to me,
> Touching from head to foot :—which Touch I feel,
> And with it take the rest, this Life of ours ! "
> —*Browning.*

# CHAPTER IX

## A GREAT EDUCATIONALIST

### (*A REVIEW*)

**We look to Germany for Educational Reform.**—We in England require, every now and then, to pull ourselves together, and to ask what they are doing on the Continent in the way of education. We still hark back to the older German educational reformers. We may not know much of Comenius, Basedow, Ratich; we do know something of Pestalozzi and Froebel; but how much do we know of the thought of Johann Friedrich Herbart, the lineal successor of these, who has largely displaced his predecessors in the field of Pedagogics?

**Herbartian Thought the most advanced on the Continent.**—How entirely German educators work upon Herbart, and Herbart only, is proved by the existence of a Herbartian educational literature greatly more extensive than the whole of our English educational literature put together.

A little volume on the *Outlines of Pedagogics*,[1] by Professor W. Rein, of the University of Jena, is offered to us by the translators, C. C. and Ida J. Van Liew, as a brief introduction to the study of Herbart

[1] Sonnenschein & Co. ; 3s.

and his school, the author making due allowance for the advances that have been made in the decades that have elapsed since Herbart's death.

As Herbart and his interpreters represent the most advanced school of educational thought on the Continent, it will, perhaps, be interesting to the reader to make a slight comparison between the educational philosophy I am trying to set forth, and the school of thought which exercises such immense influence in Germany.

**Comparison with P.N.E.U. Thought.**—One of the most characteristic features of Herbart's thinking, and that feature of it which constitutes a new school of educational thought, is, that he rejects the notion of separate mental faculties. The earlier reformers, notably Pestalozzi and Froebel, divide the faculties up with something of the precision of a phrenologist, and a chief business of education is, according to them, ' to develop the faculties.'

**The Development of the Faculties.**—There is a certain pleasing neatness in this idea which is very attractive. We want to know, definitely, what we have to do. Why, develop the perceptive faculties here, with the conceptive there, the judgment in this lesson, the affections in the other, until you have covered the whole ground, giving each so-called faculty its due share of developmental exercise! But, say the followers of Herbart, we have changed all that. The mind, like Wordsworth's cloud, moves altogether when it moves at all.

**We, like Herbart, discard the 'Faculties.'**— Now this appears to be but a slight fundamental difference, but it is one upon the recognition of which education changes front. The whole system of beauti-

fully organised lessons, whose object is to develop
this or that faculty, is called in question ; for the *raison
d'être* of specialised intellectual gymnastics is gone
when we no longer recognise particular 'muscles' of
the mind to be developed.   The aim of education must
be something quite other, and, if the aim is other, the
methods must be altered, for what is method but *a
way to an end* ?   So far we are entirely with Herbart ;
we do not believe in the 'faculties' ; therefore we do
not believe in the 'development of the faculties' ;
therefore we do not regard lessons as instruments for
this 'development' : in fact, our whole method of
procedure is altered.

**Pervasiveness of Dominant Ideas.**—Again, we
are with the philosopher in his recognition of the
force of an idea, and especially of those ideas which
are, as we phrase it, in the air at any given moment.
" Both the circle of the family and that of social intercourse are subjected to forces that are active in the
entire social body, and that penetrate the entire
atmosphere of human life in invisible channels.   No
one knows whence these currents, these ideas arise ;
but they are there.   They influence the moods, the
aspirations, and the inclinations of humanity, and no
one, however powerful, can withdraw himself from their
effects ; no sovereign's command makes its way into
their depths.   They are often born of a genius to be
seized upon by the multitude that soon forgets their
author ; then the power of the thought that has thus
become active in the masses again impels the
individual to energetic resolutions : in this manner it
is constantly describing a remarkable circle.   Originating with those that are highly gifted, these thoughts
permeate all society, reaching, in fact, not only its

adult members, but also through these its youth, and appearing again in other highly gifted individuals in whom they will perhaps have been elevated to a definite form.

"Whether the power of these dominant ideas is greater in the individual, or in the body of individuals as a whole, is a matter of indifference here. Be that as it may, it cannot be denied that their effect upon the one is manifested in a reciprocal action upon the other, and that their influence upon the younger generation is indisputable."

The Zeitgeist.—We entirely agree that no one can escape the influence of this Zeitgeist, and that the Zeitgeist is, in fact, one of the most powerful of the occult educational influences, and one which parents and all who have the training of children will do well to reckon with in the adjustment of their work.

The Child's Schoolmasters. — Nature, family, social intercourse, this Zeitgeist, the Church and the State, thus Professor Rein, as interpreting Herbart, sums up the schoolmasters under whose influences every child grows up; a suggestive enumeration we should do well to consider. '*Erziehung ist Sache der Familien; von da geht sie aus und dahin kehrt sie grössenteils zurück*,' says Herbart. He considers, as do we, that by far the most valuable part of education is carried on in the family, because of the union of all the members under a common parentage, of the feeling of dependence upon a head, of the very intimate knowledge to be gained of the younger members.

A Noble Piety.—"The members of the family look confidently to the head ; and this sense of dependence favours, at the same time, the proper reception of that which is dearest to mankind, namely, the religious feeling. If the life of the family is permeated by a noble piety, a sincere religious faith will take root in the hearts of the children. Faithful devotion to the guide of the youth also calls forth faithful devotion to Him who controls human destinies —a thought which Herbart expresses so beautifully in the words—' To the child, the family should be the symbol of the order in the world ; from the parents one should derive by idealisation the characteristics of the deity.' "

A Mediæval Conception of Education.—This idea of all education springing from and resting upon our relation to Almighty God is one which we have ever laboured to enforce. We take a very distinct stand upon this point. We do not merely give a *religious* education, because that would seem to imply the possibility of some other education, a secular education, for example. But we hold that all education is divine, that every good gift of knowledge and insight comes from above, that the Lord the Holy Spirit is the supreme educator of mankind, and that the culmination of all education (which may, at the same time, be reached by a little child) is that personal knowledge of and intimacy with God in which our being finds its fullest perfection. We hold, in fact, that great conception of education held by the mediæval Church, as pictured upon the walls of the Spanish chapel in Florence. Here we have represented the descent of the Holy Ghost upon the Twelve, and directly under them, fully under the illuminating rays, are the noble figures of the seven liberal arts, Grammar, Rhetoric, Logic, Music, Astronomy, Geometry, Arithmetic, and under these again the men who received and expressed, so far as the artist knew, the initial idea in each of these subjects; such men as Pythagoras, Zoroaster, Euclid, whom *we* might call pagans, but whom the earlier Church recognised as divinely taught and illuminated.

**The Family Principle.**—Here follows a passage which we do more than endorse, for it contains the very *raison d'être* of our society. " The education of the children will always remain the holiest and highest of all family duties. The welfare, civilisation, and culture of a people depend essentially upon the degree of success that attends the education in the homes. The family principle is the point at which both the religious and educational life of a people centres, and about which it revolves. It is a force in comparison with which every sovereign's command appears powerless."

By the way, we are inclined to think that Dr Rein's mention of Rousseau is a little misleading. It is true that in *Emil* the parents are supplanted, but, notwithstanding that fact, perhaps no other educationalist has done so much to awaken parents to their great work as educators. After investigating the conditions of home training, Dr Rein proceeds to a discussion of schools (*a*) as they exist in Germany; (*b*) as they exist in his own ideal, a discussion which should be most interesting to parents.

**Uncertainty as to the Purpose of Education.**— Teleology, *i.e.* the theory of the purpose of education, falls next under discussion in an extremely instructive chapter. It is well we should know the vast uncertainty which exists on this fundamental point. As a matter of fact, few of us know definitely what we propose to ourselves in the education of our children. We do not know what it is possible to effect, and, as a man does not usually compass more than he aims at, the results of our education are very inadequate and unsatisfactory.

Some Attempts to fix the Purpose of Education. —" Shall the educator follow Rousseau and educate a man of nature in the midst of civilised men? In so doing, as Herbart has shown, we should simply repeat from the beginning the entire series of evils that have already been surmounted. Or shall we turn to Locke and prepare the pupil for the world which is customarily in league with worldlings? We should then arrive at the standpoint of Basedow, and aim to educate the pupil so that he would become a truly useful member of human society. Of course we should always be harassed with the secret doubt as to whether this is the ideal purpose after all, and whether we are not at times directly enjoined to place the pupil at variance with the usage and customary dealings of the world. If we reflect that an endless career is open to man for his improvement, we realise that only that education, whose aims are always the highest, can hope to reach the lofty goals that mark this career.

" Therefore an ideal aim must be present in the mind of the educator. Possibly he can obtain information and help from Pestalozzi, whose nature evinced such ideal tendencies. Pestalozzi wished the welfare of mankind to be sought in the harmonious cultivation of *all* powers. If one only knew what is to be understood by a multiplicity of mental powers, and what is meant by the *harmony* of various powers. These phrases sound very attractive, but give little satisfaction. The purely *formal* aims of education will appeal just as little to the educator: 'Educate the pupil to independence'; or, 'Educate the pupil to be his own educator'; or, 'Educate the pupil so that "it" will become better than "its" educator.' (*Hermann and Dorothea*, Hector and Astyanax in the *Iliad*.) Such and similar attempts to fix the purpose of education are abundant in the history of pedagogy; but they do not bring us nearer the goal. In their formal character they do not say, for example, of what kind the independence shall be, what content it shall have, what aims it shall have in view, or in what directions its course shall lie. For the pupil that has become independent can use his freedom rightly for good just as well as misuse it for evil."

**Herbart's Theory, Ethical.** — Herbart's own theory of education, so far as we may venture to formulate it, is strictly ethical as opposed to intellectual, that is, the development and sustenance of the intellect is of secondary importance to the educator for two reasons: character building is the matter of first importance to human beings; and this because, (*a*) train character and intellectual 'development' largely takes care of itself, and (*b*) the lessons designed for intellectual culture have high ethical value, whether stimulating or disciplinary. This is familiar ground to us: we too have taught, in season and out of season, that the formation of character is the aim of the educator. So far, we are at one with the philosopher; but, may we venture to say it? we have arrived, through the study of Physiology, at the definiteness of aim which he desires but does not reach.

**Obscurity of Psychology.** — We must appeal, he says, to Psychology, but then, he adds, "of course we cannot expect a concordant answer from all psychologists; and in view of the obscurity which still prevails in this sphere, the different views as to the nature of the human soul and the extraordinary difficulty with which the empirical method of investigation meets, an absolutely indubitable explanation can hardly be expected."

**Two Luminous Principles.**—This is doubtless true of Psychology alone, but of Psychology illuminated by Physiology we have another tale to tell. It is the study of that border-land betwixt mind and matter, the brain, which yields the richest results to the educator. For the brain is the seat of habit : the culture of habit is, to a certain extent, physical culture : the discipline of habit is at least a third part of the great whole which we call education, and here we feel that the physical science of to-day has placed us far in advance of the philosopher of fifty years ago. We hold with him entirely as to the importance of great formative ideas in the education of children, but we add to our ideas, habits, and we labour to form habits upon a physical basis. Character is the result not merely of the great ideas which are given to us, but of the habits which we labour to form *upon those ideas.* We recognise both principles, and the result is a wide range of possibilities in education, practical methods, and a definite aim. We labour to produce a human being at his best physically, mentally, morally, and spiritually, with the enthusiasms of religion, of the good life, of nature, knowledge, art, and manual work ; and we do *not* labour in the dark.

I have ventured to indicate in a former chapter what appears to me the root-defect of the educational philosophy of this great thinker—that it tends to eliminate personality, and therefore leads to curious

futilities in teaching.   It is therefore the more gratifying to observe that certain fundamental ideas, long
the property of the world, which we have embraced
in our scheme of thought, appealed with equal force
to so great and original a thinker as Herbart.

## CHAPTER X

### SOME UNCONSIDERED ASPECTS OF PHYSICAL TRAINING

PERHAPS never since the days of the Olympian games has more attention been paid to physical culture than it receives in England to-day. But possibly this physical cult suffers from the want of unity and sanctity of purpose which nullifies to a considerable extent most of our educational efforts.

Does our Physical Culture make Heroes?—We want to turn out 'a fine animal,' a man or woman with a fine physique and in good condition, and we get what we lay ourselves out for. The development, in women especially, within the last twenty years, is amazing. I heard it remarked the other day that the stiff little brocaded dresses of our great-grandmothers, which are kept here and there, appear to have belonged to little women, while the grandmothers we are rearing to-day promise to be daughters of Anak. So far, so good. All the same, it is question-able whether we are making heroes; and this was the object of physical culture among the early Greeks, anyway. Men must be heroes, or how could they fulfil the heavy tasks laid upon them by the gods? Heroes are not made in a day; therefore, the boy

was trained from his infancy in heroic exercises, and
the girl brought up to be the mother of heroes.
Flashes of the heroic temper seem to remain to this
day in that little country with a great history. 'Your
son has behaved like a hero,' was said to the mother
of a soldier who fell some years ago. 'That's what
I bore him for,' was the reply. Englishmen, too,
can die, but it is not so certain that they can live,
like heroes. The object of the fine physical culture
that English youths and maidens receive is, too
often, the poor and narrow one that they may get
the most, especially the most of physical enjoyment, out of life; and so young people train their
bodies to hardships, and pamper them with ease
and self-indulgence, by turns, the one and the other
being for their own pleasure; the pampering being
the more delightful after the period of training, the
training itself rather a pleasant change from the
softness of pampering.

**A Serviceable Body, the End of Physical
Culture.**—Some of our young people prefer to endure
hardness all the time, and go off in the Berserker
spirit to find adventures; but even this is not the best
that might be done. The object of athletics and
gymnastics should be kept steadily to the front;
enjoyment is good by the way, but is not the end;
the end is the preparation of a body, available from
crown to toe, for whatever behest 'the gods' may lay
upon us. It is a curious thing that we, in the full
light of Revelation, have a less idea of vocation and
of preparation for that vocation than had nations of
the Old World with their 'few, faint and feeble' rays
of illumination as to the meaning and purpose of life.
'Ye *are* your own,' is perhaps the unspoken thought

of most young persons—your own, and free to do what you like with your own.  Therefore, excess in sports, excess in easy-going pleasure, excess in study, excess in desultory reading, excess of carelessness in regard to health, any excess that we have a mind to, is lawful to us if only it is expedient.  This loose morality with regard to our physical debts, without touching actual vice, which is probably on the decline, is the reason why the world does not get all that it should out of splendid material.

**Ye are not Your Own.**—But if children are brought up from the first with this magnet—'Ye are *not* your own'; the divine Author of your being has given you life, and a body finely adapted for His service; He gives you the work of preserving this body in health, nourishing it in strength, and training it in fitness for whatever special work He may give you to do in His world,—why, young people themselves would readily embrace a more Spartan regimen; they would desire to be available, and physical transgressions and excesses, however innocent they seem, would be self-condemned by the person who felt that he was trifling with a trust.

It would be good work to keep to the front this idea of living under authority, training under authority, serving under authority, a discipline of life readily self-embraced by children, in whom the heroic impulse is always strong.  We would not reduce the pleasures of childhood and youth by an iota ; rather we would increase them, for the disciplined life has more power of fresh enjoyment than is given to the unrestrained. Neither is it lawful for parents to impose any un-necessary rigours upon their children; this was the error of the eighteenth century and of the early decades of our own age, when hunger, cold, and denial, which was by no means self-denial, were supposed wholesome for children. All we claim is that every young person shall be brought up under the sense of *authority* in the government, management, and training of his body. The sense that health is a duty, and that any trifling with health, whether vicious or careless, is really of the nature of suicide, springs from this view—that life is held in trust from a supreme Authority.

Direct teaching or reading on such subjects as the following might be profitable to parents and teachers on the one hand and to boys and girls on the other :—

Greek games and Greek heroes.

How a child may be trained to his physical responsibilities.

The vocation of the body.

'Innocent' excesses.

Unlawful and lawful home discipline.

The heroic impulse.

The training afforded by games.

Athletics, their use and abuse.

Parental authority in physical matters.

The right uses of self-denial.

The government, management, and training of the body.

The duty of health.

**Use of Habit in Physical Training.**—It is well that a child should be taught to keep under his body and bring it into subjection, first, to the authority of his parents and, later, to the authority of his own will ; and always, because no less than this is due, to the divine Authority in whom he has his being. But to bring ourselves under authority at all times would

require a constantly repeated effort of thought and
will which would make life too laborious. Authority
must be sustained by habit. We all know something
of the genesis of a habit, and most of us recognise its
physical basis, *i.e.* that frequently-repeated thoughts
or acts leave some sort of register in the brain tissue
which tends to make the repetition of such thoughts,
at first easy, and at last automatic. In all matters
of physical exercise it is obvious to us that—do a
thing a hundred times and it becomes easy, do
a thing a thousand times and it becomes mechanical,
as easy to do as not. This principle is abundantly
applied in cricket, boating, golf, cycling, all the
labours we delight in. But there is an outfit of half-
physical, half-moral habits of life which the playing-
field tends to form, but which are apt to be put on
ard off with the flannels if they are not steadily and
regularly practised in the home life also. These are
the habitudes which it is the part of parents to give
their children, and, indeed, they do form part of the
training of all well brought-up young people ; but it is
well not to lose sight of this part of our work.

Self-restraint.—Self-restraint in indulgences is a
habit which most educated mothers form with care.
Children are well and agreeably fed, and they do not
hanker after a bit of this and a taste of the other.
Whether one or two sweetmeats a day are allowed,
or whether they go without any, well brought-up
children do not seem to mind. It is the children of
cottage homes who, even when they are comfortably
fed and clothed, keep the animal instinct of basking
in the heat of the fire. But there is perhaps danger
lest the habits of the nursery and schoolroom should
lapse in the case of older boys and girls. It is easy

to get into the way of lounging in an arm-chair with a novel in the intervals between engagements which are, in fact, amusements. This sort of thing was a matter of conscience with an older generation ; lethargic, self-indulgent intervals were not allowed. When people were not amusing themselves health-fully, they were occupying themselves profitably ; and, little as we may think of the crewel-work our grand-mothers have left behind, it was better for them morally and physically than the relaxed muscles and mind of the novel and the lounge. No doubt the bodily fatigue which follows our more active exercises has something to say in the matter, but it is a grave question whether bodily exercises of any kind should be so frequent and so excessive as to leave us without mental and moral vigour in the intervals.

Self-control. — Self-control in emergencies is another habit of the disciplined life in which a child should be trained from the first ; it is the outcome of a general habit of self-control. We all see how ice accidents, boat accidents, disasters by fire (like a late melancholy event in Paris), might be minimised in their effects if only one person present were under perfect self-control, which implies the power of organising and controlling others. But the habit of holding oneself well in hand, the being impervious to small annoyances, cheerful under small inconveniences, ready for action with what is called 'presence of mind' in all the little casualties of the hour—this is a habit which should be trained in the nursery. If children were sent into the world with this part of their panoply complete, we should no longer have the spectacle of the choleric Briton and of the nervous and fussy British lady at every foreign *doûane* ;

people would not jostle for the best places at a public
function ; the mistresses of houses would not be
fretted and worn out by the misdoings of their maids ;
the thousand little sorenesses of social life would be
soothed, if children were trained to bear little hurts
to body and mind without sign.  ' If you are vexed,
don't show it,' is usually quite safe teaching, because
every kind of fretfulness, impatience, resentfulness,
and nervous irritability generally, grows with expression and passes away under self-control.  It is worth
while to remember that the physical signs promote
the mental state just as much as the mental state
causes the physical signs.

Self-discipline.—The discipline of habit is never
complete until it becomes self-discipline in habits.    It
is not a trifle that even the nursery child messes his
feeder, spills his milk, breaks his playthings, dawdles
about his small efforts.   The well-trained child delights
to bring himself into good habits in these respects.
He knows that to be cleanly, neat, prompt, orderly,
is so much towards making a man of him, and man
and hero are in his thought synonymous terms.
Supposing that good habits have not been set up at
home, parents look to school life to supply the
omission; but the habits practised in school and
relaxed at home, because 'it's holidays now, you
know,' do not really become habits of the life.

Local Habits. — The fact that habits have a
tendency to become local, that in one house a child
will be neat, prompt, diligent; in another untidy,
dawdling, and idle, points to the necessity for self-
discipline on the part of even a young child.

> " Self-reverence, self-knowledge, self-control,
> These three alone lead life to sovereign power."

This subject of training in becoming habits is so well understood amongst us that I need only add that such habits are not fully formed so long as supervision is necessary. At first, a child wants the support of constant supervision, but, by degrees, he is left to do the thing he ought of his own accord. Habits of behaviour, habits of deportment, habits of address, tones of voice, etc., all the habits of a gentleman-like bearing and a kind and courteous manner, fall under this head of self-discipline in bodily habits.

> " When first thou camest—such a courtesy
> Spake through the limbs and in the voice—I knew
> For one of those who eat in Arthur's hall."

Alertness.—Many a good man and woman thinks regretfully of the opportunities in life they have let slip through a certain physical inertness. They missed the chance of doing some little service, or some piece of courtesy, because they did not see in time. It is well to bring up children to think it is rather a sad failure if they miss a chance of going a message, opening a door, carrying a parcel, any small act of service that presents itself. They should be taught to be equally alert to seize opportunities of getting knowledge ; it is the nature of children to regard each grown-up person they meet as a fount of knowledge on some particular subject; let their training keep up the habit of eager inquiry. Success in life depends largely upon the cultivation of alertness to seize opportunities, and this is largely a physical habit. We all know how opportunity is imaged — a figure flying past so rapidly that there is no means of catching him but,

in advance, by the forelock which overhangs his
brow.

Quick Perception.—Closely connected with that
of alertness is the habit of quick perception as to all
that is to be seen, heard, felt, tasted, smelt in a world
which gives illimitable information through our five
gateways of knowledge.    Mr Grant, in his most
interesting studies of Neapolitan character, describes
the training of a young Camorrist (the Camorra is
a dangerous political faction ; and, ill as we may
think of the ends of such training, the means are
well worth recording).    " The great object of this
part of his training was to teach him to observe
habitually with minuteness and accuracy, and it was
conducted in something like the following manner.
When walking through the city the Camorrist would
suddenly pause and ask, ' How was the woman
dressed who sat at the door of the fourth house in
the last street ?' or, ' What were the two men talking
about whom we met at the corner of the last street
but three ?' or, ' Where was cab 234 ordered to drive
to ?' or perhaps it would be, ' What is the height
of that house and the breadth of its upper window ?'
or, ' Where does that man live ?'"    This habit, again
largely a physical habit, of quick perception has
been dwelt upon in other aspects.    All that now need
be urged is that the quickness of observation natural
to a child should not be relied upon; in time, and
especially as school studies press upon him, his early
quickness deserts the boy, but the trained habit of
seeing all that is to be seen, hearing all that is to be
heard, remains through life.    I have not space to go
further into these habitudes of body, which become
also, mental and moral habitudes, but perhaps reading

and reflection and direct teaching on such subjects
as the following would be useful:—

Self-control in emergencies.

Self-restraint in indulgences.

Self-discipline in habits.

Alertness to seize opportunities.

Promptness and vigour in bodily exercises.

Quick perception as to that which is to be seen,
heard, felt, tasted, smelt.

Stimulating Ideas.—A habit becomes morally
binding in proportion to the inspiring power of the
*idea* which underlies it. When I was a child I used
to have a book full of moral aphorisms from the
Greek and Latin classics, translated. These fine rolling
sentences, full of matter, made, I recollect, a great
impression on me; and one can understand that the
Greek or Roman boy, brought up on this strong
meat, developed virtues in regard to which we are a
little slack. In like manner the early Church per-
sonified and typified in a thousand ways the three
evangelical and four cardinal virtues and the opposing
seven deadly sins. We shall have to revive this kind
of teaching if we would have children undertake the
labour of the discipline of habit, a discipline that we
can do no more than initiate.

Fortitude.—Touch the right spring and children
are capable of an amazing amount of steady effort.
I know a little boy of ten who set himself the task
of a solitary race of three miles every day in the hot
summer holidays because he was to compete in a
race when he went back to school; and this, not
because he cared much about sports, but because his
eldest brother had always distinguished himself in
them, and he must do the same. When we think

how little power we have to do the tiresome things
we set ourselves to do every day, we appreciate the
self-compelling power a child can use, given a strong
enough impulse.  The long name, Fortitude, would
have its effect on the little boy in the dentist's hands.
It is good to know that it is a manly and knightly
virtue to be strong to bear pain and inconvenience
without making any sign.  The story of the Spartan
boy and the fox will still wake an echo ; and the
girl who finds it a fine thing to endure hardness will
not make a fuss about her physical sensations.  She
will be pained for the want of fortitude which called
forth the reproof, ' Could ye not watch with me one
hour ? ' and will brace herself to bear, that she may
be able to serve.  Portia, the wife of Brutus, gave a
fair test of her quality when she wounded her tender
flesh to prove that she was fit to share her husband's
counsels.

Service.—Service is another knightly quality which
a child should be nerved for by heroic examples until
he grudges to let slip an opportunity.

Courage.—Courage, too, should be something more
than the impulse of the moment ; it is a natural fire
to be fed by heroic example and by the teaching that
the thing to be done is always of more consequence
than the doer.

Prudence.—Prudence, too, is a condition of knightly
service, whether to our kind or to our kin, and courage
without prudence is recklessness ; but, in this connection
of bodily service, prudence is largely concerned with
the duty of health.  I have heard of a boy at a school
where a good deal of hygienic teaching was given,
getting quite anxious and overcharged with the care
of his own health.  This meaner kind of caution is

not worthy to be called prudence, which should regard every physical power as a means of service and of conflict, and should think it a shame by any fool-hardiness to make any part of the body unable for its due service.

**Chastity.**—For Chastity we can have no impulse higher than ' Your bodies are the temples of the Holy Ghost'; but how inadequately do we present the thought! The inspiring ideas which should sustain all physical culture and training are very numerous, and teaching on such subjects as Chastity, Fortitude, Courage, Constancy, Prudence, Temperance, with the consideration of heroic examples, should strengthen the hands of parents and teachers for the better physical culture of their charges. Parents would do well to see to it that they turn out their children fit for service, not only by observing the necessary hygienic conditions, but by bringing their bodies under rule, training them in habits and inspiring them with the ideas of knightly service.

# CHAPTER XI

## SOME UNCONSIDERED ASPECTS OF INTELLECTUAL TRAINING

**We are Law-abiding in Matters Physical and Moral.**—We all recognise that we are under the reign of law so far as our bodies go. We know that 'put your finger in the fire and it will be burnt,' 'sit in a draught and you will catch cold,' 'live a vigorous and temperate life and health will be your reward.' That law attends our steps with its penalties and rewards in all matters physical we know very well. Some of us go further and have a personal sense of the Lawgiver in matters of sickness and health. In sickness especially we feel that God is dealing with us, and we endeavour to lay ourselves open to the lesson of the hour. In moral matters, too, we live under the law. We may forget ourselves, but we have compunctions and are aware of penalties.

**Not so in Matters Intellectual.**—But in matters intellectual we are disposed to stand upon our rights. Here we recognise no authority, abide by no law. Every man is free to his own opinion, however casually formed. Every man kindles his own 'lights,' and thinks that no more is expected of him than to live up to those lights. In fact our attitude with regard to our own intellectual processes leads to that disturbing sense of duality which causes the shipwreck of many lives, the distressing unrest of others, and the easy drifting of many more. Our thinking is not a separate thing from our conduct and our prayers, or even from our bodily well-being. Man is not several entities. He is one spirit (visibly expressed in bodily form), with many powers. He can work and love and pray and live righteously, but all these are the outcome of the manner of thoughts he thinks.

**Three Ultimate Facts—Not open to Question.** —There are two directions in which we commit intellectual offences against the law, and oppose ourselves to authority. In the first place we are disposed to regard everything by turns as an open question. We forget that there are three ultimate postulates which the thought of man can neither prove nor disprove, though in every age it has played uneasily about one or the other. God, Self, and the World, are the three fixed points of thought. The active Western mind, with each new evolution of scientific thought, finds again and again that there is no place for God in the world ; nay, so active and pleasant is the conception of self that an important school of philosophy has demonstrated that the real world is no more than a simulacrum, a mirage, as it were, projected from the conscious self. The more passive Eastern mind, is, on the contrary, inclined to regard selfhood as a passing phase in a state of absorption or reabsorption by deity. But when we learn to realise that—God is, Self is, the World is, with all that these existences imply, quite untouched by any thinking of ours, unprovable, and self-proven, —why, we are at once put into a more humble attitude of mind. We recognise that above us, about us, within us, there are 'more things . . . . than are dreamt of in our philosophy.' *We realise ourselves as persons, we have a local habitation, and we live and move and have our being in and under a supreme authority.* It is not well we should take it for granted that everybody knows these things. Perhaps we all have a hearsay acquaintance with, but very few of us have a realising knowledge of, these ultimate facts.

Limitations of Reason.—A second direction in which it is well that we should recognise our limitations is with regard to the nature and function of what we call our reason, and should, perhaps, describe more accurately as our power of reasoning. We all know how often we go to bed with a difficult question to settle. We say we will sleep upon it, and, in the morning, behold, the whole question has worked itself into shape : we see all its bearings and know just how to act. We are so accustomed to take wonders as matters of course, mere everyday events, that it does not occur to us to be surprised. We even say, the mind is clearer after sleep, regardless of the fact that we have no labour of thinking at all in the morning ; all comes straight of itself. When we come to think of it, most of our decisions arrive in this un-laborious way. We really cannot say that we have thought such and such a matter out : the decision comes to us in a flash, by an intuition, what you will. The subject is a large one, but all I care to stipulate for here is that children should be taught to know that much of our reasoning and so-called thinking is involuntary,—is as much a natural function as is the circulation of our blood, and that this very fact points to the limitations of reason.

**Reason brings Logical Proof of any Idea we Entertain.**—We, personally, might or might not be trusted to come to a morally right conclusion from any premise we entertain. But the reasoning power, acting in a more or less mechanical and involuntary manner, does not necessarily work towards the morally right conclusion. All that reason does for us is to prove, logically, any idea we choose to entertain. For example, as we have said, important schools (Eastern and Western) of philosophy entertain the idea that there is no actual real world independent of man's conception thereof. The logical proofs of this premise pour in upon their minds in such volume that a considerable literature exists to prove an idea which on the face of it appears absurd. We all know that, entertain a notion that a servant is dishonest, that a friend is false, that a dress is unbecoming, and some power within us, unconsciously to us, sets to work to collect evidence and bring irrefragable proof of the position we have chosen to take up. This is the history of wars and persecutions and family feuds all over the world. How necessary then that a child should be instructed to understand the limitations of his own reason, so that he will not confound logical demonstration with eternal truth, and will know that the important thing to him is the ideas he permits himself to entertain, and not by any means the conclusions he draws from these ideas, because these latter are self-evolved.

**A Third Fallacy—Intellect Man's Peculiar Sphere, Knowledge his Proper Discovery.**—A third fallacy which lies at the root of our thinking, and therefore, of our education, is, that while nature, morals, and theology may be more or less divine in

their origin and relations, not only is intellect man's
proper and peculiar sphere, but knowledge, — the
knowledge of witty inventions, of man and nature, of
art and literature, of the heavens above and the earth
beneath,—all this knowledge is man's proper discovery.   He has found it out himself, thought it out
for himself, observed, reasoned, collected, laboured,
gathered his forces, altogether of his own will and for
his own ends and as an independent agent.   Now,
this pride of intellect also comes of the arrogance of
man ; not only in our age, which, I venture to think,
is the very best age the world has ever seen, but in
all time, it is our nature to lift up our heads and say,
'We are the people; before us there were none like
unto us, neither shall there be any more after us.'
But when we come to ourselves we realise that our
Author and Father has not in this way made over
any single vast realm of our lives into our own hands.

Great Eras come from Time to Time.—The
knowledge that comes to us is given us in repasts,
so to speak.   Great eras of scientific discovery or
literary activity or poetic insight or artistic interpretation come to the world from time to time ; and then
there is a long interval for the assimilation of the new
knowledge or the new thought.   After that, the world
is taken by storm by the rise of another constellation
of its great intellects; and yet we do not discern the
signs of the times nor realise that thus our God is
bringing us up in knowledge, which is also divine,
just as much as in the nurture and admonition of the
Lord.   The mediæval Church recognised this great
truth—as Mr Ruskin has eloquently pointed out,
showing how the 'Captain Figures,' the inventors, as
it were, of grammar and music, astronomy and

geometry, arithmetic and logic, all spake that which was in them under the direct outpouring of the Holy Spirit, even though none of them had any such revelation of the true God as we recognise. What a revolution should we have in our methods of education if we could once conceive that dry-as-dust subjects like grammar and arithmetic should come to children, living with the life of the Holy Spirit, who, we are told, 'shall teach you all things.'

**Nothing so Practical as Great Ideas.**—It may occur to some readers to consider that such lines of thought as I have suggested are perhaps interesting but not practical. Believe me, nothing is so practical as a great idea, because nothing produces such an abundant outcome of practical effort. We must not turn the cold shoulder to philosophy. Education is no more than applied philosophy—our effort to train children according to the wisdom that is in us ; and not according to the last novelty in educational ideas.

'Man, know thyself,' is a counsel which we might render, 'Child, know thyself, and thy relations to God and man and nature' ; and to give their children this sort of preparation for life it is necessary that parents should know something of the laws of mind and of the source of knowledge.

**The Formation of Intellectual Habits.**—The second part of our subject—the formation of intellectual habits—need not occupy us long. We know that the possession of some half-dozen such habits makes up what is well called ability. They make a man able to do that which he desires to do with his mental powers, and to labour at the cost of not a tenth part of the waste of tissue which the same work would exact of a person of undisciplined mental

habits. We know, too, that the habits in question
are acquired through training and are not bestowed
as a gift. Genius itself, we have been told, is an
infinite capacity for taking pains ; we would rather
say, is the habit of taking infinite pains, for every
child is born with the capacity.

**We trust blindly to Disciplinary Subjects.**—
We trust perhaps a little blindly to the training
which certain subjects give in certain mental habits.
The classics, we consider, cultivate in one direction,
the mathematics, in another, science, in a third. So
they do, undoubtedly, so far as each of these subjects
is concerned ; but possibly not in forming the general
habits of intellectual life which we expect to result.
Remove the mathematician from his own field and he
is not more exact or more on the spot than other
men ; indeed he is rather given to make a big hole
for the cat and a little hole for the kitten ! The
humanities do not always make a man humane, that
is, liberal, tolerant, gentle, and candid, as regards the
opinions and status of other men. The fault does
not lie in any one of these or in any other of the
disciplinary subjects, but in our indolent habit of
using each of these as a sort of mechanical contrivance
for turning up the soil and sowing the seed. There
is no reprieve for parents. It rests with them, even
more than with the schoolmaster and his curriculum, to
form those mental habits which shall give intellectual
distinction to their children throughout their lives.

**Some Intellectual Habits.**—I need not refer
again to the genesis of a habit ; but perhaps most of
us set ourselves more definitely to form physical and
moral than we do to form intellectual habits. I will
only mention a few such, which should be matters of

careful training during the period of childhood:—
*Attention*, the power of turning the whole force of
the mind upon the subject brought before it : *Concen-
tration*, which differs from attention in that the mind
is actively engaged on some given problem rather
than passively receptive : *Thoroughness*, the habit of
dissatisfaction with a slipshod, imperfect grasp of a
subject, and of mental uneasiness until a satisfying
measure of knowledge is obtained ;—this habit is
greatly encouraged by a reference to an encyclopædia,
to clear up any doubtful point, when it turns up :
*Intellectual Volition*, the power, that is, of making ourselves think of a given subject at a given time ;—most
of us know how trying our refractory minds are in
this matter, but, if the child is accustomed to take
pleasure in the effort as effort, the man will find it
easy to make himself think of what he will : *Accuracy*,
which is to be taught, not only through arithmetic,
but through all the small statements, messages, and
affairs of daily life : *Reflection*, the ruminating power
which is so strongly developed in children and is
somehow lost with much besides of the precious cargo
they bring with them into the world. There is
nothing sadder than the way we allow intellectual
impressions to pass over the surface of our minds,
without any effort to retain or assimilate.

Meditation.—I can mention only one more invalu-
able habit. Mr Romanes consulted Darwin about
the conduct of his intellectual life. ' Meditate,' was
the answer, and we are told that the younger scientist
set great store on this advice. Meditation is also
a habit to be acquired, or rather preserved, for we
believe that children are born to meditate, as they are
to reflect ; indeed, the two are closely allied. In

reflecting we ruminate on what we have received. In meditating we are not content to go over the past, we allow our minds to follow out our subject to all its issues. It has long been known that progress in the Christian life depends much upon meditation ; intellectual progress, too, depends, not on mere reading or the laborious getting up of a subject which we call study, but on that active surrender of all the powers of the mind to the occupation of the subject in hand, which is intended by the word meditation. It would be easy for any of us to suggest to himself a dozen more important intellectual habits, the consideration of which should be profitable and stimulating.

**The Sustenance of Living Ideas.**—The intellectual life, like every manner of spiritual life, has but one food whereby it lives and grows—the sustenance of living ideas. It is not possible to repeat this too often or too emphatically, for perhaps we err more in this respect than any other in bringing up children. We feed them upon the white ashes out of which the last spark of the fire of original thought has long since died. We give them second-rate story books, with stale phrases, stale situations, shreds of other people's thoughts, stalest of stale sentiments. They complain that they know how the story will end ! But that is not all ; they know how every dreary page will unwind itself. I saw it stated the other day that children do not care for poetry, that a stirring narrative in verse is much more to their taste. They do like the tale, no doubt, but poetry appeals to them on other grounds, and Shelley's *Skylark* will hold a child entranced sooner than any moving anecdote. As for children's art, we hang the nursery with 'Christmas Number' pictures, and their books are illustrated on a lower level still.    In regard to book illustrations, we are improving a little, but still there is room.

Children's Literature.—The subject of ' Children's Literature ' has been well threshed out, and only one thing remains to be said,—children have no natural appetite for twaddle, and a special literature for children is probably far less neccessary than the booksellers would have us suppose.    Out of any list of 'the hundred best books,' I believe that seventy-five would be well within the range of children of eight or nine.     They would delight in *Rasselas, Eöthen* would fascinate them as much as *Robinson Crusoe*, the *Faëry Queen*, with its allegory and knightly adventures and sense of free moving in woodland scenery, would exactly fall in with their humour.    What they want is to be brought into touch with living thought of the best, and their intellectual life feeds upon it with little meddling on our part.

Independent  Intellectual  Development  of Children.—We do not sufficiently recognise the independent intellectual development of children which it is our business to initiate and direct, but not to control or dominate.    I know a little girl of nine who pined every day because the poems of Tennyson which she loved best were not to be found in the volumes of the larger works, which were all the house she was visiting at afforded.    She literally missed her favourite poems as a child would miss a meal ; and why not ? The intellectual appetite is just as actual and just as exigeant as bodily hunger ; more so, alas, in some cases.    Miss Martineau has a charming story [1] of the intellectual awakening of "a schoolboy of *ten* who laid himself down, back uppermost, with Southey's

[1] Quoted by Mr Lewis in *The Child and its Spiritual Nature.*

*Thalaba* before him, on the first day of the Easter
holidays, and turned over the leaves, notwithstanding
his inconvenient position, as fast as if he were looking
for something, till in a few hours it was done, and
he was off with it to the public library, bringing back
the *Curse of Kehama*.    Thus he went on with all
Southey's poems and some others through his short
holidays, scarcely moving voluntarily all those days
except to run to the library.    He came out of the
process so changed that none of his family could
help being struck by it.    The expression of his eye,
the cast of his countenance, his use of words, and
his very gait were changed.    In ten days he had
advanced years in intelligence ; and I have always
thought that this was the turning-point of his life.
His parents wisely and kindly let him alone, aware
that school would presently put an end to all excess
in the new indulgence."

As there is no religious conversion for the child
who has always been brought up in the conscious
presence of God, so parents who have always satisfied
the intellectual craving of their children must needs
forego the delight of watching a literary awakening.
A little girl brought up on temperance principles,
who said, ' I am so sorry my father isn't a drunkard,'
that she might rejoice in his reformation, put the case
for us very plainly.

**Self-selection and Self-appropriation.**—Given
a bountiful repast of ideas, the process of natural
selection soon begins.    Tennyson with his—

Our elm tree's ruddy-hearted blossom-flake is fluttering down,"

" Ruby-budded lime,"

" Black as ash-buds in the front of March,"

has done more to make field botanists than ever the Science and Art Department was able to undo with its whole apparatus of lectures and examinations.

Here, again, Browning gives us a poet's impulse to a nature student :—

> " By boulder stones where lichens mock
> The marks on a moth, and small ferns fit
> Their teeth to the polished block."

Ideas of nature, of life, love, duty, heroism,—these children find and choose for themselves from the authors they read, who do more for their education than any deliberate teaching; just for this reason, that these vital ideas are self-selected and self-appropriated.

I shall touch later upon the burning question of a curriculum which shall furnish children, not with dry bones of fact, but with fact clothed upon with the living flesh, breathed into by the vital spirit of quickening ideas. A teacher objected the other day that it was difficult to teach from Freeman's *Old English History*, because there were so many stories ; not perceiving that the stories were the living history, while all the rest was dead.

**Inherited Parsimony in Lesson-Books.**—I should like to say here that a sort of unconscious, inherited parsimony, coming down to us from the days when incomes were smaller and books were fewer, sometimes causes parents to restrict their children unduly in the matter of lesson-books—living books, varied from time to time, and not thumbed over from one school-room generation to another until the very sight of them is a weariness to the flesh. But the subject of the intellectual sustenance of children upon ideas is so large and important that I must content myself with bald suggestions. Further considered, such subjects as the following might be useful :—

(1) Children's tastes in Fiction, in Poetry, in books of Travel and Adventure, in History, in Biography (most stimulating subject).

(2) Ideas of life and conduct that children assimilate from their reading.

(3) Ideas of duty assimilated in the same way.

(4) Ideas of nature that children seize.

(5) The leading, vitalising ideas in subjects of school study, as geography, grammar, history, astronomy, Cæsar's Commentaries, etc., etc.

Let me again refer the reader to Mr Ruskin's description of the 'Captain Figures' at the head of each of the Liberal Arts, in his account of the Spanish Chapel ; and conclude with a wise sentence of Coleridge's concerning the method of Plato, which should be always present to the minds of persons engaged in the training of children :—

Plato's Educational Aim.—" He desired not to assist in storing the passive mind with the various sorts of knowledge most in request, as if the human soul were a mere repository or banqueting room, but to place it in such relations of circumstance as should gradually excite its vegetating and germinating powers to produce new fruits of thought, new conceptions and imaginations and ideas."

# CHAPTER XII

## SOME UNCONSIDERED ASPECTS OF MORAL
## TRAINING

**Three Foundation Principles.**—Three principles
which underlie the educational thought of the Union,[1]
and the furtherance of which some of us have deeply
at heart, are :—(*a*) The recognition of authority as a
fundamental principle, as universal and as inevitable
in the moral world as is that of gravitation in the
physical ; (*b*) the recognition of the physical basis
of habits and of the important part which the formation of habits plays in education ; (*c*) the recognition
of the vital character and inspiring power of ideas.

**Authority, the Basis of Moral Teaching.**—
First let us consider the principle of authority, which
is the basis of moral as it is of religious teaching.
'Ought' is part of the verb 'to owe,' and that which
we owe is a personal debt to a Lawgiver and Ruler,
however men name the final authority. If they choose
to speak of Buddha or Humanity, they do not escape
from the sense of a moral authority. They know
that that which they *ought* is that which they *owe* to
do, a debt to some power or personality external to
themselves. God has made us so that, however
much we may be in the dark as to the divine Name,
we can never for a minute escape from the sense of

---

[1] The Parents' National Educational Union.

'Ought,' the law, which becomes flesh-torturing and spirit-quelling in proportion as we are removed from the light of Revelation.   To us, who know the name of God and have the revelation of the Scriptures, authority carries no vague terror.   We know what is required of us, and that the requirements are never arbitrary, but necessary in the nature of things, both for the moral government of the world and to gratify the unquenchable desire of every human soul to rise into a higher state of being.   Perhaps parents, great as they are and should be in the eyes of their children, should always keep well to the front the fact that their authority is derived.

Principles, not Rules.—'God does not allow' us to do thus and thus should be a rarely expressed but often present thought to parents who study the nature of the divine authority where it is most fully revealed, that is, in the Gospels.   They see there that authority works by principles and not by rules, and as they themselves are the deputy authorities set over every household, it becomes them to consider the divine method of government.   They should discern the signs of the times too ; the tendency is to think that a man can only act according to his 'lights,' and, therefore, that it is right for him to do that which is right in his own eyes ; in other words, that every man is his own final authority in questions of right and wrong.   It is extremely important that parents should keep in view, and counteract if need be, this tendency of the day.

Limitations of Authority.—On the other hand, it is well that they should understand the limitations of authority.   Even the divine authority does not compel.   It indicates the way and protects the wayfarer, and strengthens and directs self-compelling power. It permits a man to make free choice of obedience rather than compels him to obey. In the moral training of children arbitrary action almost always produces revolt. Parents believe that they are doing well to *rule* their households, without considering the pattern, the principles, and the limitations of parental authority.

**Duty can exist only as that which we owe.** —An American writer on the moral instruction of children states that 'it is the business of the moral instructor in the school to deliver to his pupils the subject-matter of morality, but not to deal with the sanctions of it.' Here we have a contention at least two thousand years old. Socrates combated it as expressed in the formulæ :—' Man is the measure of all things'; 'Just as each thing appears to each man, so it is to him'; 'All truth is relative.' We say to-day that a man can but live up to his ' lights '; in other words, there is no authority, no truth, and no law beyond what every man carries in his own bosom. The necessary issue of this teaching is the doctrine of the unknowable God—the God who, if He exists, does not exist for us, because we have no relations with Him. It is in their early years at home that children should be taught to realise that duty can exist only as that which we *owe* to God ; that the law of God is exceeding broad and encompasses us as the air we breathe, only more so, for it reaches to our secret thoughts ; and this is not a hardship but a delight. That mothers should love their little children and make them happy all day long—this is part of the law of God : that children are glad when they are good, and sad when they are naughty—this, too, is the law of God : that, if Tommy drops his spoon, it falls to the ground, is a law of God too, of a different kind. Mother or teacher cannot give children a better inheritance than the constant sense of being ruled and encompassed by law, and that law is another name for the will of God.

**Morals do not come by Nature.**—No doubt every child is born with a conscience, that is, with a sense that he ought to choose the right and refuse the wrong ; but he is not born with the power to discern good and evil. An educated conscience is a far rarer possession than we imagine ; we are all startled now and then by the laxities of right-minded neighbours in matters the right and wrong of which is patent to ourselves; but probably our own moral eccentricities are equally startling to our friends. The blame rests on our faulty moral education, which has hardly made us aware of fallacious thought and insincere speech ; we believe that Latin and Greek must be taught, but that morals come by nature. A certain rough-and-ready kind of morality, varying with our conditions, does come by heredity and environment ; but that most delicate and beautiful of human possessions, an educated conscience, comes only by teaching with authority and adorning by example.

**Children born neither Moral nor Immoral.**— It is curious how educated people are still at sea as regards the moral status of children. Some time ago I was present at an interesting discussion, among the members of an educational society, on the subject of children's lies. It was interesting to notice that the meeting, consisting of able, educated people, divided itself into those who held that children were born true and those who held that they were born false;

it did not occur to anybody to recall his own childhood, or even to reflect on his own condition at the present moment. The question lay between children being born moral and born immoral. Nobody reflected that every human being comes into the world with infinite possibilities for good; and, alas! infinite possibilities for evil; possibly with evil hereditary tendencies which may be rectified by education, or with good tendencies which his bringing-up may nullify.

**Moral Teaching.**—We need go no further than the Ten Commandments and our Lord's exposition of the moral law to find corrective teaching for the spasmodic, impulsive moral efforts which tend to make up our notion of what the children call 'being good,' and nowhere shall we find a more lucid and practical commentary on the moral law than is set forth in the Church Catechism. It was the practice of a venerable Father of the Church, Bishop Ken, to recite the 'duty towards God,' and the 'duty towards my neighbour' every day. It is a practice worth imitating, and it would not be amiss to let all children of whatever communion learn these short abstracts of the whole duty of man.

**Of the Poets.**—The poets give us the best help in this kind of teaching; as, for example, Wordsworth's *Ode to Duty* :—

> "Stern lawgiver! yet thou dost wear
>  The Godhead's most benignant grace;
>  Nor know we anything so fair
>  As is the smile upon thy face;
>  Flowers laugh before thee on their beds;
>  And fragrance in thy footing treads;
>  Thou dost preserve the stars from wrong;
>  And the most ancient heavens, through thee, are
>      fresh and strong."

Or Matthew Arnold's lines on *Rugby Chapel*—

> "Servants of God !—or sons
> Shall I not call you? because
> Not as servants ye knew
> Your Father's innermost mind,
> His, who unwillingly sees
> One of His little ones lost—
> Yours is the praise, if mankind
> Hath not as yet in its march
> Fainted, and fallen, and died !"

Or this, again, of Tennyson—

> "Not once or twice in our fair island story
> The path of duty was the way to glory :
> He, that ever following her commands,
> On with toil of heart and knees and hands,
> Thro' the long gorge to the far light, has won
> His path upward and prevail'd,—
> Shall find the toppling crags of duty, scaled,
> Are close upon the shining table-lands
> To which our God Himself is moon and sun."

Or Matthew Arnold's *Morality*—

How, "Tasks in hours of insight willed
> Can be through hours of gloom fulfilled."

Possibly we could hardly do better than lead children to reflect on some high poetic teaching, adding love to law and devotion to duty, so that children shall know themselves, by duty as by prayer,

"Bound by gold chains about the feet of God."

In the matter of the ideas that inspire the virtuous life, we miss much by our way of taking things for granted.

**Ethical Teaching of the Middle Ages.**—The mediæval Church preserved classical traditions. It endeavoured to answer the Socratic inquiry : "What

ought we to do and what do we mean by the words
'ought' and 'doing' or 'acting'?" and it answered,
as far as might be by way of object-lessons, visible
signs of spiritual things signified.

In the Arena Chapel at Padua, we have Giotto's
Faith and Infidelity, Love and Envy, Charity and
Avarice, Justice and Injustice, Temperance and
Gluttony, Hope and Despair, pictured forth in un-
mistakable characters for the reading of the un-
learned and ignorant. We have the same theme,
treated with a difference, in what Mr Ruskin calls
the 'Bible of Amiens,' where we may study Humility
and Pride, Temperance and Gluttony, Chastity
and Lust, Charity and Avarice, Hope and Despair,
Faith and Idolatry, Perseverance and Atheism, Love
and Discord, Obedience and Rebellion, Courage
and Cowardice, Patience and Anger, Gentleness and
Churlishness,—in pairs of quatrefoils, an upper and
a lower, each under the feet of an Apostle, who was
held to personify the special virtue. But *we* know
nothing about cardinal virtues and deadly sins.

We have no Authoritative Teaching.—We
have no teaching by authoritative utterance strong
in the majesty of virtue. We work out no schemes
of ethical teaching in marble; we paint no scale of
virtues on our walls, and no repellent vices. Our
poets speak for us, it is true; but the moral aphorisms,
set like jewels though they be on the forefinger of
time, are scattered here and there, and we leave it
serenely to happy chance whether our children shall
or shall not light upon the couple of lines which
should fire them with the impulse to virtuous living.
It may be said that we neglect all additional ethical
teaching because we have the Bible; but how far and

*how* do we use it? Here we have indeed the most
perfect ethical system, the most inspiring and heart-
enthralling, that the world has ever possessed ; but it
is questionable whether we attempt to set a noble
child's heart beating with the thought that he is
required to be perfect as his Father which is in
Heaven is perfect.

**High Ideals.**—It is time we set ourselves seriously
to this work of moral education which is to be done,
most of all, by presenting the children with high
ideals. ' Lives of great men all remind us we can
make our lives sublime,' and the study of the lives of
great men and of the great moments in the lives of
smaller men is most wonderfully inspiring to children,
especially when they perceive the strenuousness of
the childhood out of which a noble manhood has
evolved itself. As one grows older no truth strikes
one more than that ' the child is father to the man.'
It is amazing how many people of one's own acquaintance have fulfilled the dreams of their childhood and early youth, and have had their days indeed
' bound each to each in natural piety.'

**Value of Biography.**—The Bible is, of course, a
storehouse of most inspiring biographies ; but it would
be well if we could manage our teaching so as to
bring out in each character the master-thought of all
his thinking. The late Queen has done this with
singular tact and power in the Albert Memorial
Chapel, where, as we know, Prophets and Patriarchs
are presented, each showing in action that special
virtue or form of endeavour which seemed to her the
keynote of his character. This is a happy effort to
revive the mediæval object teaching of which I have
already spoken. The same thing occurs again in the

School of Song of the Edinburgh Cathedral, where Mrs Traquair has frescoed the walls to illustrate the *Benedicite*, where 'holy and humble men of heart,' for example, is illustrated by three men of our own day of different schools of thought—Cardinal Newman is the only one I recollect. The force of this kind of master-idea, and the unity it gives to life, cannot be better illustrated than by the perhaps apocryphal 'I will be good' of our late beloved Queen. There are few children in the kingdom whose hearts have not thrilled to the phrase. Perhaps she will one day know how much was done to give moral impulse to this great Empire by that simple child-like promise so abundantly fulfilled.

**Of Patriotic Poems.**—Next in value to biographies from the point of view of inspiration are the burning words of the poets,—Tennyson's *Ode to the Iron Duke*, for example. Perhaps no poet has done more to stir the fire of patriotism amongst us than Mr Rudyard Kipling: " We learn from our wistful mothers to call Old England 'home,'" opens the door to a flood of patriotic feeling ; as indeed do the whole of the poems, *The Native-born* and *The Flag of England* :—

> " Never was isle so little,
> Never were seas so lone,
> But over the scud and the palm trees
> The English flag has flown."

From another point of view, how this (of Browning's) makes the heart quick with patriotic emotions !—

> " Buy my English posies,
> Kent and Surrey may,
> Violets of the undercliff
> Wet with Channel spray,

> Cowslips of the Devon combe,
> Midland furze afire ;
> Buy my English posies
> And I'll sell you heart's desire."

**Mottoes.**—In the reading of the Bible, of poetry, of the best prose, the culling of mottoes is a delightful and most stimulating occupation, especially if a motto book be kept, perhaps under headings, perhaps not.   It would not be a bad idea for children to make their own year-book, with a motto for every day in the year culled from their own reading.  What an incentive to a good day it would be to read in the morning as a motto of our very own choice and selection, and not the voice of an outside mentor : ' Keep ye the law ; be swift in all obedience ' !  The theme suggests endless subjects for consideration and direct teaching : for example, lives with a keynote ; Bible heroes ; Greek heroes; poems of moral inspiration ; poems of patriotism, duty, or any single moral quality ; moral object-lessons; mottoes and where to find them, etc.

**The Habit of Sweet Thoughts.**—Moral habits, the way to form them and the bounden duty of every parent to send children into the world with a good outfit of moral habits, is a subject so much to the front in our thoughts, that I need not dwell further upon it here.  The moral impulse having been given by means of some such inspiring idea as we have considered, the parent's or teacher's next business is to keep the idea well to the front, with tact and delicacy, and without insistence, and to afford apparently casual opportunities for moral effort on the lines of the first impulse.  Again, let us keep before the children that it is the manner of thoughts we think which matters; and, in the early days, when a child's face is an open book to his parents, the habit of sweet thoughts must be kept up, and every selfish, resentful, unamiable movement of children's minds observed in the countenance must be changed before consciousness sets in.

**Virtues in which Children should be Trained.** —One more point: parents should take pains to have their own thoughts clear as to the manner of virtues they want their children to develop. Candour, fortitude, temperance, patience, meekness, courage, generosity, indeed the whole rôle of the virtues, would be stimulating subjects for thought and teaching, offering ample illustrations. One caution I should like to offer. A child's whole notion of religion is 'being good.' It is well that he should know that being good is not his whole duty to God, although it is so much of it; that the relationship of love and personal service, which he owes as a child to his Father, as a subject to his King, is even more than the 'being good' which gives our Almighty Father such pleasure in His children.

# CHAPTER XIII

## SOME UNCONSIDERED ASPECTS OF RELIGIOUS EDUCATION

**Authority in Religious Education.**—I should like to preface my remarks on Religious Education by saying that there is not the slightest pretence that they are exhaustive. My treatment has for its object the indication of practical lines for religious education, and I very earnestly hope that the reader will find I have left out things I ought to have said, or said things I ought not to have said.

Let us first consider how the principle of authority bears on religious teaching. The sense of duty, more or less illuminated, or more or less benighted, is always relative to a ruler with whom it rests to say 'Thou shalt' or 'Thou shalt not.' It is brought home, too, to most of us who are set in authority, that we ourselves are acting under a higher, and finally, under the highest rule. A child cannot have a lasting sense of duty until he is brought into contact with a supreme Authority, who is the source of law, and the pleasing of whom converts duty into joy. In these rather latitudinarian days, there is perhaps no part of religious teaching more important than to train children in the sense of the immediate presence and continual going forth of the supreme Authority.

'Thou art about my path and about my bed and spiest out all my ways,' should be a thought, not of fear, but of very great comfort to every child. This constant recognition of authority excites the twofold response of docility and of reverence. It is said that the children of our day are marked by wilfulness and a certain flippancy and want of reverence; if this is so, and in so far as it is so, it is because children are brought up without the consciousness of their relation to God, whom we are taught to call 'Our Father.' This divine name reminds us that authority is lodged in the Author of our being, and is tender, pitiful, preventive, strong to care for and wise to govern ; as we see it feebly shown forth even in the best of human fathers.

Questions in the Air.—But there are questions in the air about the authenticity of the Scriptures and what not, and we are all more or less at the mercy of words ; and, because the so-called higher criticism finds much to question as to the verbal accuracy of passages of the Scriptures, we get a dim idea that the divine authority itself is in question. One part of the work of this Union [1] is, no doubt, to strengthen the hands of parents by comforting them with the sense of the higher Power behind theirs and always supporting them in the exercise of the deputed powers they hold as heads of families. There is another notion in the air which tells against the recognition of authority, and that is, the greatly increased respect for individual personality and for the right of each individual to develop on the lines of his own character. But it is a mistake to suppose that the exercise of authority runs counter to any

[1] The Parents' Union.

individual development that is not on morally wrong
lines.

**How Authority Works.**—The supreme authority
(and all deputed authority) works precisely as does a
good and just national government, whose business it
is to defend the liberties of the subject at all points,
even by checking, repressing, and punishing the
licence which interferes with the rights of others and
with the true liberty of the transgressor. The law
(that is, the utterance of authority) is for the punishment of evil-doers, but for the praise of them that do
well ; and the association of harshness, punishment,
force, arbitrary dealings, with the idea of authority,
human and divine, is an example of the confusion of
thought to which most of our errors in conduct are
traceable. It is not authority which punishes : the
penalties which follow us through life, of which those
in the family are a faint foretaste, are the inevitable
consequences of broken law, whether moral or
physical, and from which authority, strong and
benign, exists to save us by prevention, and, if needs
be, by lesser and corrective penalties.

It seems to me that reading and teaching on the
following subjects, for example, might help to focus
thought on a subject of vital importance :—our
relation to the supreme authority, not a relation of
choice, but as inevitable as the family relationships into
which we are born ; the duty of loyalty and the shame
of infidelity ; the duty of reverence; the duty of docility
to indications of the divine will ; scriptural revelations
of God, as the ruler of men, as saying to Abraham, ' Go,
and he goeth ' ; to Cyrus, ' Do this, and he doeth it ' ;
revelations which history affords of God as the ruler
of nations, and as the benign ruler of men who

prospers the ways of His servants; how the sense of
the divine authority may be imparted in the home;
how reverence for holy things may be taught;
definite Bible teaching on this head.—Indeed, the
subject is capable of great amplification, and suggests
trains of thought very important in these days.

The Habits of the Religious Life.—The next
point we must set ourselves to consider is the laying
down of lines of *habit* in the religious life. We need
not enter again into the physiological reasons for the
compelling power of habit. My present purpose is to
consider how far this power can be employed in the
religious development of a child. Let us consider the
subject as it bears upon habits of thought and of
attitude, of life and of speech; though indeed all
these are one, for every act and attitude is begotten
of a thought, however unaware we be of thinking.

Habit of the Thought of God.—It is said of the
wicked that 'God is not in all their thoughts.' Of
the child it should be said that God is in all his
thoughts; happy-making, joyous thoughts, restful and
dutiful thoughts, thoughts of loving and giving and
serving, the wealth of beautiful thoughts with which
every child's heart overflows. We are inclined to
think that a child is a little morbid and precocious
when he asks questions and has imaginings about
things divine, and we do our best to divert him.
What he needs is to be guided into true, happy
thinking; every day should bring him 'new thoughts
of God, new hopes of heaven.' He understands things
divine better than we do, because his ideas have not
been shaped to a conventional standard; and thoughts
of God are to him an escape into the infinite from the
worrying limitations, the perception of the prison

bars, which are among the bitter pangs of childhood.
To keep a child in this habit of the thought of God—
so that to lose it, for even a little while, is like coming
home after an absence and finding his mother out—is
a very delicate part of a parent's work.

Reverent Attitudes.—The importance of reverent
attitudes is a little apt to be overlooked in these days.
We are, before all things, sincere, and are afraid to
insist upon 'mere forms,' feeling it best to leave the
child to the natural expression of his own emotions.
Here perhaps we are wrong, as it is just as true to
say that the form gives birth to the feeling as that
the feeling should give birth to the form. Children
should be taught to take time, to be reverent at grace
before meals, at family prayers, at their own prayers,
in church, when they are old enough to attend.
Perhaps some of us may remember standing daily
by our mother's knee in reverent attitude to recite
the Apostles' Creed, and the recollection of the
reverence expressed in that early act remains with
one through a lifetime. 'Because of the angels'
should be a thought to repress unbecoming behaviour
in children. It is a mistake to suppose that the
forms of reverence need be tiresome to them. They
love little ceremonies, and to be taught to kneel
nicely while saying their short prayers would help
them to a feeling of reverence in after life. In
connection with children's behaviour in church, the
sentiment and forms of reverence cannot be expected
if they are taken to church too young, or to too long
services, or are expected to maintain their attention
throughout. If children must be taken to long
services, they should be allowed the resource of a
Sunday picture-book, and told that the hymns and

the 'Our Father,' for example, are the parts of the service for them. But in these days of bright short services especially adapted for children the difficulty need not arise.

**Regularity in Devotions.**—The habit of regularity in children's devotions is very important. The mother cannot always be present, but I have known children far more punctual in their devotions when away from their mother, because they know it to be her wish, than if she were there to remind them. They may say, like a little friend of mine, aged four, 'Mother, I always worship idols.' 'Do you indeed, Margaret? when?' 'Why, when I say my prayers to the chair.' But it is a great thing for all of us to get the habit of 'saying our prayers' at a given time and in a given place, which comes to be to us as a holy place. The chair, or the bedside, or the little prayer-table, or, best of all, the mother's knee, plays no small part in framing the soul to a habit of devotion. In this connection it is worth while to remark that the evening prayers of children and of school girls and boys should not be left until the children are tired and drop asleep over their evening exercises. After tea is a very good set time for prayers when it can be managed.

**The Habit of Reading the Bible.**—The habit of hearing, and later, of reading the Bible, is one to establish at an early age. We are met with a difficulty — that the Bible is, in fact, a library containing passages and, indeed, whole books which are not for the edification of children ; and many parents fall back upon little collections of texts for morning and evening use. But I doubt the wisdom of this plan. We may believe that the narrative teaching of the Scriptures is far more helpful to children, anyway, than the stimulating moral and spiritual texts picked out for them in little devotional books. The twopenny single books of the Bible, published by the Bible Society, should be a resource for parents. A child old enough to take pleasure in reading for himself would greatly enjoy reading through the Gospel of St Mark, bit by bit, for example, in a nice little book, as part of his morning's devotions.

**Children Formalists by Nature.** — But while pressing the importance of habits of prayer and devotional reading, it should be remembered that children are little formalists by nature, and that they should not be encouraged in long readings or long prayers with a notion of any merit in such exercises.

**The Habit of Praise.**—Perhaps we do not attach enough importance to the habit of praise in our children's devotions. Praise and thanksgiving come freely from the young heart; gladness is natural and holy, and music is a delight. The singing of hymns at home and of the hymns and canticles in church should be a special delight ; and the habit of soft and reverent singing, of offering our very best in praise, should be carefully formed. Hymns with a story, such as : ' A little ship was on the sea,' ' I think when I read that sweet story of old,' ' Hushed was the evening hymn,' are perhaps the best for little children.

Children should be trained in the habits of attention and real devotion during short services or parts of services. The habit of finding their places in the prayer-book and following the service is interesting and aids attention, but perhaps it would be well to tell children, of even ten or eleven, that during the litany, for example, they might occupy themselves by saying over silently hymns that they know.

**The Habit of Sunday-keeping.**—The habit of Sunday observances, not rigid, not dull, and yet peculiar to the day, is especially important. Sunday stories, Sunday hymns, Sunday walks, Sunday talks, Sunday painting, Sunday knitting even, Sunday card-games, should all be special to the day,—quiet, glad, serene. The people who clamour for a Sunday that shall be as other days little know how healing to the jaded brain is the change of thought and occupation the seventh day brings with it. There is hardly a more precious inheritance to be handed on than that of the traditional English Sunday, stripped of its austerities, we hope, but keeping its character of quiet gladness and communion with Nature as well as with God. But I cannot pursue the subject further. The field of the habits of the religious life should afford many valuable matters for reflection and teaching; as, for example, the habitual thought of God in a family; the habit of reverence in thought, attitude, act, and speech; the habit of prayer as regards time, place, manner, matter; the habit of praise and thanksgiving; the habits of attention and devotion during a service (or part of a service); aids to devout habits; the habit of devotional reading.

**Inspiring Ideas of the Religious Life.**—The most important part of our subject remains to be considered—the inspiring ideas we propose to give children in the things of the divine life. This is a matter we are a little apt to leave to chance; but when we consider the vitalising power of an idea, and how a single great idea changes the current of a life, it becomes us to consider very carefully what ideas of the things of God we may most fitly offer children, and how these may be most invitingly presented. It is a very sad fact that many children get their first ideas of God in the nursery, and that these are of a Being on the watch for their transgressions and always ready to chastise. It is hard to estimate the alienation which these first ideas of the divine Father set up in the hearts of His little children. Another danger is, lest the things of the divine life should be made too familiar and hackneyed, that the name of our blessed Lord should be used without reverence; and that children should get the notion that the Lord God exists for their uses, and not they, for His service.

**The Fatherhood of God.** — Perhaps the first vitalising idea to give children is that of the tender Fatherhood of God; that they live and move and have their being within the divine embrace. Let children grow up in this joyful assurance, and, in the days to come, infidelity to this closest of all relationships will be as shameful a thing in their eyes as it was in the eyes of the Christian Church during the age of faith.

**The Kingship of Christ.**—Next, perhaps, the idea of Christ their King is fitted to touch springs of conduct and to rouse the enthusiasm of loyalty in children, who have it in them, as we all know, to bestow heroic devotion on that which they find heroic. Perhaps we do not make enough of this principle of hero-worship in human nature in our teaching of religion. We are inclined to make our religious aims subjective rather than objective. We are tempted to look upon Christianity as a 'scheme of salvation' designed and carried out for our benefit; whereas the very essence of Christianity is passionate devotion to an altogether adorable Person.

**Our Saviour.**—But, recognising this, there is still a danger in these days of adopting a rose-water treatment in our dealings with children. Few grown-up people, alas! have so keen and vivid a sense of sin as a little transgressor say of six or seven. Many a naughty, passionate, or sulky and generally hardened little offender is so, simply because he does not know, with any personal knowledge, that there is a Saviour of the world, who has for him instant forgiveness and waiting love. But here again, the thoughts of a child should be turned outwards to Jesus, our Saviour, and not inward to his own thoughts and feelings towards our blessed Saviour.

**The Indwelling of the Holy Ghost.**—One more salient truth of the Christian verity I have space to touch upon. Most Christian parents teach their children to recognise the indwelling of the Holy Ghost, the Comforter ; they expand the ideas expressed in—

> " Enable with perpetual light
>   The dulness of our blinded sight."

> " Anoint and cheer our soiled face
>   With the abundance of Thy grace."

But it would be well if we could hinder in our children's minds the rise of a wall of separation between things sacred and things so-called secular, by making them feel that all 'sound learning,' as well as all 'religious instruction,' falls within the office of God, the Holy Spirit, the supreme educator of mankind.

Many other inspiring ideas concerning the religious life will occur to every parent and teacher, ideas of more value than any I can suggest. Teaching, reading, and meditation, for example, on any one of the several clauses of the Lord's Prayer and of the Apostles'

Creed, or, again, on the clauses of that Duty towards God in the Church Catechism which all who receive the Old and the New Testament Scriptures must accept, should be profitable.

I have touched very inadequately, not upon all that is necessary to bring up children in 'the nurture and admonition of the Lord,' but on a few of the principles which seem to me essential.

# CHAPTER XIV

## A MASTER-THOUGHT

**A Motto.**—Some of my readers will know the Parents' Union motto, 'Education is an atmosphere, a discipline, a life,' especially well in the neat diagrammatic form in which it appears on the covers of our Library books. I am told that we, as a society, are destined to live by our motto. A notable educationalist writes to me, in connection with public education : 'There is more need than ever for such a view of education as that embodied in the memorable words which are the motto of the *Parents' Review.*' An inspiring motto must always be a power, but to live *upon* the good repute of our motto, and to live *up* to it and *in* it, are two different things, and I am afraid the Parents' Union has much and continual thinking and strenuous living to face, if it proposes to stand before the world as interpreting and illustrating these 'memorable words.' But we are not a faint-hearted body; we *mean*, and mean intensely ; and to those who purpose the best, and endeavour after the best, the best arrives.

**Nineteenth-Century Formula, Education is an Atmosphere.**—Meantime, we sometimes err, I think, in taking a part for the whole, and a part of a part

for the whole of that part.   Of the three clauses of our
definition, that which declares that 'education is an
atmosphere' pleases us most, perhaps, because it is
the most inviting to the *laissez aller* principle of
human nature.   By the way, we lose something by
substituting 'environment' (that blessed word, Meso-
potamia!) for atmosphere.   The latter word is
symbolic, it is true, but a symbol means more to us
all than the name of the thing signified.   We think
of fresh air, pure, bracing, tonic,—of the definite act
of breathing which must be fully accomplished ; and
we are incited to do more and mean more in the
matter of our children's surroundings if we regard the
whole as an atmosphere, than if we accept the more
literal 'environment.'

**Results in Inanition.** — But, supposing that
'Education is an atmosphere' brings a fresh and
vigorous thought to our minds, suppose that it
means to us, for our children, sunshine and green
fields, pleasant rooms and good pictures, schools
where learning is taken in by the gentle act of
inspiration, followed by the expiration of all that
which is not wanted, where charming teachers compose the children by a half-mesmeric effluence which
inclines them to do as others do, be as others are,—
suppose that all this is included in our notion of
'Education is an atmosphere,' may we not sit at our
ease and believe that all is well, and that the whole
of education has been accomplished ?   No ; because
though we cannot live *without* air, neither can we live
*upon* air, and children brought up upon 'environment'
soon begin to show signs of inanition ; they have little
or no healthy curiosity, power of attention, or of
effort ; what is worse, they lose spontaneity and

initiative; they expect life to drop into them like drops into a rain-tub, without effort or intention on their part.

**And Ennui.**—This notion, that education is included in environment, or, at the best, in atmosphere, has held the ground for a generation or two, and it seems to me that it has left its mark upon our public and our private lives. We are more ready to be done unto than to do; we do not care for the labour of ordering our own lives in this direction or in that; they must be conducted for us; a press of engagements must compel us into what next, and what next after. We crave for spectacular entertainment, whether in the way of pageants in the streets, or spectacles on the boards. Even Shakespeare has come to be so much the occasion for gorgeous spectacles that what the poet says is of little moment compared with the show a play affords. There is nothing intentionally vicious in all this; it is simply our effort to escape from the *ennui* that results from a one-sided view of education,—that education is an atmosphere *only*.

**Eighteenth-Century Formula, Education is a Life, results in Intellectual Exhaustion.**—A still more consuming *ennui* set in at the end of the eighteenth century, and that also was the result of a partial view of education. 'Education is a life' was the (unconscious) formula then; and a feverish chase after ideas was the outcome. It is pathetic to read how Madame de Staël and her coterie, or that 'blue-stocking' coterie which met at the Hôtel Rambouillet, for example, went little to bed, because they could not sleep; and spent long nights in making character sketches of each other, enigmas, anagrams, and other futilities of the intellect, and met again (some of them) at early breakfast to compose and sing little airs, upon little themes. We may be as much inclined to yawn in each other's faces as they were, but, anyway, if we sin as they did by excess in one direction, there is less wear and tear in a succession of shows than in their restless pursuit of inviting notions. Still, the beginning of the nineteenth century has its lessons for the beginning of the twentieth. They erred, as we do, because they did not understand the science of the proportion of things. We are inclined to say, 'Education is environment'; they would say, 'Education is ideas.' The truth includes both of these, and a third definition introducing another side, a third aspect, of education.

**Education is the Cultivation of Faculties, leads to Abnormal Developments.**—The third conceivable view, 'Education is a discipline,' has always had its votaries, and has them still. That the discipline of the habits of the good life, both intellectual and moral, forms a good third of education, we all believe. The excess occurs when we imagine that certain qualities of character and conduct run out, a prepared product like carded wool, from this or that educational machine, mathematics or classics, science or athletics; that is, when the notion of the development of the so-called faculties takes the place of the more physiologically true notion of the formation of intellectual habits. The difference does not seem to be great; but two streams that rise within a foot of one another may water different countries and fall into different seas, and a broad divergence in practice often arises from what appears to be a small difference in conception, in matters educational. The father of

Plutarch had him learn his Homer that he might get heroic ideas of life. Had the boy been put through his Homer as a classical grind, as a machine for the development of faculty, a pedant would have come out, and not a man of the world in touch with life at many points, capable of bringing men and affairs to the touchstone of a sane and generous mind. It seems to me that this notion of the discipline which should develop 'faculty' has tended to produce rather one-sided men, with the limitations which belong to abnormal development. An artist told me the other day that the condition of successful art is absorption in art, that the painter must think pictures, paint pictures, nothing but pictures. But when art was great, men were not mere artists. Quentin Matsys wrought in iron and painted pictures and did many things besides. Michael Angelo wrote sonnets, designed buildings, painted pictures; marble was by no means his only vehicle of expression. Leonardo wrote treatises, planned canals, played instruments of music, did a hundred things, and all exquisitely. But then, the idea of the development of faculty, and the consequent discipline, had not occurred to these great men or their guardians.

Education has Three Faces. — Having safeguarded ourselves from the notion that education has only one face, we may go on to consider how 'education is a life,' without the risk of thinking that we are viewing more than one side of the subject.

Education is a Life, one of these. —It has been said that 'man doth not live by bread alone, but by every word that proceedeth out of the mouth of God'; and the augustness of the occasion on which the words were spoken has caused us to confine

their meaning to what we call the life of the soul;
when, indeed, they include a great educational
principle which was better understood by the
mediæval Church than by ourselves. May I be
allowed once again to describe a painting in which the
educational creed of many of us is visibly expressed?
The reader is, probably, familiar with the frescoes
on the walls of the so-called Spanish Chapel of the
church of S. Maria Novella. The philosophy of the
Middle Ages dealt, as we know, with theology as its
subject-matter; and, while there is much ecclesiastical
polity with which we have little sympathy pictured
on the remaining walls, on one compartment of wall
and roof we have a singularly satisfying scheme of
educational thought. At the highest point of the
picture we see the Holy Ghost descending in the
likeness of a dove; immediately below, in the upper
chamber are the disciples who first received His
inspiration; below, again, is the promiscuous crowd
of all nationalities who are brought indirectly under
the influence of that first outpouring; and in the
foreground are two or three dogs, showing that the
dumb creation was not excluded from benefiting by
the new grace. In the lower compartment of the great
design are angelic figures of the cardinal virtues,
which we all trace more or less to divine inspiration,
floating above the seated figures of apostles and
prophets, of whom we know that they 'spake as they
were moved by the Holy Ghost.' So far, this
mediæval scheme of philosophy reveals no new
thought to persons instructed in the elements of
Christian truth. But below the prophets and
apostles are a series of pictured niches, those to the
right being occupied by the captain figures, the ideal

representations, of the seven Liberal Arts, figures of
singular grace and beauty, representing such familiar
matters as grammar, rhetoric, logic, music, astronomy,
geometry, and arithmetic, all of them under the
outpouring of the Spirit of God. Still more liberal is
the philosophy which places at the foot of each of
these figures him who was then accepted as the leader
and representative of each several science,—Priscian,
Cicero, Aristotle, Tubal Cain, Zoroaster, Euclid,
Pythagoras; men whom a narrower and later
theology would have placed beyond the pale of
the Christian religion, and therefore of the teaching
of the Spirit of God. But here all are represented as
under the same divine outpouring which illuminated
the disciples in the upper chamber.

**A Creed which unifies Life.**—Our nature craves
after unity. The travail of thought, which is going on
to-day and has gone on as long as we have any record
of men's thoughts, has been with a view to establishing some principle for the unification of life. Here
we have the scheme of a magnificent unity. We are
apt to think that piety is one thing, that our intellectual and artistic yearnings are quite another matter,
and that our moral virtues are pretty much matters of
inheritance and environment, and have not much tc
do with our conscious religion. Hence, there come
discords into our lives, discords especially trying to
young and ardent souls who want to be good and
religious, but who cannot escape from the overpower-
ing drawings of art and intellect and mere physical
enjoyment; they have been taught to consider that
these things are, for the most part, alien to the
religious life, and that they must choose one or the
other; they do choose, and the choice does not

always fall upon those things which, in our un-
scriptural and unphilosophical narrowness, we call
the things of God.   Let us bless Taddeo Gaddi and
Simone Memmi for placing before our eyes a creed
(copies[1] of which we might all hang upon our walls),
which shows that our piety, our virtue, our intellectual
activities, and, let us add, our physical perfections, are
all fed from the same source, God Himself; are all
inspired by the same Spirit, the Spirit of God.   The
ages which held this creed were ages of mighty
production in every kind; the princely commerce of
Venice was dignified and sobered by this thought of
the divine inspiration of ideas—ideas of trade, ideas
of justice and fair balance and of utility; Columbus
went out to discover a new world, informed by the
divine idea, as our own philosopher, Coleridge, points
out, adding that 'great inventions and Ideas of Nature
presented to chosen minds by a higher power than
nature herself, suddenly unfold as it were in prophetic
succession systematic views destined to produce the
most important revolutions in the state of man.'
When Columbus came back, his new world discovered, people and princes took it as from God and
sang *Te Deum.*

  The Diet of Great Ideas.—Michael Angelo writes
to his friend Vittoria Colonna, that 'good Christians
always make good and beautiful figures.   In order to
represent the adored image of our Lord, it is not
enough that a master should be great and able.   I
maintain that he must also be a man of good morals
and conduct, if possible a saint, in order that the Holy

---

[1] 'La Discessa dello Spirito Santo' and 'Allegoria filosofica della
Religione Cattolica,' to be had from Mr G. Cole, 1 Via Torna Buoni,
Florence (shilling size, Nos. 4077 and 4093).

Ghost may give him inspiration.' In truth, a nation or a man becomes great upon one diet only, the diet of great ideas communicated to those already prepared to receive them by a higher Power than Nature herself.

Science, the Teaching vouchsafed to Men to-day.—I think we [1] hold amongst us the little leaven which is able to leaven the whole lump. Let us set ourselves to labour with purpose and passion to restore to the world, enriched by the additions of later knowledge, that great scheme of unity of life which produced great men and great work in the past. Nor need we fear that in endeavouring after some such doctrine of ideas as may help us in the work of education, we are running counter to science. Many of us feel, and, I think, rightly, that the teaching of science is *the* new teaching which is being vouchsafed to mankind in our age. Some of us are triumphant, and believe that the elements of moral and religious struggle are about to be eliminated from life, which shall run henceforth, whether happy or disastrous, on the easy plane of the inevitable; others are bewildered and look in vain for a middle way, a place of reconciliation for science and religion; while others of us, again, take refuge in repudiating 'evolution' and all its works and nailing our colours to religion, interpreted on our own narrow lines. Whichever of these lines we take, we probably err through want of faith.

Let us first of all settle it with ourselves that science and religion cannot, to the believer in God, by any possibility be antagonistic. Having assured ourselves of this, we shall probably go on to perceive that the evolution of science is in fact a process of

[1] Of 'The Parents' Union.'

revelation, being brought about in every case, so far as I am aware, by the process which Coleridge has so justly described; that is, "that the *Ideas* of Nature, presented to chosen minds by a higher power than Nature herself, suddenly unfold as it were in prophetic succession systematic views destined to produce the must important revolutions in the state of man." Huxley defines the utility of Biology "as helping to give right ideas in this world, which is, after all," he goes on to say, "absolutely governed by ideas, and very often by the wildest and most hypothetical ideas." Again, he writes, "those who refuse to go beyond the fact rarely get as far as the fact; and anyone who has studied the history of science knows that almost every great step therein has been made by the 'anticipation of nature,' that is, by the invention of hypotheses." One cannot help thinking that scientific men would find the unifying principle they are in search of in the fine saying of Coleridge's which I have quoted more than once or twice; so would they stand revealed to themselves as the mouthpieces, not merely of *the truth*, for which they are so ready to combat and suffer, but also as the chosen and prepared servants of Him who is the Truth.

**Evolution, the Master-thought of the Age.—** Few of us can forget Carlyle's incomparable picture of the *Tiers État* waiting for organisation : " Wise as serpents ; harmless as doves : what a spectacle for France ! Six hundred inorganic individuals, essential for its regeneration and salvation, sit there, on their elliptic benches, longing passionately towards life." Less picturesque, but otherwise very much on a par with this, is Coleridge's description of Botany, as that science existed in his own day, waiting for the unify‧

ing idea which should give it organisation. " What," he says, " is Botany at this present hour ? Little more than an enormous nomenclature ; a huge catalogue, *bien arrangé*, yearly and monthly augmented, in various editions, each with its own scheme of technical memory and its own conveniences of reference ! The innocent amusement, the healthful occupation, the ornamental accomplishment of *amateurs* ; it has yet to expect the devotion and energies of the philosopher." The keyword for the interpretation of life, both animal and vegetable, has been presented to our generation, and we cannot make too much of it.

The Ages have sought for a Unifying Principle. —We cannot overrate the enormous repose and satisfaction to the human mind contained in the idea of evolution. But it is well to remember that for three thousand years thinkers have been occupied with attempts to explain the world by means of a single principle, which should also furnish an explanation of reason and the human soul. Herakleitos and his age thought they had laid hold of the informing idea in the phrase, ' The true Being is an eternal Becoming ' : the ' universal flux of things ' explained all. Demokritos and his age cried—Eureka ! solved the riddle of the universe, with the saying that ' nothing exists except atoms moving in vacancy.' Many times since, with each epoch-making discovery, has science cried—Eureka ! over the one principle which should explain all things and eliminate Personality.

But Personality Remains.— But some little knowledge of history and philosophy will give us pause. We shall see that each great discovery, each luminous idea of nature that the world has received hitherto, is like a bend in a tortuous lake which appears final until your boat approaches it, and then —behold an opening into further and still further reaches beyond! And the knowledge of God will give us something more than the wider outlook which comes of a knowledge of history—the knowledge that there *is* what Wordsworth calls the 'stream of tendency,' a stream of immeasurable force in shaping character and events ; but there is also Personality, a power able to turn the 'stream of tendency' to its uses, if also liable to be carried away in its current.

**Attitude of Parents and Teachers towards Evolution.**—If I appear to dwell on a subject which at first sight appears to have little to do with the bringing up of children, it is because I think that his attitude towards the great idea, great lesson, set for his age to grasp, is a vital part of a parent's preparation. If parents take no heed of the great thoughts which move their age, they cannot expect to retain influence over the minds of their children. If they fear and distrust the revelations of science, they introduce an element of distrust and discord into their children's lives. If, with the mere neophyte of science, they rush to the conclusion that the last revelation is final, accounts for all that is in man, and, to say the least, makes God unnecessary and unknowable, or negligible, they may lower the level of their children's living to that struggle for existence—without aspiration, consecration, and sacrifice—of which we hear so much. If, lastly, parents recognise every great idea of nature as a new page in the progressive revelation made by God to men already prepared to receive such idea ; if they realise that the new idea, however comprehensive, is not final nor all-inclusive,

nor to be set in opposition with that personal
knowledge of God which is the greatest knowledge,
why, then, their children will grow up in that attitude
of reverence for science, reverence for God, and open-
ness of mind, which befits us for whom life is a pro-
bation and a continual education. So much for the
nutriment of ideas laid on the table of the world
during this particular course of its history.

Education is a World Business.—Next, we may
have poetry, or art, or philosophy ; we cannot tell ;
but two things are incumbent upon us,—to keep ourselves and our children in touch with the great
thoughts by which the world has been educated in
the past, and to keep ourselves and them in the right
attitude towards the great ideas of the present. It is
our temptation to make too personal a matter of
education, to lose sight of the fact that education is a
world business, that the lessons of the ages have been
duly set, and that each age is concerned, not only
with its own particular page, but with every preceding
page. For who feels that he has mastered a book
if he is familiar with only the last page of it ? This
brings me to a point I am anxious to bring forward.

We do not sufficiently realise the need for unity of
principle in education. We have no Captain Idea
which shall marshal for us the fighting host of educational ideas which throng the air ; so, in default of
a guiding principle, a leading idea, we feel ourselves
at liberty to pick and choose. This man thinks he is
free to make science the sum of his son's education,
the other chooses the classics, a third prefers a
mechanical, a fourth, a commercial programme, a
fifth makes bodily health his cult, and chooses a
school which makes the care of health a special

feature of its programme (not that we must allow health to be neglected, but that, given good general conditions, the less obvious attention their health receives the better for the boys and girls); and everyone feels himself at liberty to do that which is right in his own eyes with regard to the education of his children.

Let it be our negative purpose to discourage in every way we can the educational faddist, that is, the person who accepts a one-sided notion in place of a universal idea as his educational guide. Our positive purpose is to present, in season and out of season, one such universal idea; that is, that education is the science of relations.

**A Captain Idea for us,— Education is the Science of Relations.**—A child should be brought up to have relations of force with earth and water, should run and ride, swim and skate, lift and carry; should know texture, and work in material; should know by name, and where and how they live at any rate, the things of the earth about him, its birds and beasts and creeping things, its herbs and trees; should be in touch with the literature, art and thought of the past and the present. I do not mean that he should *know* all these things; but he should feel, when he reads of it in the newspapers, the thrill which stirred the Cretan peasants when the frescoes in the palace of King Minos were disclosed to the labour of their spades. He should feel the thrill, not from mere contiguity, but because he has with the past the relationship of living pulsing thought; and, if blood be thicker than water, thought is more quickening than blood. He must have a living relationship with the present, its historic movement, its science, literature, art, social needs and aspirations. In fact, he must have a wide outlook, intimate relations all round; and force, *virtue*, must pass out of him, whether of hand, will, or sympathy, wherever he touches. This is no impossible programme. Indeed it can be pretty well filled in by the time an intelligent boy or girl has reached the age of thirteen or fourteen; for it depends, not upon *how much* is learned, but upon *how* things are learned.

**A Wider Curriculum.**—Give children a wide range of subjects, with the end in view of establishing in each case some one or more of the relations I have indicated. Let them learn from first-hand sources of information—really good books, the best going, on the subject they are engaged upon. Let them get at the books themselves, and do not let them be flooded with a warm diluent at the lips of their teacher. The teacher's business is to indicate, stimulate, direct and constrain to the acquirement of knowledge, but by no means to be the fountain-head and source of all knowledge in his or her own person. The less parents and teachers talk-in and expound their rations of knowledge and thought to the children they are educating, the better for the children. Peptonised food for a healthy stomach does not tend to a vigorous digestion. Children must be allowed to ruminate, must be left alone with their own thoughts. They will ask for help if they want it.

**We may not Choose or Reject Subjects.**—You will see at a glance, with this Captain Idea of establishing relationships as a guide, the unwisdom of choosing or rejecting this or that subject, as being more or less useful or necessary in view of a child's future. We decide, for example, that Tommy, who is eight, need not waste his time over the Latin

Grammar. We intend him for commercial or scientific pursuits,—what good will it be to him? But we do not know how much we are shutting out from Tommy's range of thought besides the Latin Grammar. He has to translate, for example,—' *Pueri formosos equos vident.*' He is a ruminant animal, and has been told something about that strong Roman people whose speech is now brought before him. How their boys catch hold of him! How he gloats over their horses! The Latin Grammar is not mere words to Tommy, or rather Tommy knows, as we have forgotten, that the epithet 'mere' is the very last to apply to words. Of course it is only now and then that a notion catches the small boy, but when it does catch, it works wonders, and does more for his education than years of grind.

Let us try, however imperfectly, to make education a science of relationships—in other words, try in one subject or another to let the children work upon living ideas. In this field small efforts are honoured with great rewards, and we perceive that the education we are giving exceeds all that we intended or imagined.

## CHAPTER XV

### SCHOOL-BOOKS AND HOW THEY MAKE
### FOR EDUCATION

**Line upon Line.** —The theme of 'School-Books'
is not a new one, and I daresay the reader will find
that I have said before what I shall say now. But
we are not like those men of Athens who met to hear
and to tell some new thing; and he will, I know,
bear with me because he will recognise how necessary
it is to repeat again and again counsels which are
like waves beating against the rock of an accepted
system of things. But, in time, the waves prevail and
the rock wears away; so we go to work with good
hope. Let me introduce what I have to say about
school-books by a little story from an antiquated
source.

**An Incident of School-Girl Life.**—Frederika
Bremer, in her novel of *The Neighbours* (published
1837), tells an incident of school-girl life (possibly a
bit of autobiography), with great spirit. Though it
is rather long, I think the reader will thank me for
it—the little episode advances what I have to say
better than could any duller arguments of my own.

The heroine says:—" I was then sixteen, and,
fortunately for my restless character, my right

shoulder began to project at the time.  Gymnastics were then in fashion as remedies against all manner of defects, and my parents determined to let me try gymnastics.    Arrayed in trimmed pantaloons, a *Bonjour* coat of green cloth and a little morning cap with pink ribbon, I made my appearance one day in an assemblage of from thirty to forty figures dressed almost the same as myself, who were merrily swarming about a large saloon, over ropes, ladders, and poles.  It was a strange and novel scene.  I kept myself in the background the first day, and learned from my governess the ' bending of the back ' and the ' exercises of the arms and legs.'  The second day I began to be intimate with some of the girls, the third I vied with them on ropes and ladders, and ere the close of the second week I was the leader of the second class, and began to encourage them to all manner of tricks.

"At that time I was studying Greek history ; their heroes and their heroic deeds filled my imagination even in the gymnastic school.  I proposed to my band to assume masculine and antique names and, in this place, to answer to no other than such as Agamemnon, Epaminondas, etc.  For myself I chose the name of Orestes, and called my best friend in the class, Pylades.   There was a tall thin girl, with a Finlandish accent, whom I greatly disliked, chiefly on account of the disrespect for me and my ideas which she manifested without reserve ; . . . . from this arose fresh cause for quarrels.

"Although in love with the Greek history, I was no less taken with the Swedish.  Charles XII. was my idol, and I often entertained my friends in my class with narration of his deeds till my own soul was on fire with the most glowing enthusiasm. Like a shower of cold water, Darius (the tall girl, whose name was Britsa) one day came into the midst of us, and opposed me with the assertion that the Czar Peter I. was a much greater man than Charles XII. I accepted the challenge with blind zeal and suppressed rage. My opponent brought forward a number of facts with coolness and skill, in support of her opinion, and when I, confuting all her positions, thought to exalt my victorious hero to the clouds, she was perpetually throwing Bender and Pultawa in my way. O Pultawa! Pultawa! many tears have fallen over thy bloody battlefield, but none more bitter than those which I shed in secret when I, like Charles himself, suffered a defeat there. Fuel was added to the flame until—'I challenge you, I demand satisfaction,' cried I to Darius, who only laughed and said, 'Bravo, bravo!' . . . . I exclaimed, 'You have insulted me shamefully, and I request that you ask my pardon in the presence of the whole class, and acknowledge that Charles XII. was a greater man than Czar Peter, or else you shall fight with me, if you have any honour in your breast and are not a coward.' Britsa Kaijsa blushed, but said with detestable coolness: 'Ask pardon indeed? I should never dream of such a thing. Fight? O, yes, I have no objection! but where and with what? With pins, think you, or'—'With the sword if you are not afraid, and on this very spot. We can meet here half an hour before the rest; arms I shall bring with me; Pylades is my second and you shall appoint your own!' . . . . Next morning when I had entered the spacious saloon, I found my enemy already there with her second. Darius and I saluted each other proudly

and distantly. I gave her the first choice of the
swords. She took one and flourished it about quite
dexterously, as if she had been accustomed to the
use of it. I saw myself (in imagination) already
stabbed to the heart. . . . . . 'Czar Peter *was* a great
man,' cried Darius. 'Down with him! long life to
Charles XII.!' I cried, bursting into a furious rage.
I placed myself in an attitude of defence. Darius
did the same. . . . . Our swords clashed one against
the other, and in the next moment I was disarmed
and thrown on the ground. Darius stood over me
and I believed my last hour had arrived. How
astonished was I, however, when my enemy threw
her sword away from her, took me by the hand and
lifted me up, whilst she cheerfully cried : 'Well, now
you have satisfaction ; let us be good friends again ;
you are a brave little body !' At this moment a
tremendous noise was heard at the door and in rushed
the fencing master and three teachers. My senses
now forsook me."

I hope the reader is not among the naughty
children who read the fable and skip the moral ; for,
whatever is to follow, is, in fact, the moral of this
pretty incident.

**How did the Girls get their Enthusiasm ?—**
What was it, we wonder, in their school-books that
these Swedish maidens found so exciting ? There is
no hint of other than *school* reading. In the first
place we may conclude it was *books*. The oral lesson
for young children, the lecture for older, had not been
invented in the earlier years of the last century. We
use books in our schoolrooms ; but one does not hear
of wild enthusiasm, ungovernable excitement, over the
tabulated events of the history books, the tabulated

facts of the science primers. Those Swedish girls
must have used books of another sort; and it is to our
interest to find out of what sort. As records would
be hard to come by, we must look for information to
the girls themselves; not that we can summon them
to give a direct answer, but if we can get at what
*they* were, we shall be able to make a good guess
at what should fire their souls.

**What manner of Book sustains the Life of
Thought?**—The story discloses no more than that
they were intelligent girls, probably the children of
intelligent parents. But that is enough for our
purpose. The question resolves itself into—What
manner of book will find its way with upheaving
effect into the mind of an intelligent boy or girl?
We need not ask what the girl or boy likes. *She*
very often likes the twaddle of goody-goody story
books, *he* likes condiments, highly-spiced tales of
adventure. We are all capable of liking mental food
of a poor quality and a titillating nature; and
possibly such food is good for us when our minds
are in need of an elbow-chair; but our spiritual life is
sustained on other stuff, whether we be boys or girls,
men or women. By spiritual I mean that which is
not corporeal; and which, for convenience' sake, we
call by various names—the life of thought, the life of
feeling, the life of the soul.

It is curious how every inquiry, superficial as it
may seem to begin with, leads us to fundamental
principles. This simple-seeming question — what
manner of school-books should our boys and girls
use?— leads us straight to one of the two great
principles which bottom educational thought.

**The School - Books of the Publishers. —** I

believe that spiritual life, using spiritual in the sense
I have indicated, is sustained upon only one manner
of diet—the diet of ideas—the living progeny of
living minds. Now, if we send to any publisher for
his catalogue of school books, we find that it is
accepted as the nature of a school-book that it be
drained dry of living thought. It may bear the name
of a thinker, but then it is the abridgment of an
abridgment, and all that is left for the unhappy
scholar is the dry bones of his subject denuded of
soft flesh and living colour, of the stir of life and
power of moving. Nothing is left but what Oliver
Wendell Holmes calls the 'mere brute fact.'

It cannot be too often said that information is
not education. You may answer an examination
question about the position of the Seychelles and
the Comoro Islands without having been anywise
nourished by the fact of these island groups existing
in such and such latitudes and longitudes ; but if you
follow Bullen in *The Cruise of the Cachelot*, the names
excite that little mental stir which indicates the
reception of real knowledge.

**Reason for Oral Teaching.**—Intelligent teachers
are well aware of the dry-as-dust character of school
books, so they fall back upon the 'oral' lesson, one
of whose qualities must be that it is not *bookish*.
Living ideas can be derived only from living minds,
and so it occasionally happens that a vital spark is
flashed from teacher to pupil. But this occurs only
when the subject is one to which the teacher has
given *original* thought. In most cases the oral lesson,
or the more advanced lecture, consists of information got up by the teacher from various books,
and imparted in language, a little pedantic, or a little

commonplace, or a little reading-made-easy in style. At the best, the teacher is not likely to have vital interest in, and, consequently, original thought upon, a wide range of subjects.

Limitations of Teachers.—We wish to place before the child open doors to many avenues of instruction and delight, in each one of which he should find quickening thoughts. We cannot expect a school to be manned by a dozen master-minds, and even if it were, and the scholar were taught by each in turn, it would be much to his disadvantage. What he wants of his teacher is moral and mental discipline, sympathy and direction ; and it is better, on the whole, that the training of the pupil should be undertaken by one wise teacher than that he should be passed from hand to hand for this subject and that.

Our aim in Education is to give a Full Life.— We begin to see what we want. Children make large demands upon us. We owe it to them to initiate an immense number of interests. 'Thou hast set my feet in a large room,' should be the glad cry of every intelligent soul. Life should be all *living*, and not merely a tedious passing of time ; not all doing or all feeling or all thinking—the strain would be too great—but, all living ; that is to say, we should be in touch wherever we go, whatever we hear, whatever we see, with some manner of vital interest. We cannot *give* the children these interests ; we prefer that they should never say they have learned botany or conchology, geology or astronomy. The question is not,—how much does the youth *know* ? when he has finished his education—but how much does he *care* ? and about how many orders of things does he care? In fact, how large is the room in which he finds his feet set? and, therefore, how full is the life he has before him?

I know you may bring a horse to the water, but you cannot make him drink. What I complain of is that we do *not* bring our horse to the water. We give him miserable little text-books, mere compendiums of facts, which he is to learn off and say and produce at an examination; or we give him various knowledge in the form of warm diluents, prepared by his teacher with perhaps some grains of living thought to the gallon. And all the time we have books, books teeming with ideas fresh from the minds of thinkers upon every subject to which we can wish to introduce children.

**We undervalue Children.**—The fact is, we undervalue children. The notion that an infant is a huge oyster, who by slow degrees, and more and more, develops into that splendid intellectual and moral being, a full-grown man or woman, has been impressed upon us so much of late years that we believe intellectual spoon-meat to be the only food for what we are pleased to call 'little minds.' It is nothing to us that William Morris read his first Waverley Novel when he was four and had read the whole series by the time he was seven. He did not die of it, but lived and prospered; unlike that little Richard, son of John Evelyn, who died when he was five years and three days old, a thing not to be wondered at when we read that he had 'a strong passion for Greek, could turn English into Latin and *vice versâ* with the greatest ease,' had 'a wonderful disposition to Mathematics, having by heart divers propositions of Euclid'; but I quote little

Richard (nobody could ever have called him Dick) by way of warning and not of example.

Macaulay seems to have begun life as a great reader. We know the delightful story of how, when Hannah More called on his parents, he, a little boy of four, came forward with pretty hospitality to say that if she 'would be good enough to come in' he would bring her 'a glass of old spirits.' He explained afterwards that 'Robinson Crusoe often had some.'

**Children of the Last Generation.**—But we may dismiss these precocious or exceptional children. All we ask of them is to remind us that our grandfathers and grandmothers recognised children as reasonable beings, persons of mind and conscience like themselves; but, needing their guidance and control, as having neither knowledge nor experience. Witness the queer old children's books which have come down to us; these addressed children as, before all things, reasonable, intelligent, and responsible persons. This is the note of home-life in the last generation. So soon as the baby realised his surroundings, he found himself morally and intellectually responsible.

**Children as they are.**—And children have not altered. This is how we find them—with intelligence more acute, logic more keen, observing powers more alert, moral sensibilities more quick, love and faith and hope more abounding; in fact, in all points like as we are, only more so; but absolutely ignorant of the world and its belongings, of us and our ways, and, above all, of how to control and direct and manifest the infinite possibilities with which they are born.

**Our Work, to give vitalising Ideas.**—Knowing that the brain is the physical seat of habit and that conduct and character, alike, are the outcome of the habits we allow ; knowing, too, that an inspiring idea initiates a new habit of thought, and hence, a new habit of life; we perceive that the great work of education is to inspire children with vitalising ideas as to every relation of life, every department of knowledge, every subject of thought ; and to give deliberate care to the formation of those habits of the good life which are the outcome of vitalising ideas.    In this great work we seek and assuredly find the co-operation of the Divine Spirit, whom we recognise, in a sense rather new to modern thought, as the supreme Educator of mankind in things that have been called secular, fully as much as in those that have been called sacred.

# CHAPTER XVI

## HOW TO USE SCHOOL-BOOKS

**Disciplinary Subjects of Instruction.**—Having cleared our minds as to the end we have in view, we ask ourselves—' Is there any fruitful *idea* underlying this or that study that the children are engaged in ? ' We divest ourselves of the notion that to develop the faculties is the chief thing, and a ' subject ' which does not rise out of some great thought of life we usually reject as not nourishing, not fruitful; while we retain those studies which give exercise in habits of clear and orderly thinking. Mathematics, grammar, logic, etc., are not purely disciplinary, they do develop (if a bull may be allowed) intellectual muscle. We by no means reject the familiar staples of education in the school sense, but we prize them even more for the record of intellectual habits they leave in the brain tissue, than for their distinct value in developing certain ' faculties.'

**'Open, Sesame.'**—I think we should have a great educational revolution once we ceased to regard ourselves as assortments of so-called faculties, and realised ourselves as persons whose great business it is to get in touch with other persons of all sorts and conditions, of all countries and climes, of all times,

past and present. History would become entrancing,
literature a magic mirror for the discovery of other
minds, the study of sociology a duty and a delight. We
should tend to become responsive and wise, humble
and reverent, recognising the duties and the joys of
the full human life. We cannot of course overtake
such a programme of work, but we can keep it in view ;
and I suppose every life is moulded upon its ideal.

The Bible, the great Storehouse of Moral
Impressions.—Valuable as are some compendiums
of its moral teaching, it is to the Bible itself we must
go as to the great storehouse of moral impressions.
Let us hear De Quincey on this subject :—

" It had happened, that among our vast nursery
collection of books was the Bible, illustrated with
many pictures. And in long dark evenings, as my
three sisters with myself sat by the firelight round
the guard of our nursery, no book was so much in
request amongst us. It ruled us and swayed us as
mysteriously as music. Our younger nurse, whom
we all loved, would sometimes, according to her
simple powers, endeavour to explain what we found
obscure. We, the children, were all constitutionally
touched with pensiveness ; the fitful gloom and
sudden lambencies of the room by firelight suited our
evening state of feelings; and they suited also, the
divine revelations of power and mysterious beauty
which awed us. Above all, the story of a just man—
man and yet *not* man, real above all things, and yet
shadowy above all things—who had suffered the
passion of death in Palestine, slept upon our minds
like early dawn upon the waters. The nurse knew
and explained to us the chief differences in oriental
climates ; and all these differences (as it happens)

express themselves, more or less, in varying relation to the great accidents and powers of summer. The cloudless sunlights of Syria—these seemed to argue everlasting summer ; the disciples plucking the ears of corn—that *must* be summer ; but, above all, the very name of Palm Sunday (a festival in the English Church) troubled me like an anthem."

**Effect of our Liturgy on a Child.**—I cannot refrain from adding De Quincey's beautiful words describing the effect of our liturgy upon him as a child. " On Sunday mornings I went with the rest of my family to church : it was a church on the ancient model of England, having aisles, galleries, organ, all things ancient and venerable, and the proportions majestic. Here, whilst the congregation knelt through the long litany, as often as we came to that passage, so beautiful amongst many that are so, where God is supplicated on behalf of 'all sick persons and young children,' and that He would 'show His pity upon all prisoners and captives,' I wept in secret ; and raising my streaming eyes to the upper windows of the galleries, saw, on days when the sun was shining, a spectacle as affecting as ever prophet can have beheld. The *sides* of the windows were rich with stained glass; through the deep purples and crimsons streamed the golden light; emblazonries of heavenly illumination (from the sun) mingling with the earthly emblazonries (from art and its gorgeous colouring) of what is grandest in man. *There* were the apostles that had trampled upon earth, and the glories of earth, out of celestial love to man. *There* were the martyrs that had borne witness to the truth through flames, through torments, and through armies of fierce, insulting faces. *There* were the saints who, under intolerable pangs,

had glorified God by meek submission to His will."
"God speaks to children, also, in dreams and by the
oracles that lurk in darkness. But in *solitude*, above all
things, when made vocal to the meditative heart by
the truths and services of a national church, God holds
with children 'communion undisturbed.' *Solitude*,
though it may be silent as light, is, like light, the
mightiest of agencies; for solitude is essential to man.
All men come into this world *alone*; all leave it *alone*."

Principles on which to select School-Books.—
In their power of giving impulse and stirring emotion
is another use of books, the right books; but that is
just the question—which *are* the right books?—a point
upon which I should not wish to play Sir Oracle. The
'hundred best books for the schoolroom' may be put
down on a list, but not by me. I venture to propose
one or two principles in the matter of school-books,
and shall leave the far more difficult part, the application of those principles, to the reader. For example,
I think we owe it to children to let them dig their
knowledge, of whatever subject, for themselves out of
the fit book; and this for two reasons: What a child
*digs for* is his own possession; what is poured into his
ear, like the idle song of a pleasant singer, floats out
as lightly as it came in, and is rarely assimilated. I
do not mean to say that the lecture and the oral lesson
are without their uses; but these uses are, to give
impulse and to *order* knowledge; and not to convey
knowledge, or to afford us that part of our education
which comes of fit knowledge, fitly given.

Again, as I have already said, ideas must reach us
directly from the mind of the thinker, and it is chiefly
by means of the books they have written that we get
into touch with the best minds.

**Marks of a Fit Book.**—As to the distinguishing marks of a book for the school-room, a word or two may be said. A fit book is not necessarily a big book. John Quincy Adams, aged nine, wrote to his father for the fourth volume of Smollett for his private reading, though, as he owned up, his thoughts were running on birds' eggs; and perhaps some of us remember going religiously through the many volumes of Alison's *History of Europe* with a private feeling that the bigness of the book swelled the virtue of the reader. But, now, big men write little books, to be used with discretion; because sometimes the little books are no more than abstracts, the dry bones of the subjects; and sometimes the little books are fresh and living. Again, we need not always insist that a book should be written by the original thinker. It sometimes happens that second-rate minds have assimilated the matter in hand, and are able to give out what is their own thought (only because they have *made* it their own) in a form more suitable for our purpose than that of the first-hand thinkers. We cannot make any hard and fast rule—a big book or a little book, a book at first-hand or at second-hand; either may be right provided we have it in us to discern a *living* book, quick, and informed with the ideas proper to the subject of which it treats.

**How to use the Right Books.**—So much for the right books; the right use of them is another matter. The children must enjoy the book. The ideas it holds must each make that sudden, delightful impact upon their minds, must cause that intellectual stir, which mark the inception of an idea. The teacher's part in this regard is to see and feel for himself, and then to rouse his pupils by an appreciative look or word ; but to beware how he deadens the impression by a flood of talk. Intellectual sympathy is very stimulating ; but we have all been in the case of the little girl who said, " Mother, I think I could under-stand if you did not explain *quite* so much." A teacher said of her pupil, " I find it so hard to tell whether she has really grasped a thing or whether she has only got the mechanical hang of it." Children are imitative monkeys, and it is the ' mechanical hang ' that is apt to arrive after a douche of explanation.

**Children must Labour.**—This, of getting ideas out of them, is by no means all we must do with books. ' In all labour there is profit,' at any rate in some labour ; and the labour of thought is what his book must induce in the child. He must generalise, classify, infer, judge, visualise, discriminate, labour in one way or another, with that capable mind of his, until the substance of his book is assimilated or rejected, according as he shall determine ; for the determination rests with him and not with his teacher.

**Value of Narration.**—The simplest way of dealing with a paragraph or a chapter is to require the child to narrate its contents after a single attentive reading, —*one* reading, however slow, should be made a condition ; for we are all too apt to make sure we shall have another opportunity of finding out ' what 'tis all about.' There is the weekly review if we fail to get a clear grasp of the news of the day ; and, if we fail a second time, there is a monthly or a quarterly review or an annual summing up : in fact, many of us let present-day history pass by us with easy minds, feeling sure that, in the end, we shall be *compelled* to see the bearings of events. This is a bad habit to get into ; and we should do well to save our children by not giving them the vague expectation of second and third and tenth opportunities to do that which should have been done at first.

**A Single Careful Reading.**—There is much difference between intelligent reading, which the pupil should do in silence, and a mere parrot-like cramming up of contents; and it is not a bad test of education to be able to give the points of a description, the sequence of a series of incidents, the links in a chain of argument, correctly, after a single careful reading. This is a power which a barrister, a publisher, a scholar, labours to acquire; and it is a power which children can acquire with great ease, and once acquired, the gulf is bridged which divides the reading from the non-reading community.

**Other Ways of using Books.**—But this is only *one* way to use books: others are to enumerate the statements in a given paragraph or chapter; to analyse a chapter, to divide it into paragraphs under proper headings, to tabulate and classify series; to trace cause to consequence and consequence to cause; to discern character and perceive how character and circumstance interact; to get lessons of life and conduct, or the living knowledge which makes for science, out of books; all this is possible for school boys and girls, and *until* they have begun to use books for themselves in such ways, they can hardly be said to have begun their education.

**The Teacher's Part.**—The teacher's part is, in the first place, to see what is to be done, to look over the work of the day in advance and see what mental discipline, as well as what vital knowledge, this and that lesson afford; and then to set such questions and such tasks as shall give full scope to his pupils' mental activity. Let marginal notes be freely made, as neatly and beautifully as may be, for books should be handled with reverence. Let numbers, letters, underlining be used to help the eye and to save the needless fag of writing abstracts. Let the pupil write for himself half a dozen questions which cover the passage studied; he need not write the answers if he be taught that the mind can know nothing but what it can produce in the form of an answer to a question put by the mind to itself.

**Disciplinary Devices must not come between Children and the Soul of the Book.**—These few hints by no means cover the disciplinary uses of a good school-book; but let us be careful that our disciplinary devices, and our mechanical devices to secure and tabulate the substance of knowledge, do not come between the children and that which is the *soul* of the book, the living thought it contains. Science is doing so much for us in these days, nature is drawing so close to us, art is unfolding so much meaning to us, the world is becoming so rich for us, that we are a little in danger of neglecting the art of deriving sustenance from books. Let us not in such wise impoverish our lives and the lives of our children; for, to quote the golden words of Milton: " Books are not absolutely dead things, but do contain a potency of life in them to be as active as that soul was, whose progeny they are; nay, they do preserve, as in a vial, the purest efficacy and extraction of that living intellect that bred them. As good almost kill a man, as kill a good book; who kills a man kills a good reasonable creature, God's image; but he who destroys a good book, kills reason itself—kills the image of God, as it were, in the eye."

# CHAPTER XVII

## EDUCATION, THE SCIENCE OF RELATIONS: WE ARE EDUCATED BY OUR INTIMACIES: THE *PRELUDE* AND *PRÆTERITA*

> " But who shall parcel out
> His intellect by geometric rules,
> Split like a province into round and square?
> Who knows the individual hour in which
> His habits were first sown, even as a seed?
> Who that shall point as with a wand and say,
> ' This portion of the river of my mind
> Came from yon fountain'?"—*Prelude.*

I NEED not again insist upon the nature of our educational tools. We know well that " Education is an atmosphere, a discipline, a life." In other words, we know that parents and teachers should know how to make sensible use of a child's *circumstances* (atmosphere) to forward his sound education ; should train him in the discipline of the *habits* of the good life; and should nourish his life with *ideas*, the food upon which personality waxes strong.

**Only Three Educational Instruments.**—These three we believe to be the only instruments of which we may make lawful use in the upbringing of children; and any short cut we take by trading on their sensibilities, emotions, desires, passions, will bring us and our children to grief. The reason is plain ; habits, ideas, and circumstances are external, and we may all help each other to get the best that is to be had of these ; but we may not meddle directly with the personality of child or man. We may not work upon his vanity, his fears, his love, his emulation, or any-thing that is his by very right, anything that goes to make him a person.

**Our Limitations.**—Most thinking people are in earnest about the bringing up of children ; but we are in danger of taking too much upon us, and of not recognising the limitations which confine us to the outworks of personality. Children and grown-up persons are the same, with a difference ; and a thoughtful writer has done us good service by care-fully tracing the method of our Lord's education of the Twelve.

" Our Lord," says this author, " reverenced what-ever the learner had in him of his own, and was tender in fostering this native growth. . . . . Men, in His eyes, were not mere clay in the hands of the potter, matter to be moulded to shape. They were organic beings, each growing from within, with a life of his own—a personal life which was exceedingly precious in His and His Father's eyes—and He would foster this growth so that it might take after the highest type." [1]

**We temper Life too much for Children.**—I am not sure that we let life and its circumstances have free play about children. We temper the wind too much to the lambs ; pain and sin, want and suffering, disease and death—we shield them from

[1] *Pastor Pastorum*, by H. Latham, M.A., page 6.

the knowledge of these at all hazards. I do not say that we should wantonly expose the tender souls to distress, but that we should recognise that life has a ministry for them also; and that Nature provides them with a subtle screen, like that of its odour to a violet, from damaging shocks. Some of us will not even let children read fairy tales because these bring the ugly facts of life too suddenly before them. It is worth while to consider Wordsworth's experience on this point. Indeed I do not think we make enough use of two such priceless boons to parents and teachers as the educational autobiographies we possess of the two great philosophers, Wordsworth and Ruskin.

**Fairy Lore a Screen and Shelter.**—The former tells us how, no sooner had he gone to school at Hawkshead, than the body of a suicide was recovered from Esthwaite Lake; a ghastly tale, but full of comfort as showing how children are protected from shock. The little boy was there and saw it all ;—

> " Yet no soul-debasing fear,
> Young as I was, a child not nine years old,
> Possessed me, for my inner eye had seen
> Such sights before, among the shining streams
> Of fairyland, the forests of romance :
> Their spirit hallowed the sad spectacle
> With decoration of ideal grace ;
> A dignity, a smoothness, like the works
> Of Grecian art, and purest poesy."

It is delightful to know, on the evidence of a child who went through it, that a terrible scene was separated from him by an atmosphere of poetry— a curtain woven of fairy lore by his etherealising imagination.

But we may run no needless risks, and must keep

a quiet, matter-of-fact tone in speaking of fire, ship-wreck, or any terror. There are children to whom the thought of Joseph in the pit is a nightmare; and many of us elders are unable to endure a ghastly tale in newspaper or novel. All I would urge is a natural treatment of children, and that they be allowed their fair share of life, such as it is; prudence and not panic should rule our conduct towards them.

**Spontaneous Living.**—The laws of habit are, we know, laws of God, and the forming of good and the hindering of evil habits are among the primary duties of a parent. But it is just as well to be reminded that habits, whether helpful or hindering, only come into play occasionally, while a great deal of spontaneous living is always going on towards which we can do no more than drop in vital ideas as opportunity occurs. All this is old matter, and I must beg the reader to forgive me for reminding him again that our educational instruments remain the same. We may not leave off the attempt to form good habits with tact and care, to suggest fruitful ideas, without too much insistence, and to make wise use of circumstances.

**On what does Fulness of Living depend?**—What is education after all? An answer lies in the phrase—*Education is the Science of Relations.* I do not use this phrase, let me say once more, in the Herbartian sense—that things are related to each other, and we must be careful to pack the right things in together, so that, having got into the brain of a boy, each thing may fasten on its cousins, and together they may make a strong clique or 'apperception mass.' What we are concerned with is the fact that we personally have relations with all that there is in the present, all that there has been in the past, and all that there will be in the future—with all above us and all about us—and that fulness of living, expansion, expression, and serviceableness, for each of us, depend upon how far we apprehend these relationships and how many of them we lay hold of.

George Herbert says something of what I mean :—

> " Man is all symmetry,
> Full of proportions, one limb to another,
>     And *all to all the world besides* ;
>     Each part may call the farthest brother,
> For head with foot hath private amity,
>     And *both with moons and tides*." [1]

Every child is heir to an enormous patrimony, heir to all the ages, inheritor of all the present. The question is, what are the formalities (educational, not legal) necessary to put him in possession of that which is his? You perceive the point of view is shifted, and is no longer subjective, but objective, as regards the child.

**The Child a Person.**—We do not talk about developing his faculties, training his moral nature, guiding his religious feelings, educating him with a view to his social standing or his future calling. The joys of 'child-study' are not for us. We take the child for granted, or rather, we take him as we find him—a person with an enormous number of healthy affinities, embryo attachments ; and we think it is our chief business to give him a chance to make the largest possible number of these attachments valid.

**An Infant's Self-Education.**—An infant comes into the world with a thousand such embryonic

---

[1] The italics are mine.

feelers, which he sets to work to fix with amazing energy :—

> "The Babe,
> Nursed in his Mother's arms, who sinks to sleep
> Rocked on his Mother's breast ; who with his soul
> Drinks in the feelings of his Mother's eye !
> For him, in one dear Presence, there exists
> A virtue which irradiates and exalts
> Objects through widest intercourse of sense.
> No outcast he, bewildered and depressed :
> Along his infant veins are interfused
> The gravitation and the filial bond
> Of nature that connects him with the world."[1]

He attaches his being to mother, father, sister, brother, 'nanna,' the man in the street whom he calls 'dada,' cat and dog, spider and fly; earth, air, fire, and water attract him perilously; his eyes covet light and colour, his ears sound, his limbs movement ; everything concerns him, and out of everything he gets—

> "That calm delight
> Which, if I err not, surely must belong
> To those first-born affinities that fit
> Our new existence to existing things,
> And, in our dawn of being, constitute
> The bond of union between life and joy."[1]

He gets also, when left to himself, the real knowledge about each thing which establishes his relation with that particular thing.

**Our Part, to remove Obstructions and to give Stimulus.**—Later, we step in to educate him. In proportion to the range of living relationships we put in his way, will he have wide and vital interests, fulness of joy in living. In proportion as he is made

[1] *The Prelude.*

aware of the laws which rule every relationship, will his life be dutiful and serviceable : as he learns that no relation with persons or with things, animate or inanimate, can be maintained without strenuous effort, will he learn the laws of work and the joys of work.    Our part is to remove obstructions and to give stimulus and guidance to the child who is trying to get into touch with the universe of things and thoughts which belongs to him.

Our Error.—Our deadly error is to suppose that we are his showman to the universe ; and, not only so, but that there is no community at all between child and universe unless such as we choose to set up. We are the people! and if we choose that a village child's education should be confined to the 'three R's,' why, what right has he to ask for more? If *life* means for him his Saturday night in the ale-house, surely that is not our fault! If our own boys go through school and college and come out without quickening interests, without links to the things that are worth while, we are not sure that it is our fault either.    We resent that they should be called 'muddied oafs' because we know them to be fine fellows.    So they are, splendid stuff which has not yet arrived at the making!

Business and Desire.—Quoth Hamlet,—

"Every man hath business and desire."

Doubtless that was true in the spacious days of great Elizabeth ; for us, we have business, but have we desire?    Are there many keen interests soliciting us outside of our necessary work?    Perhaps not, or we should be less enslaved by the vapid joys of Ping-Pong, Patience, Bridge, and their like.    The fact is that 'interests' are not to be taken up on the spur of the moment; they spring out of affinities we have found and laid hold of. Or, in the words of an old writer: "In worldly and material things, what is Used is spent; in intellectual and spiritual things, what is not Used is not Had."

Supposing we have realised that we must make provision for the future of our children otherwise than by safe investments, the question remains, how to set about it.

**The Setting-up of Dynamic Relations.**—We say a child should have what we will call *Dynamic Relations* with earth and water, must run and leap and dance, must ride and swim. This is how *not* to do it, as set forth in *Præterita*:—

"And so on to Llanberis and up Snowdon. . . . . And if only then my father and mother had seen the real strengths and weaknesses of their little John; if they had given me but a shaggy scrap of a Welsh pony, and left me in charge of a good Welsh guide, and of his wife, if I needed any coddling, they would have made a man of me there and then. . . . . If only! But they could no more have done it than thrown me like my cousin Charles into Croydon Canal, trusting me to find my way out by the laws of nature. Instead, they took me back to London; my father spared time from his business hours, once or twice a week, to take me to a four-square, sky-lighted, saw-dust floored prison of a riding school in Moorfields, the smell of which, as we turned in at the gate of it, was a terror and horror and abomination to me : and there I was put on big horses that jumped and reared, and circled, and sidled, and fell off them regularly whenever they did any of these things ; and was a disgrace to my family, and a burning shame and misery to myself, till at last the riding school was given up on my spraining my right hand fore-finger (it has never come straight again since) ; and a well-broken Shetland pony bought for me, and the two of us led about the Norwood roads by a riding master with a leading string.

" I used to do pretty well as long as we went straight, and
then get thinking of something and fall off as we turned a corner.
I might have got some inkling of a seat in heaven's good time,
if no fuss had been made about me, nor inquiries instituted
whether I had been off or on ; but as my mother the moment
I got home made searching scrutiny into the day's disgraces, I
merely got more nervous and helpless after every tumble ; and
this branch of my education was at last abandoned, my parents
consoling themselves as best they might, in the conclusion that
my not being able to learn to ride was the sign of my being a
singular genius."

### Ruskin's Indictment of the Limitations of his Condition.

—Ruskin suffered from the malady of
his condition.  He was of the suburban dwellers of
the rich middle class who think, not wisely but too
much, about the bringing up of their children, who
choke a good deal of life with care and coddling, and
are apt to be persuaded that their children want no
outlets but such as it occurs to them to provide.
Suburban life is a necessity, but it is also a misfortune,
because, in a rich suburb, people live too much with
their own sort.  They are cut off from the small
and the great, from labour, adventure, and privation.
Let me recommend all rich educated parents who
live in suburbs to read *Præterita*.  With all his
chivalrous loyalty to his parents, Ruskin has left
here a grave indictment, not of them, but of the
limitations of his condition.  One hears the cry of
the child, like that of Laurence Sterne's caged
starling—' I can't get out, I can't get out '—repeated
from page to page.

You will say, whatever were the faults of his
education, *Ruskin* emerged from it, such as it was ;
and *we* look for no more.  But it is not for us to
say how much greater an apostle among men even

Ruskin would have become had he been allowed his right of free living as a child. And it may be, on the other hand, safe to admit that not every child, born and bred in a villa, will certainly be another Ruskin !

We cannot follow Mr Ruskin further in the setting up of the dynamic relations proper to him, because his parents forbade, and nothing happened. His mother, he says, 'never allowed me to go to the edge of a pond or be in the same field with a pony.' But he notes 'with thankfulness the good I got out of the tadpole-haunted ditch in Croxted Lane.' Camberwell Green had a pond, and, he says, 'it was one of the most valued privileges of my early life to be permitted by my nurse to contemplate this judicial pond with awe from the other side of the way.'

**Wordsworth's Recognition of his Opportunities.**—Wordsworth tells us of a much more rough-and-tumble bringing up. When he was nine, he was sent to the Grammar School in the little village of Hawkshead and lodged with Dame Tyson in the cottage many of us know ; and found most things, at home and abroad, congenial to his soul. He had no lessons in riding and skating, hockey and tennis; but no doubt the other boys made it plain to the little chap that he must do as they did or be thought a fool. But then he went to school a hardy youngster ; his mother had let her little boy *live* :—

> "Oh, many a time have I, a five years' child,
> In a small mill-race severed from his stream,
> Made one long bathing of a summer's day ;
> Basked in the sun, and plunged, and basked again."

Of his childhood, he says :—

> "Fair seed-time had my soul, and I grew up
> Fostered alike by beauty and by fear."

Ere he had told ten birthdays, he was transplanted
to that 'belovèd Vale' of which he says :—

> "There were we let loose
> For sports of wider range."

What was there those Hawkshead boys did not
do!   He tells us of times,—

> "When I have hung
> Above the raven's nest, by knots of grass
> And half-inch fissures in the slippery rock
> But ill-sustained, and almost (so it seemed)
> Suspended by the blast that blew amain,
> Shouldering the naked crag."

The boys skated :—

> "All shod with steel,
> We hissed along the polished ice in games
> Confederate, imitative of the chase
> And woodland pleasures,—the resounding horn,
> The pack loud chiming, and the hunted hare."

They played :—

> "From week to week, from month to month, we lived
> A round of tumult.   Duly were our games
> Prolonged in summer till the daylight failed."

They boated :—

> "When summer came,
> Our pastime was, on bright half-holidays,
> To sweep along the plain of Windermere
> With rival oars. . . . .
>         In such a race
> So ended disappointment could be none,
> Uneasiness, or pain, or jealousy :
> We rested in the shade, all pleased alike,
> Conquered and conqueror."

The young Wordsworth, too, had his essays on
horseback when he and his schoolmates came back

rich from the half-yearly holidays and hired horses from 'the courteous innkeeper,' and off they went, 'proud to curb, and eager to spur on, the galloping steed'; and then, the home-coming :—

> "Through the walls we flew
> And down the valley, and, a circuit made
> In wantonness of heart, through rough and smooth
> We scampered homewards."

# CHAPTER XVIII

## WE ARE EDUCATED BY OUR INTIMACIES

### PART II.—*FURTHER AFFINITIES*

**Affinity for Material: Ruskin's Opportunities.**
—Of the *Affinity for Material*, the joy of handling and
making, Wordsworth says little, but Ruskin sent out
feelers in this direction which began with 'two boxes
of well-cut wooden bricks' and culminated, perhaps,
in the road-making of the Oxford days:—

> "I was afterwards," he says, "gifted with a two-arched bridge,
> admirable in fittings of voussoir and keystone, and adjustment
> of the level courses of masonry with bevelled edges, into which
> they dovetailed in the style of Waterloo Bridge. Well-made
> centrings, and a course of inlaid steps down to the water, made
> this model largely, as accurately, instructive : and I was never
> weary of building, *un*-building—(it was too strong to be thrown
> down, but had always to be *taken* down)—and re-building it."

We know how he busied himself with making a
small dam and reservoir at both the Herne Hill and
Denmark Hill homes ; and how, while still a boy, he
scrubbed down, with pail of water and broom, the
dirty steps of an Alpine hotel, because they offended
his mother. We feel that in this direction, again, his
nature cried aloud for opportunities.

**Intimacy with Natural Objects.**—We do not

hear much of the intimacy of either boy with *Natural
Objects*, such as birds and flowers ; but here, again, we
feel that Ruskin was deprived of opportunity.    His
flower friends were garden dwellers ; and could anything be more pathetic than this : " My chief prayer
for the kindness of heaven, in its flowerful seasons, was
that the frost might not touch the almond blossom." [1]

Wordsworth appears to have waited for his
intimacy with wild-flowers until he could say of his
sister Dorothy, " She gave me eyes, she gave me
ears."    Birds, as we have seen, he knew through the
wicked joy of birdsnesting ; but not only so, that day
when the wild cavalcade rode to Furness Abbey, he
marked—

> "That simple wren
> Which one day sang so sweetly in the nave
> Of the old church, that . . . .
> I could have made
> My dwelling-place, and lived for ever there
> To hear such music."

**Ruskin's Flower Studies.**—If Ruskin had not, as
a child, a wide acquaintance with the flowers of the
field, he made up, perhaps, by the enormous attention
he gave to such as came in his way ; and, just as his
toy bricks and his bridge gave him his initiation in
the principles of architecture, so, perhaps, his early
flower studies resulted in his power of seeing and
expressing detail.    He says of flowers : " My whole
time passed in staring at them or into them.    In no
morbid curiosity, but in admiring wonder, I pulled
every flower to pieces till I knew all that could be
seen of it with a child's eyes ; and used to lay up

[1] Students of *Love's Meinie* and *Proserpine* will know what rich
compensations later life brought for the child's disadvantages.

little treasures of seeds, by way of pearls and beads,—
never with any thought of sowing them." He com-
plains that books on Botany were harder than the
Latin Grammar.

**His Pebble Studies.**—" Had there been anybody
then to teach me anything about plants or pebbles," he
says, " it had been good for me." He loved the pebbles
of the Tay, and followed up his acquaintance with
pebbles at Matlock. " In the glittering white broken
spar, speckled with galena, by which the walks of the
hotel garden were made bright, and in the slopes
of the pretty village, and in many a happy walk
along its cliffs, I pursued my mineralogical studies
on fluor, calcite, and the ores of lead, and with in-
describable rapture when I was allowed to go into
a cave."

**A Life-shaping Intimacy.**—Later we find him
going up Snowdon, " of which ascent I remember, as
the most exciting event, the finding for the first time
in my life a real 'mineral' for myself, a piece of
copper pyrites ! " This eagerly sought acquaintance
with pebbles resulted in the life-shaping intimacy with
minerals to which we owe *The Ethics of the Dust.*

**Insatiate Delight in a Book—Ruskin's.**—As
for *Books*, we are told how Ruskin grew up upon the
Waverley Novels, on Pope's Homer's *Iliad,* many of
Shakespeare's plays, and much else that is delightful ;
but he does not give us an instance of the sort of thing
we are looking for—the sudden keen, insatiate delight
in a book which means kinship—until he is introduced to Byron. His first acquaintance with Byron
he puts " about the beginning of the teen period " :—

" But very certainly, by the end of this year 1834, I knew
my Byron pretty well all through, all but Cain, Werner, the

Deformed Transformed, and Vision of Judgment, none of which I could understand, nor did papa and mamma think it would be well I should try to. . . . . So far as I could understand it, I rejoiced in all the sarcasm of Don Juan. But my firm decision, as soon as I got well into the later cantos of it, that Byron was to be my master in verse, as Turner in colour, was made of course in that gosling (or say cygnet) epoch of existence, without consciousness of the deeper instincts that prompted it : only two things I consciously recognised, that his truth of observation was the most exact, and his chosen expression the most concentrated, that I had yet found in literature. . . . . But the thing wholly new and precious to me in Byron was his measured and living *truth*—measured, as compared with Homer ; and living, as compared with everybody else. . . . . He taught me the meaning of Chillon and of Meillerie, and bade me seek first in Venice—the ruined homes of Foscari and Falieri. . . . . Byron told me of, and reanimated for me, the real people whose feet had worn the marble I trod on."

**Wordsworth's.**—This is how Wordsworth took to his books :—

> "A precious treasure had I long possessed,
> A little yellow canvas-covered book,
> A slender abstract of the Arabian tales ;
> And, from companions in a new abode,
> When first I learnt, that this dear prize of mine
> Was but a block hewn from a mighty quarry—
> That there were four large volumes, laden all
> With kindred matter, 'twas to me, in truth,
> A promise scarcely earthly. . . . .
> And when thereafter to my father's house
> The holidays returned me, there to find
> That golden store of books which I had left,
> What joy was mine ! How often . . . .
>                     have I lain
> Down by thy side, O Derwent ! murmuring stream,
> On the hot stones, and in the glaring sun,
> And there have read, devouring as I read,
> Defrauding the day's glory, desperate !"

### "They must have their Food" of Romance.—
Nor can I omit the counsel that follows :—

"A gracious spirit o'er this earth presides,
   And o'er the heart of man : invisibly
   It comes, to works of unreproved delight,
   And tendency benign, directing those
   Who care not, know not, think not what they do.
   The tales that charm away the wakeful night
   In Araby romances ; legends penned
   For solace by dim light of monkish lamps ;
   Fictions, for ladies of their love, devised
   By youthful squires ; adventures endless, spun
   By the dismantled warrior in old age,
   Out of the bowels of those very schemes
   In which his youth did first extravagate ;
   These spread like day, and something in the shape
   Of these will live till man shall be no more.
   Dumb yearnings, hidden appetites, are ours,
   And *they must* have their food.   Our childhood sits,
   Our simple childhood, sits upon a throne
   That hath more power than all the elements."

### Children must range at will among Books.—
And this other counsel :—

"Rarely and with reluctance would I stoop
   To transitory themes ; yet I rejoice,
   And, by these thoughts admonished, will pour out
   Thanks with uplifted heart, that I was reared
   Safe from an evil which these days have laid
   Upon the children of the land, a pest
   That might have dried me up, body and soul. . . . .
   Where had we been, we two, belovèd Friend !
   If in the season of unperilous choice,
   In lieu of wandering, as we did, though vales
   Rich with indigenous produce, open ground
   Of fancy, happy pastures ranged at will,
   We had been followed, hourly watched, and noosed.
   Each in his several melancholy walk."

Words, 'a Passion and a Power.'—Later,
follows the story of his first enthralment by poetry :—

> "Twice five years
> Or less I might have seen, when first my mind
> With conscious pleasure opened to the charm
> Of words in timeful order, found them sweet
> For their own *sakes*, a passion and a power ;
> And phrases pleased me chosen for delight,
> For pomp, or love.  Oft, in the public roads
> Yet unfrequented, while the morning light
> Was yellowing the hill tops, I went abroad
> With a dear friend, and for the better part
> Of two delightful hours we strolled along
> By the still borders of the misty lake,
> Repeating favourite verses with one voice,
> Or conning more, as happy as the birds
> That round us chaunted."

**Ruskin's Local Historic Sense.**—The awakening
of the *Historic Sense* in Ruskin appears to be always,
and here is a great lesson for us, connected with
places : that historic interest and æsthetic delight
are one with him, is another thing to take note of.
We have seen how Byron served him in this way.
Again, he tells us of the "three centres of my life's
thought, Rouen, Geneva, and Pisa, which have been
tutoresses of all I know and were mistresses of all I
did from the first moments I entered their gates."
These came later, but Abbeville "was entrance for
me into immediately healthy labour and joy. . . . .
My most intense happinesses have of course been
among mountains.  But for cheerful, unalloyed,
unwearying pleasure, the getting sight of Abbeville
on a fine summer afternoon, jumping out in the
courtyard of the Hôtel de l'Europe and rushing
down the street to see St Wulfran again before the

sun was off the towers, are things to cherish the past for—to the end."

**Living Touch with the Past necessary.**—But Ruskin's want of living touch with the past, except as such touch was given by the newly discovered history of a place he happened to be in, is shown in his first impressions of Rome :—

"My stock of Latin learning, with which to begin my studies of the city, consisted of the two first books of Livy, never well known, and the names of places remembered without ever looking where they were on a map ; Juvenal, a page or two of Tacitus, and in Virgil the burning of Troy, the story of Dido, the episode of Euryalus, and the last battle. Of course, I had nominally read the whole Æneid, but thought most of it nonsense. Of later Roman history, I had read English abstracts of the imperial vices, and supposed the malaria in the Campagna to be the consequence of the Papacy. I had never heard of a good Roman Emperor, or a good Pope ; was not quite sure whether Trajan lived before Christ or after, and would have thanked, with a sense of relieved satisfaction, anybody who might have told me that Marcus Antoninus was a Roman philosopher contemporary with Socrates. . . . . We of course drove about the town, and saw the Forum, Coliseum, and so on. I had no distinct idea what the Forum was or ever had been, or how the three pillars, or the seven, were connected with it, or the Arch of Severus. . . . . What the Forum or Capitol had been, I did not in the least care ; the pillars of the Forum I saw were on a small scale, and their capitals rudely carved, and the houses above them nothing like so interesting as the side of any close in the 'auld toun' of Edinburgh."

**Wordsworth and Ruskin, aloof from the Past.**
—Wordsworth, too, stood aloof. He was aware of

> "Old, unhappy, far-off things
> And battles long ago ; "

but the past of nations did not enthral him ; even the throes of the French Revolution, to judge by what he

tells us in the *Prelude*, hardly shook him to his foundation, though he took a walking tour on the Continent
at the moment when, as he himself says—

> "As if awaked from sleep, the nations hailed
>    Their great expectancy."

But for him—

> "I looked upon these things
> As from a distance ; heard and saw and felt,
> Was touched, but with no intimate concern."

**Knowledge learned in Schools.**—As for the
*Knowledge learned in Schools*, Ruskin gives us rather
dry details of his experiences in Euclid, the Latin
grammar, and the like, but neither boy appears to
have been 'stung with the rapture of a sudden
thought' in the course of his lessons, unless Hawkshead Grammar School can take this to itself :—

> "Many are our joys
> In youth, but oh ! what happiness to live
> When every hour brings palpable access
> Of knowledge, when all knowledge is delight,
> And sorrow is not there !"

But the praise of the unfolding of the seasons follows,
and I am afraid it is the lore they brought with them
that the poet had in his mind's eye.

**Comradeship.**—We have all been interested in
the late Mr Rhodes's illuminating will, and I suppose
most mothers and most masters have pondered the
four groups of qualifications for scholarships. In (3)
we have 'fellowship,' in (4) 'instincts to lead and take
an interest in his schoolmates.' It is well that a talent
for *Comradeship* should be brought before us in this
prominent way as a *sine quâ non*. Here is the rock

upon which Ruskin's education split, as he was sadly aware; he never knew the joys of comradeship. Having spoken of 'peace, obedience, faith; these three for chief good; next to these the habit of fixed attention with both eyes and mind,' as the main blessings of his childhood, he goes on to enumerate 'the equally dominant calamities':—

"First, that I had nothing to love. My parents were—in a sort—visible powers of nature to me, no more loved than the sun and the moon : only I should have been annoyed and puzzled if either of them had gone out ; (how much, now, when both are darkened !)—still less did I love God ; not that I had any quarrel with Him, or fear of Him ; but simply found what people told me was His service, disagreeable ; and what people told me was His book, not entertaining. I had no companions to quarrel with neither ; nobody to assist, and nobody to thank. Not a servant was ever allowed to do anything for me, but what it was their duty to do ; and why should I have been grateful to the cook for cooking, or the gardener for gardening? . . . . My present verdict, therefore, on the general tenor of my education at that time, must be, that it was at once too formal and too luxurious ; leaving my character at the most important moment for its construction, cramped indeed, but not disciplined ; and only by protection innocent, instead of by practice virtuous."

Wordsworth, on the contrary, as we have seen, lived the life of his school-fellows with entire *abandon*. He was with a crowd of his mates or he was with a friend, and was only alone in those moments of deeper intimacy which we shall speak of presently. The simple life of his 'belovèd Vale' took such hold on his tenacious northern nature that not Cambridge, nor London, nor (as we have seen) Europe in its time of convulsion, could displace the earlier images or give new direction to his profoundest thought.

Scott laid claim to 'intimacy with all ranks of my countrymen from the Scottish peer to the Scottish

ploughman,' and — we get the Waverley Novels.
Wordsworth was satisfied to know the fine-natured
peasant folk of his own dales, and poet-souls like his
own. Perhaps such limitations went to the making
of the poet of plain living and high thinking; but
limitations are hazardous.

# CHAPTER XIX

## WE ARE EDUCATED BY OUR INTIMACIES

### PART III.—*VOCATION*

I might trace the consummation of various other affinities in these two illustrious subjects, but space fails; I can only indicate the joy of pursuing the acquaintanceship, followed by the endless occupation for mind and heart, in that high intimacy which we call the *Vocation* of each of these men of genius.

**Turner's Call to Ruskin.**—Ruskin's 'career,' to use our own common and expressive figure, began when,—

"On my thirteenth (?) birthday, 8th February 1832, my father's partner, Mr Henry Telford, gave me Rogers's Italy, and determined the main tenor of my life. . . . . I had no sooner cast my eyes on the Turner vignettes than I took them for my only masters, and set myself to imitate them as far as I possibly could by fine pen shading. . . . .

"My father at last gave me, not for a beginning of a Turner collection, but for a specimen of Turner's work, which was all—as it was supposed—I should ever need or aspire to possess, the 'Richmond Bridge, Surrey.'"

Again, anent his purchase of Turner's 'Harlech':—

"Whatever germs of better things remained in me, were then all centred in this love of Turner. It was not a piece of painted paper, but a Welsh castle and village, and Snowdon in blue cloud, that I bought for my seventy pounds."

**Sincere Work.**—Not until he is twenty-two does he produce what he considers his first sincere drawing :—

"One day on the road to Norwood, I noticed a bit of ivy round a thorn stem, which seemed, even to my critical judgment, not 'ill-composed,' and proceeded to make a light and shade pencil study of it in my grey paper pocket-book, carefully, as if it had been a bit of sculpture, liking it more and more as I drew. When it was done, I saw that I had virtually lost all my time since I was twelve years old, because no one had ever told me to draw what was really there !"

**Initiation.**—Later, follows the story of his true initiation :—

"I took out my book and began to draw a little aspen tree, on the other side of the cart-road, carefully. . . . . Languidly, but not idly, I began to draw it ; and as I drew, the langour passed away, the beautiful lines insisted on being traced, without weariness. More and more beautiful they became as each rose out of the rest and took its place in the air. With wonder increasing every instant, I saw that they composed themselves by finer laws than any known of men. At last the tree was there, and everything that I had thought before about trees nowhere. . . . . 'He hath made everything beautiful in His time' became for me thenceforward the interpretation of the bond between the human mind and all visible things."

**Nature a Passion.**—Let us intrude into the consummation of one more intimacy. Already the boy has made acquaintance with mountains ; he is now to have his first sight of the Alps. He, his father, his mother, and his cousin Mary, went out to walk the first Sunday evening after their arrival on the garden terrace of Schaffhausen, and—

"Suddenly—behold—beyond ! There was no thought in any of us for a moment of their being clouds. They were clear as crystal, sharp on the pure horizon sky, and already tinged with rose by the setting sun. Infinitely beyond all that we had ever thought or dreamed—the seen walls of lost Eden could not have been more beautiful to us ; not more awful, round heaven, the walls of sacred death. It is not possible to imagine, in any time of the world, a more blessed entrance into life, for a child of such temperament as mine."

How shall we venture to trace the growth of that austere, most gracious and enthralling intimacy with Nature which was to Wordsworth the master-light of all his seeing ? He unfolds to us—

"The simple ways in which my childhood walked ;
    Those chiefly that first led me to the love
    Of rivers, woods, and fields. The passion yet
    Was in its birth, sustained as might befall
    By nourishment that came unsought."

We cannot trace every step of the growth of this ethereal passion, but only take a phase of it here and there. The boy and some of his schoolfellows were boating on Windermere in the late evening, and they left one of their number, 'the Minstrel of the Troop,' on a small island :—

"And rowed off gently, while he blew his flute
    Alone upon the rock—oh, then, the calm
    And dead still water lay upon my mind
    Even with a weight of pleasure, and the sky,
    Never before so beautiful, sank down
    Into my heart, and held me like a dream !
    Thus were my sympathies enlarged, and thus
    Daily the common range of visible things
    Grew dear to me : already I began
    To love the sun ; a boy, I loved the sun,
    Not as I since have loved him, as a pledge
    And surety of our earthly life, a light
    Which we behold and feel we are alive ;
    Not for his bounty to so many worlds--
    But for this cause, that I had seen him lay
    His beauty on the morning hills, had seen
    The western mountain touch his setting orb."

**The Calling of a Poet.**—We may take one more look at this marvellous boy, who, become a man, held that every child, as he, is born a poet :—

> " My seventeenth year was come ,
> . . . . I, at this time,
> Saw blessings spread around me like a sea.
> Thus while the days flew by, and years passed on,
> From nature and her overflowing soul
> I had received so much, that all my thoughts
> Were steeped in feeling ; I was only then
> Contented, when with bliss ineffable
> I felt the sentiment of Being spread
> O'er all that moves and all that seemeth still ;
> O'er all that, lost beyond the reach of thought
> And human knowledge, to the human eye
> Invisible, yet liveth to the heart ;
> O'er all that leaps and runs, and shouts and sings,
> Or beats the gladsome air ; o'er all that glides
> Beneath the wave, yea, in the wave itself,
> And mighty depth of waters.
> . . . . If I should fail with grateful voice
> To speak of you, ye mountains, and ye lakes
> And sounding cataracts, ye mists and winds
> That dwell among the hills where I was born.
> If in my youth I have been pure in heart,
> If, mingling with the world, I am content
> With my own modest pleasures, and have lived
> With God and nature communing, removed
> From little enmities and low desires,
> The gift is yours."

**The Education of the Little Prig.**—Before taking leave of the *Prelude*, may I introduce Wordsworth's sketch of the 'child-studied' little prig of his days—days of much searching of heart and of many theories on the subject of education ?—

> " That common sense
> May try this common system by its fruits,
> Leave let me take to place before her sight

A specimen pourtrayed with faithful hand.
Full early trained to worship seemliness,
This model of a child is never known
To mix in quarrels ; that were far beneath
Its dignity ; with gifts he bubbles o'er
As generous as a fountain ; selfishness
May not come near him, nor the little throng
Of flitting pleasures tempt him from his path ;
The wandering beggars propagate his name,
Dumb creatures find him tender as a nun,
And natural or supernatural fear,
Unless it leaps upon him in a dream,
Touches him not.  To enhance the wonder, see
How arch his notices, how nice his sense
Of the ridiculous ; . . . . he can read
The inside of the earth, and spell the stars ;
He knows the policies of foreign lands ;
Can string you names of districts, cities, towns,
The whole world over, tight as beads of dew
Upon a gossamer thread ; he sifts, he weighs ;
All things are put to question ; he must live
Knowing that he grows wiser every day,
Or else not live at all, and seeing too
Each little drop of wisdom as it falls
Into the dimpling cistern of his heart :
For this unnatural growth the trainer blame,
Pity the tree. . . . .
Meanwhile old grandame earth is grieved to find
The playthings, which her love designed for him,
Unthought of : in their woodland beds the flowers
Weep, and the river sides are all forlorn.
Oh ! give us once again the wishing-cap
Of Fortunatus, and the invisible coat
Of Jack the Giant-killer, Robin Hood,
And Sabra in the forest with St George !
The child, whose love is here, at least, doth reap
One precious gain, that he forgets himself."

**Children have Affinities and should have
Relations.**—I cannot stop here to gather any more

of the instruction and edification contained in those
two great educational books, *The Prelude* and
*Præterita*. It is enough for the present if they have
shown us in what manner children attach themselves
to their proper affinities, given opportunity and liberty.
Our part is to drop occasion freely in the way, whether
in school or at home. Children should have relations
with earth and water, should run and leap, ride and
swim, should establish the relation of maker to material
in as many kinds as may be; should have dear and
intimate relations with persons, through present intercourse, through tale or poem, picture or statue; through
flint arrow-head or modern motor-car: beast and bird,
herb and tree, they must have familiar acquaintance
with. Other peoples and their languages must not
be strange to them. Above all they should find that
most intimate and highest of all Relationships,—the
fulfilment of their being.

This is not a bewildering programme, because, in
all these and more directions, children have affinities;
and a human being does not fill his place in the
universe without putting out tendrils of attachment
in the directions proper to him. We must get rid
of the notion that to learn the 'three R's' or the
Latin grammar well, a child should learn these and
nothing else. It is as true for children as for ourselves that, the wider the range of interests, the more
intelligent is the apprehension of each.

**Education not Desultory.**—But I am not
preaching a gospel for the indolent and proclaiming that education is a casual and desultory
matter. Many great authors have written at least one
book devoted to education; and *Waverley* seems to
me to be Scott's special contribution to our science.

Edward Waverley, we are told, 'was permitted in a great measure to learn as he pleased, when he pleased, and what he pleased.' That he did please to learn and that his powers of apprehension were uncommonly quick, would appear to justify this sort of education. But wavering he was allowed to grow up, and 'Waverley' he remained; instability and ineffectiveness marked his course. The manner of his education and its results are thus shortly set forth :—

"Edward would throw himself with spirit upon any classical author of which his preceptor proposed the perusal, make himself master of the style so far as to understand the story, and, if that pleased or interested him, he finished the volume. But it was in vain to attempt fixing his attention on critical distinctions of philology, upon the difference of idiom, the beauty of felicitous expression, or the artificial combinations of syntax. 'I can read and understand a Latin author,' said young Edward, with the self-confidence and rash reasoning of fifteen, 'and Scaliger or Bentley could not do much more.' Alas! while he was thus permitted to read only for the gratification of his amusement, he foresaw not that he was losing for ever the opportunity of acquiring habits of firm and assiduous application, of gaining the art of controlling, directing, and concentrating the powers of his mind for earnest investigation—an art far more essential than even that intimate acquaintance with classical learning which is the primary object of study."

*Waverley* but illustrates, what Mr Ruskin says in plain words; that our youth—whatever we make of it —abides with us to the end:—

"But so stubborn and chemically inalterable the laws of the prescription were, that now, looking back from 1886 to that brook shore of 1837, whence I could see the whole of my youth, I find myself in nothing whatsoever *changed*. Some of me is dead, more of me is stronger. I have learned a few things, forgotten many. In the total of me, I am but the same youth, disappointed and rheumatic."

**Strenuous Effort and Reverence.**—We have seen in Ruskin and Wordsworth the strenuous attention —condition of receptiveness—which made each of them a producer after his kind ; and whosoever will play the game, whether it be cricket or portrait painting, must learn the rules with all diligence and get skill by his labour. It is true, 'the labour we delight in physics pain,' but it is also true that we cannot catch hold of any one of the affinities that are in waiting for us without strenuous effort and without reverence. A bird-lover, one would say, has chosen for himself an easy joy ; but no : your true bird-lover is out of doors by four in the morning to assist at the levée of the birds; nay, is he not in Hyde Park by 2.30 a.m. to see—the kingfisher, no less ! He lies in wait in secret places to watch the goings on of the feathered peoples, travels far afield to make a new acquaintance in the bird-world ; in fact, gives to the study of birds attention, labour, love, and reverence. He gets joy in return, so is perhaps little conscious of effort ; but the effort is made all the same.

**Comradeship has Duties.**—To take one more instance of an affinity—comradeship. Most of us have serious thoughts about friendship ; but we are apt to take comradeship, fellowship, very casually, and to think it is sufficiently maintained if we meet for parties, games, picnics, or what not. Public school boys generally learn better ; they know that comradeship means much cheerful give-and-take, chaff, help, unsparing criticism ; if need be, the taking or giving of serious reproof; loyalty each to each, plucky and faithful leading, staunch following, truth-speaking ; the power to see others put first without chagrin, and to bear advancement without conceit. Here, too, are calls for attention, labour, love, and reverence; but, again, labour is swallowed up in delight.

**The Angel troubles the Still Pool.**—One more point. We are steadfast to the affinities we take hold of, till death do us part, or longer. And here let me say a word as to the 'advantages' (?) which London offers in the way of masters and special classes. I think it is most often the still pool which the angel comes down to trouble: a steady unruffled course of work without so-called advantages lends itself best to that 'troubling' of the angel—the striking upon us of what Coleridge calls 'the Captain Idea,' which initiates a tie of affinity.

**The Highest Relationship.**—Neither *The Prelude* nor *Præterita* lends itself to the study of the highest Relationship, the profoundest Intimacy, which awaits the soul of man. I think I cannot do better than close with an extract from a little book[1] which tells the spiritual history of *Brother Lawrence*, a lay Brother among the barefooted Carmelites, at Paris, in the seventeenth century.

"The first time I saw *Brother Lawrence* was upon the 3rd of August, 1666. He told me that God had done him a singular favour in his conversion at the age of eighteen. That in the winter, seeing a tree stripped of its leaves, and considering that within a little time the leaves would be renewed, and after that the flower and fruit appear, he received a high view of the Providence and Power of God, which has never since been effaced from his soul. That this view had perfectly set him loose from the world, and kindled in him such a love for God, that he could not tell whether it had increased in about forty years that he had lived since. That he had been footman to M. Fieubert, the treasurer, and that he was a great awkward fellow who broke everything. That he had desired to be

[1] *The Secret of the Presence of God.* Masters.

received into a monastery, thinking he would there be made to smart for his awkwardness and the faults he should commit, and so he should sacrifice to God his life, with its pleasures : but that God had disappointed him, he having met with nothing but satisfaction in that state. . . . . That with him the set times of prayer were not different from other times ; that he retired to pray, according to the directions of his Superior, but that he did not want such retirement, nor ask for it, because his greatest business did not divert him from God. . . . . That the greatest pains or pleasures of this world were not to be compared with what he had experienced of both kinds in a spiritual state ; so that he was careful for nothing and feared nothing, desiring but one only thing of God, viz., that he might not offend Him. . . . . That he had so often experienced the ready succours of Divine Grace upon all occasions, that from the same experience, when he had business to do, he did not think of it beforehand ; but when it was time to do it he found in God, as in a clear mirror, all that was fit for him to do. That of late he had acted thus, without anticipating care ; but before the experience above mentioned he had used it in his affairs. When outward business diverted him a little from the thought of God, a fresh remembrance coming from God invested his soul, and so inflamed and transported him that it was difficult for him to contain himself, that he was more united to God in his outward employments than when he left them for devotion in retirement."

" I want,—am made for,—and must have a God,
Ere I can be aught, do aught ;—no mere Name
Want, but the True Thing, with what proves its truth,—
To wit, a relation from that Thing to me
Touching from head to foot :—which Touch I feel,
And with it take the rest, this Life of Ours !"
*—Browning.*

## AN EDUCATIONAL MANIFESTO

*" Studies serve for Delight, for Ornament, and for Ability."*

Every child has a right of entry to several fields of knowledge.

Every normal child has an appetite for such knowledge.

This appetite or desire for knowledge is a sufficient stimulus for all school work, if the knowledge be fitly given.

There are four means of destroying the desire for knowledge :—

    (a) Too many oral lessons, which offer knowledge in a diluted form, and do not leave the child free to deal with it.

    (b) Lectures, for which the teacher collects, arranges, and illustrates matter from various sources ; these often offer knowledge in too condensed and ready prepared a form.

    (c) Text-books compressed and re-compressed from the big book of the big man.

    (d) The use of emulation and ambition as incentives to learning in place of the adequate desire for, and delight in, knowledge.

Children can be most fitly educated on *Things* and *Books*. Things, *e.g.* :—

    i. Natural obstacles for physical contention, climbing, swimming, walking, etc.

    ii. Material to work in—wood, leather, clay, etc.

    iii. Natural objects *in situ*—birds, plants, streams, stones, etc.

    iv. Objects of art.

    v. Scientific apparatus, etc.

The value of this education by *Things* is receiving wide recognition, but intellectual education to be derived from *Books* is still for the most part to seek.

Every scholar of six years old and upwards should study with 'delight' *his own, living,* books on every subject in a pretty wide curriculum. Children between six and eight must for the most part have their books read to them.

This plan has been tried with happy results for the last twelve years in many home schoolrooms, and some other schools.

By means of the free use of books the mechanical difficulties of education—reading, spelling, composition, etc.—disappear, and studies prove themselves to be 'for delight, for ornament, and for ability.'

There is reason to believe that these principles are workable in all schools, Elementary and Secondary ; that they tend in the working to simplification, economy, and discipline.

## CHAPTER XX

### SUGGESTIONS TOWARDS A CURRICULUM

#### (*For Children under Fourteen*)

##### PART I

**Summary of Preceding Chapters.**—I have left the consideration of a curriculum, which is, practically, the subject of this volume, till the final chapters ; because a curriculum is not an independent product, but is linked to much else by chains of cause and consequence. The fundamental principles of docility and authority have been considered in the first place because they *are* fundamental ; but, for that very reason, they should be present but not in evidence ; we do not expose the foundations of our house. Not only so, but these principles must be conditioned by respect for the personality of children ; and, in order to give children room for free development on the lines proper to them, it is well that parents and teachers should adopt an attitude of masterly inactivity.

Having considered the relations of teachers and taught, I have touched upon those between education and current thought. Education should be in the flow, as it were, and not shut up in a watertight compartment. Perhaps, reverence for personality as such, a sense of the solidarity of the race, and a profound consciousness of evolutionary progress, are among the elements of current thought which should help us towards an educational ideal.

In considering the training of children under the convenient divisions of physical, mental, moral, and religious, I have not thought it necessary to give counsels upon matters of common knowledge and general acceptance, but have dwelt upon aspects of training under each heading which are rather likely to be overlooked. Under the phrase 'Education is a life,' I have tried to show how necessary it is to sustain the intellectual life upon ideas, and, as a corollary, that a school-book should be a medium for ideas and not merely a receptacle for facts. That normal children have a natural desire for, and a right of admission to, all knowledge, appears to me to be covered by the phrase, 'Education is the science of relations.'

These considerations clear the ground for the consideration of a curriculum, which occupies the remaining chapters; these are, in fact, a summary of what has gone before; and therefore I beg the reader's patience with such repetitions as seem to me necessary in bringing the argument to a point.

Some Preliminary Considerations.—As the following suggestions have been worked out in connection with the Parents' National Educational Union, it may perhaps be desirable to repeat here that the first effort of this society, continued through ten years of its existence, was to impress upon its members the definition of Education contained in our motto, '*Education is an Atmosphere, a Discipline, a Life.*' By this we mean that parents and teachers should know how to make sensible use of a child's circumstances (*atmosphere*), should train him in habits of good living (*discipline*), and should nourish his mind with ideas, the food of the intellectual *life*. These three we believe to be the only instruments of which we may make lawful use in bringing up children. An easier way may be found by trading on their sensibilities, emotions, desires, passions; but the result must be disastrous. And for this reason, that habits, ideas, and circumstances are external, and we may help each other to get the best that is to be had of them ; we may not, however, meddle directly with the personality of child or man ; we may not work upon his vanity, his fears, his love, his emulation, or anything that goes to make him a person. Most thinking people are in earnest about the bringing up of children ; but we are in danger of taking too much upon us, and of not recognising the limitations which confine us to the outworks of personality.

**A Definite Aim.**—The Parents' Union, having devoted, as I have said, ten years of its existence to learning how to use the three instruments of education (circumstances, habits, and ideas), took a new departure some few years ago, and asked what should be the end in view as the result of a wise use of due means. What is education ? The answer we accept is that *Education is the Science of Relations*.

We do not use this phrase in the Herbartian sense, that things or thoughts are related to each other and that teachers must be careful to pack the right things, in together, so that, having got into the pupil's brain, each may fasten on its kind, and, together, make a strong clique or apperception mass.

What concerns us personally is the fact that we

have relations with what there is in the present and
with what there has been in the past, with what is
above us, and about us; and that fulness of living
and serviceableness depend for each of us upon how
far we apprehend these relationships and how many
of them we lay hold of. Every child is heir to an
enormous patrimony. The question is, what are the
formalities necessary to put him in possession of that
which is his?

**Education Objective, not Subjective.**—The
point of view is shifted; it is no longer *subjective*
as regards the child, but *objective*. We do not
talk about developing his faculties, training his
moral nature, guiding his religious feelings, educating
him with a view to his social standing or his future
calling. We take the child as we find him, a person
with many healthy affinities and embryonic attachments, and we try to give him a chance to make the
largest possible number of these attachments valid.

An infant comes into the world with a thousand
feelers which he at once begins to fix with great
energy; and out of everything about him he gets—

"That calm delight which, if I err not, surely must belong,
To those first-born affinities that fit
Our new existence to existing things,
And in our dawn of being, constitute
The bond of union between life and joy."[1]

He gets also when left to himself that real knowledge
about each thing he comes across which establishes his
relations with that thing. Later, we step in to educate
him. In proportion to the range of living relationships we put in his way will he have wide and vital
interests and joy in living. His life will be dutiful

[1] *The Prelude.*

and serviceable if he is made aware of the laws which rule each relationship ; he will learn the laws of work and the joys of work as he perceives that no relation with persons or with things can be kept up without effort.

Our part is to remove obstructions, to give stimulus and guidance to the child who is trying to get into touch with the universe of things and thoughts. Our error is to suppose that we must act as his show-man to the universe, and that there is no community between child and universe except such as we choose to set up.

Interests.—Have we many keen interests solicit-ing us outside of our necessary work ?   If we have, we shall not be enslaved by vapid joys.

Interests are not to be taken up on the spur of the moment ; they spring out of the affinities which we have found and laid hold of.   And the object of education is, I take it, to give children the *use* of as much of the world as may be.

Influenced by such considerations as these, the phrase, ' *Education is the Science of Relations*,' gives us the advantage of a definite aim in our work.

Educational Unrest. — We have been made familiar with the phrase 'educational unrest,' and we all feel its fitness.   Never were there more able and devoted teachers, whether as the heads or on the staffs of schools of all classes.   Money, labour, and research are freely spent on education, theory is widely studied, and pains are taken to learn what is done elsewhere ; yet there is something amiss beyond that 'divine discontent' which leads to effort.   We know that a change of front is necessary ; and we are ready, provided that the change be something more

than an experiment.    Headmasters and mistresses
are, I believe, amongst the persons most ready to
fall in with a sound reform ; but, because these are
persons with wide experience and highly-trained
intellects, they are unwilling to launch changes which
have not a philosophic basis as well as a utilitarian end.

A Unifying Principle.—Hitherto we, of the
Parents' Union, have pressed on the public rather our
views on home-training than those on school-teaching,
but this is because we have been unwilling to disturb
the existing order.    We have, however, during the last
twelve years worked out in our training college and
school *a unifying principle and adequate methods* with
happy results.    We exist because we have a definite
aim, and to carry out that aim.    I need not now
speak of the few principles which form a guide to us
in the upbringing of children ; but that principle
which guides us in what is commonly called education
—the teaching of knowledge—may be found to indicate the cause of many educational failures and may
point the way to reform.

Education should give Knowledge touched
with Emotion.—To adapt a phrase of Matthew
Arnold's concerning religion,—education should aim
at giving knowledge ' *touched with emotion.*'    I have
already quoted the charming episode in Frederika
Bremer's *Neighbours*, where two school-girls fight a duel
on behalf of their heroes—Charles XII. and Peter the
Great.    Parents may be glad that we have no girl-duels
to-day !    The school-girl does not care for heroes, she
cares for marks.    Knowledge for her is not ' touched
with emotion,' unless it be those of personal acquisi-
tiveness and emulation.    The boys and girls have it
in them to be generous and enthusiastic ; that they

leave school without interests, beyond that of preparing
for further examinations or the absorbing interest of
games, is no doubt the fault of the schools. Perhaps
the 'unrest' of the public mind at home and abroad
about secondary education is due to the fact that
young people are turned out from excellent schools
*devitalised* so far as their minds go. No 'large
draughts of intellectual day' have been offered to
their thirst; and yet the thirst was there to begin
with.

Mr Benson[1] speaks very frankly. He says: " I
honestly believe that the masters of public schools
have two strong ambitions—to make boys good and to
make them healthy; but I do not think they care about
making them intellectual : intellectual life is left to
take care of itself. My belief is that a great many
masters look upon the boys' work as a question of
duty—that is, they consider it from the moral standpoint and not from the intellectual. . . . . It must
be frankly admitted that the intellectual standard
maintained at the English public schools is low; and,
what is more serious, I do not see any evidence that
it is tending to become higher."

Professor Sadler, with a perhaps wider outlook, says,
practically, the same thing—our secondary schools
have capital points, but intellectually they are behind-
hand, compared even with those of some continental
nations. Mr Benson speaks no doubt from personal
knowledge; but is it a fact that so intellectual a body
as our headmasters deliberately forego intellectual
distinction in their schools? Or is it not rather that
examinations throw them back on the pseudo-

[1] "The Schoolmaster," by H. C. Benson, of Eton College.—*Nineteenth Century*, December 1902.

intellectual work known as 'cram'? It is because cram is deadening that some of us deprecate the registration of teachers as a backward movement. Hundreds of mediocre young women set themselves to cram for a course of examinations, often a long course, to end at last in registration; and already head-mistresses feel the evil and inquire diligently for assistants who are 'not the usual sort.' Women are apt to be over-strenuous and over-conscientious, and the strain of moral effort carried on through years of preparation for successive examinations often leaves a certain dulness of apprehension. There are brilliant exceptions, but the average young woman who has undergone such an experience has little initiative, is slow of perception, not readily adaptable, not quick in the uptake; is, in fact, a little devitalised. I speak of moral effort, because the labour of preparing for examinations, of going through steady long-sustained grind, is apt to be rather a moral than an intellectual effort. With young men it is otherwise; they are commonly less strenuous, less absorbed, and therefore, perhaps, more receptive to the ideas that beset the way of their studies.

**Education is the Science of Relations.**—The idea that vivifies teaching in the Parents' Union is that *Education is the Science of Relations*; by which phrase we mean that children come into the world with a natural 'appetency,' to use Coleridge's word, for, and affinity with, all the material of knowledge; for interest in the heroic past and in the age of myths; for a desire to know about everything that moves and lives, about strange places and strange peoples; for a wish to handle material and to make; a desire to run and ride and row and do whatever the law of gravitation permits. Therefore we do not feel it is lawful in the early days of a child's life to select certain subjects for his education to the exclusion of others; to say he shall not learn Latin, for example, or shall not learn Science; but we endeavour that he shall have relations of pleasure and intimacy established with as many as possible of the interests proper to him; not learning a slight or incomplete smattering about this or that subject, but plunging into vital knowledge, with a great field before him which in all his life he will not be able to explore.   In this conception we get that 'touch of emotion' which vivifies knowledge, for it is probable that we *feel* only as we are brought into our proper vital relations.

Is there such a thing as the 'Child-Mind'?— We get courage to attack so wide a programme through a few working ideas or principles: one of these is, there is no such thing as the 'child-mind'; we believe that the ignorance of children is illimitable, but that, on the other hand, their intelligence is hardly to be reckoned with by our slower wits.   In practical working we find this idea a great power; the teachers do not talk down to the children; they are careful *not* to explain every word that is used, or to ascertain if children understand every detail.   As a girl of twelve or so the writer browsed a good deal on Cowper's poems and somehow took an interest in *Mrs Montague's Feather Hangings.*   Only the other day did the ball to fit that socket arrive in the shape of an article in *The Quarterly* on 'The Queen of the Bluestockings.'   Behold, there was Mrs Montague with her feather hangings!   The pleasure of meeting with her after all these years was extraordinary; for in no way is knowledge more enriching than in this of

leaving behind it a, so to speak, dormant appetite
for more of the kind. The recent finds at Knossos
are only to be appreciated by those who recollect how
Ulysses told Penelope about Crete with its ninety
cities, and Knossos, and King Minos. Not what
we have learned, but what we are waiting to know,
is the delectable part of knowledge. Nor should
knowledge be peptonised or diluted, but offered to
the children with some substance in it and some
vitality. We find that children can cover a large
and various field with delight and intelligence in the
time that is usually wasted over 'the three R's,'
object-lessons, and other much-diluted matter in which
the teaching is more than the knowledge.

**Knowledge** *versus* **Information.**—The distinction between *knowledge* and *information* is, I think,
fundamental. Information is the record of facts,
experiences, appearances, etc., whether in books or
in the verbal memory of the individual ; knowledge,
it seems to me, implies the result of the voluntary
and delightful action of the mind upon the material
presented to it. Great minds, a Darwin or a Plato,
are able to deal at first hand with appearances or
experiences ; the ordinary mind gets a little of its
knowledge by such direct dealing, but for the most
part it is set in action by the vivifying knowledge of
others, which is at the same time a stimulus and a
point of departure. The information acquired in the
course of education is only by chance, and here and
there, of practical value. Knowledge, on the other
hand, that is, the product of the vital action of the
mind on the material presented to it, is power ; as
it implies an increase of intellectual aptitude in new
directions, and an always new point of departure.

Perhaps the chief function of a teacher is to distinguish information from knowledge in the acquisitions of his pupils. Because knowledge is power, the child who has got knowledge will certainly show power in dealing with it. He will recast, condense, illustrate, or narrate with vividness and with freedom in the arrangement of his words. The child who has got only information will write and speak in the stereotyped phrases of his text-book, or will mangle in his notes the words of his teacher.

**Children have a Natural Craving for Knowledge.**—It is the easier for us to deal in this direct fashion with knowledge because we are not embarrassed by the necessity of cultivating faculties ; for working purposes the so-called faculties are sufficiently described as *mind*; and the normal mind is, we find, as able to deal with knowledge as are the normal digestive organs with food. Our concern is to give a child such knowledge as shall open up for him as large a share as may be of the world he lives in for his use and enjoyment. As there are gymnastics for the body, so for the mind there are certain subjects whose use is chiefly disciplinary, and of these we avail ourselves. Again, as our various organs labour without our consciousness in the assimilation of food, so judgment, imagination, and what not, deal of their own accord with knowledge, that it may be *incorporated*, which is not the same thing as 'remembered.' A further analogy—as the digestive organs are incited by appetite, so children come into the world with a few inherent desires, some with more, some less, to incite them to their proper activities. These are, roughly speaking, the desire for power, for praise, for wealth, for distinction, for society, and for *knowledge*.

It seems to me that education, which appeals to the desire for wealth (marks, prizes, scholarships, or the like), or to the desire of excelling (as in the taking of places, etc.), or to any other of the natural desires, *except that for knowledge*, destroys the balance of character ; and, what is even more fatal, destroys by inanition that desire for and delight in knowledge which is meant for our joy and enrichment through the whole of life. " A desire for knowledge," says Dr Johnson, " is the natural feeling of mankind, and every human being whose mind is not debauched will be willing to give all that he has to get knowledge." Is it possible that what has been called ' mark-hunger ' is a debauchery of the mind ? The undebauched mind takes knowledge with avidity ; and we find their studies are so interesting to children that they need no other stimulus.

**Children must be Educated on Books.**—A corollary of the principle that education is the science of relations, is, that no education seems to be worth the name which has not made children at home in the world of books, and so related them, mind to mind, with thinkers who have dealt with knowledge. We reject epitomes, compilations, and their like, and put into children's hands books which, long or short, are *living*. Thus it becomes a large part of the teacher's work to help children to deal with their books ; so that the oral lesson and lecture are but small matters in education, and are used chiefly to summarise or to expand or illustrate.

Too much faith is commonly placed in oral lessons and lectures; "to be poured into like a bucket," as says Carlyle, " is not exhilarating to any soul " ; neither is it exhilarating to have every difficulty

explained to weariness, or to have the explanation
teased out of one by questions.   " I will not be put to
the *question*.   Don't you consider, sir, that these are
not the manners of a gentleman ?   I will not be baited
with *what* and *why* ; what is this ? what is that ? why
is a cow's tail long ? why is a fox's tail bushy ? " said
Dr Johnson.   This is what children think, though they
say nothing.   Oral lessons have their occasional use,
and when they are fitly given it is the children who
ask the questions.   Perhaps it is not wholesome or
quite honest for a teacher to pose as a source of all
knowledge and to give ' lovely ' lessons.   Such lessons
are titillating for the moment, but they give children
the minimum of mental labour, and the result is much
the same as that left on older persons by the reading
of a magazine.   We find, on the other hand, that in
working through a considerable book, which may take
two or three years to master, the interest of boys and
girls is well sustained to the end ; they develop an
intelligent curiosity as to causes and consequences,
and are in fact educating themselves.

# CHAPTER XXI

## SUGGESTIONS TOWARDS A CURRICULUM

### (*For Children under Twelve*)

#### PART II.—*SCHOOL-BOOKS*

**Books that supply the Sustenance of Ideas.**—
Mr H. G. Wells has put his finger on the place
when he says that the selection of the right school-
books is a great function of the educator. I am not
at all sure that his remedy is the right one — or
that a body of experts and a hundred thousand
pounds would, in truth, provide the manner of school-
books that reach children. They are kittle cattle,
and, though they will plod on obediently over any
of the hundreds of dry-as-dust volumes issued by the
publishers under the heading of 'School Books,' or
of 'Education,' they keep all such books in the outer
court, and allow them no access to their minds. A
book may be long or short, old or new, easy or hard,
written by a great man or a lesser man, and yet be
the *living* book which finds its way to the mind of
a young reader. The expert is not the person to
choose ; the children themselves are the experts in
this case. A single page will elicit a verdict; but the
unhappy thing is, this verdict is not betrayed; it is
acted upon in the opening or closing of the door of
the mind. Many excellent and admirable school-

books appreciated by masters are on the Index Expurgatorius of the school-boy; and that is why he takes nothing in and gives nothing out. The master must have it in him to distinguish between twaddle and simplicity, and between vivacity and life. For the rest, he must experiment or test the experiments of others, being assured of one thing— that a book serves the ends of education only as it is vital. But this subject has been treated at some length in an earlier chapter.

**Books and Oral Teaching.**—Having found the right book, let the master give the book the lead and be content himself with a second place. The lecture *must be subordinated to the book*. The business of the teacher is to put his class in the right attitude towards their book by a word or two of his own interest in the matter contained, of his own delight in the manner of the author. But boys get know-ledge only as they dig for it. Labour prepares the way for assimilation, that mental process which con-verts information into knowledge; and the effort of taking in the sequence of thought of his author is worth to the boy a great deal of oral teaching.

Do teachers always realise the paralysing and stupefying effect that a flood of talk has upon the mind? The inspired talk of an orator no doubt wakens a response and is listened to with tense attention; but few of us claim to be inspired, and we are sometimes aware of the difficulty of holding the attention of a class. We blame ourselves, whereas the blame lies in the instrument we employ—the more or less diluted oral lesson or lecture, in place of the living and arresting book. We cannot do without the oral lesson—to introduce, to illustrate,

to amplify, to sum up. My stipulation is that oral
lessons should be few and far between, and that the
child who has to *walk* through life,—and has to find
his intellectual life in books or go without,—shall not
be first taught to go upon *crutches*.

The Use of Appliances.—For the same reason,
that is, that we may not paralyse the mental vigour
of children, we are very chary in the use of appliances
(except such as the microscope, telescope, magic
lantern, etc.). I once heard a schoolmaster, who had
a school in a shipbuilding town, say that he had
demanded and got from his committee a complete
sectional model of a man-of-war. Such a model would
be of use to his boys when they begin to work in the
Yards, but during their school years I believe the effect
would be stultifying, because the mind is not able to
conceive with an elaborate model as basis. I recently
visited M. Bloch's admirable ' Peace and War ' show
at Lucerne. Torpedoes were very fully illustrated by
models, sectional diagrams, and what not, but I was
not enlightened. I asked my neighbour at dinner to
explain the principle ; he took up his spectacle case
as an illustration, and after a few sentences my
intelligence had grasped what was distinctive in
a torpedo. This gentleman turned out to have been
in the War Office and to have had much concern
with torpedoes. The power in the teacher of illustrating by inkpot and ruler or any object at hand, or by
a few lines on the blackboard, appears to me to be
of more use than the most elaborate equipment of
models and diagrams ; these things stale on the
senses and produce a torpor of thought the moment
they are presented.

The Co-ordination of Studies.—Another point,

the co-ordination of studies is carefully regulated without any reference to the clash of ideas on the threshold or their combination into apperception masses ; but solely with reference to the natural and inevitable co-ordination of certain subjects. Thus, in readings on the period of the Armada, we should not devote the contemporary arithmetic lessons to calculations as to the amount of food necessary to sustain the Spanish fleet, because this is an arbitrary and not an inherent connection ; but we should read such history, travels, and literature as would make the Spanish Armada live in the mind.

**Our Aim in Education.**—Our aim in education is to give children vital interests in as many directions as possible—to set their feet in a large room—because the crying evil of the day is, it seems to me, intellectual inanition.

Believing that he is in the world to lay hold of all that he can of those possessions which endure ; that full, happy living, expansion, expression, resourcefulness, power of initiative, serviceableness—in a word, character, for him, depends upon how far he apprehends the relationships proper to him and how many of them he seizes, we should be gravely uneasy when his education leaves a young person with prejudices and caring for 'events' (in the sporting sense) rather than with interests and pursuits. Principles, we believe, the best of our young people have and bring away from their schools fully as much as from their homes. Our educational shortcomings seem to be intellectual rather than moral.

**Education by Things.**—Education should be by *Things* and by *Books*. Ten years ago education by *Things* was little thought of except in the games of public schools. To-day, a great reform has taken place, and the worth of education by *Things* is recognised everywhere. Disciplinary exercises, artistic handicrafts, are seen to make for education as truly as do geography and Latin. ' Nature study' has come in later, but has come with a rush. If that Sikh quoted by Cornelia Sorabji [1] should visit us again ten years hence, it is to be hoped he would not then say of us, "The very thoughts of the people are merchandise; they have not learned the common language of Nature." The teaching of Science is receiving enormous attention; and the importance of education in this kind need not be enforced here. Works of art are, here and there, allowed their chance with boys and girls, and we shall look more and more to this means of education. What everyone knows it is unnecessary to repeat; and such general attention is given to education by Things, and this is carried on so far on right lines, that I have nothing to add to the general knowledge of this subject.

Education by Books.—The great educational failure we have still to deal with is in the matter of *Books*. We know that *Books* store the knowledge and thought of the world; but the mass of knowledge, the multitude of books, overpower us, and we think we may select here and there, from this book and that, fragments and facts of knowledge, to be dealt out, whether in the little cram book or the oral lesson.

Sir Philip Magnus, in a recent address on Headwork and Handwork in Elementary Schools, says some things worth pondering. Perhaps he gives his workshop too big a place in the school of the future, but certainly he puts his finger on the weak point in

[1] *Spectator*, 2nd August 1902.

the work of both elementary and secondary schools—
the 'getting by heart scraps of knowledge, fragments
of so-called science.' And we are with him in the
emphasis he lays upon *reading and writing*; it is
through these that even school 'studies' shall become
'for delight.' Writing, of course, comes of reading,
and nobody can write well who does not read much.
Sir Philip Magnus says,[1] speaking of the schools of
the future:—"We shall no longer require children
to learn by constant repetition, scraps of history,
geography, and grammar, nor try to teach them
fragments of so-called science. The daily hours
devoted to these tasks will be applicable to the
creation of mental aptitudes, and will be utilised in
showing the children how to obtain knowledge for
themselves. . . . . In future the main function of
education will be to train our hands and our sense
organs and intellectual faculties, so that we may be
placed in a position of advantage for seeking knowledge. . . . . The scope of the lessons will be enlarged.
Children will be taught to read in order that they
may desire to read, and to write that they may be
able to write. . . . . It will be the teacher's aim to
create in his pupils a desire for knowledge, and
consequently a love of reading, and to cultivate in
them, by a proper selection of lessons, the pleasure
which reading may be made to yield. The main
feature of the reading lesson will be to show the use
of books, how they may be consulted to ascertain
what other people have said or done, and how they
may be read for the pleasure they afford. The
storing of the memory with facts is no part of
elementary school work. . . . It is not enough

[1] *Education*, 16th April 1903.

that a child should learn how to write, he must know *what* to write. He must learn to describe clearly what he has heard or seen, to transfer to written language his sense-impressions, and to express concisely his own thoughts."

We should like to add a word to Sir Philip Magnus's conception, emphasising the *habit* of reading as a chief acquirement of school life. It is only those who have read who do read.

**The Question of a Curriculum.**—In regard to a curriculum, may I enforce what I have said in an earlier chapter? Perhaps the main part of a child's education should be concerned with the great human relationships. History, literature, art, languages (whether ancient or modern), travel—all of these are the record or expression of persons; so is science, so far as it is the history of discoveries, the record of observations, that is, so far as it is to be got out of books. Essentially, however, science falls under the head of *Education by Things*, and is too large a subject to be dealt with, by the way. Before all these ranks *Religion*, including our relations of worship, loyalty, love and service to God; and next in order, perhaps, the intimate interpersonal relations implied in such terms as self-knowledge, self-control. Knowledge in these several kinds is due to children; for there seems reason to believe that the limit to human intelligence coincides with the limit to human interests; that is, that a normal person of poor and narrow intelligence is so because the interests proper to him have not been called into play. The curriculum which should give children their due falls into some six or eight groups—Religion, Philosophy (?), History, Languages, Mathematics, Science, Art, Physical Exercises, and Manual Crafts.

**Religion.**—For *Religion* it is, no doubt, to the Bible itself we must go, as the great storehouse of spiritual truth and moral impressions. A child might, in fact, receive a liberal education from the Bible alone, for *The Book* contains within itself a great literature.

There was a time when 'National Schools' brought up their scholars on one of the three great bodies of ancient classical literature which the Western world possesses, and which we include under the one name, Bible; and, perhaps, there has been some falling off both in national intelligence and character since the Bible has been practically deposed for the miscellaneous 'Reader.' It is not possible or desirable to revert to old ways in this matter; but we should see to it that children derive as much intellectual, as well as moral and religious, nutriment from books as they did when their studies ranged from the story of Joseph to the Epistles of St Paul.

**History.**—In History, boys and girls of twelve to fourteen should have a fairly intimate knowledge of English history, of contemporary French history, and of Greek and Roman history—the last, by way of biography;—perhaps nothing outside of the Bible has the educational value of Plutarch's *Lives*. The wasteful mistake often made in teaching English history is to carry children of, say, between nine and fourteen through several small compendiums, beginning with *Little Arthur*; whereas their intelligence between those ages is equal to steady work on one considerable book.

**Language.**—In Language, by twelve, they should have a fair knowledge of English grammar, and should have read some literature. They should have more or less power in speaking and understanding French, and should be able to read a fairly easy French book; the same with German, but considerably less progress; and in Latin, they should be reading 'Fables,' if not 'Cæsar,' and perhaps 'Virgil.'

**Mathematics.**—I need not touch upon the subject of Mathematics. It is receiving ample attention, and is rapidly becoming an instrument for living teaching in our schools.

**'Practical Instruction.'**—To turn to the question of practical instruction, under the heads of 'Science, Drawing, Manual and Physical Training,' etc., I can do no more here than repeat our convictions. We believe that education under these four heads is due to every child of whatever class; and, for boys and girls under twelve, probably the same general curriculum would be suitable for all. I have nothing to add to the sound ideas as to the teaching of each of these subjects which are now common property.

**Science.**—In *Science*, or rather, nature study, we attach great importance to *recognition*, believing that the power to recognise and name a plant or stone or constellation involves classification and includes a good deal of knowledge. To know a plant by its gesture and habitat, its time and its way of flowering and fruiting; a bird by its flight and song and its times of coming and going; to know when, year after year, you may come upon the redstart and the pied fly-catcher, means a good deal of interested observation, and of, at any rate, the material for science. The children keep a dated record of what they see in their nature note-books, which are left to their own management and are not corrected. These note-books are a source of pride and joy, and are freely illustrated by drawings (brushwork) of twig, flower, insect, etc. The knowledge necessary for these records is not given in the way of teaching. On one afternoon in the week, the children (of the Practising School) go for a 'nature walk' with their teachers. They notice for themselves, and the teacher gives a name or other information as it is asked for, and it is surprising what a range of knowledge a child of nine or ten acquires. The teachers are careful *not* to make these nature walks an opportunity for scientific instruction, as we wish the children's attention to be given to observation with very little direction. In this way they lay up that store of 'common information' which Huxley considered should precede science teaching; and, what is much more important, they learn to know and delight in natural objects as in the familiar faces of friends. The nature-walk should not be made the occasion to impart a sort of *Tit-Bits* miscellany of scientific information. The study of science should be pursued in an ordered sequence, which is not possible or desirable in a walk. It seems to me a *sine quâ non* of a living education that all school children of whatever grade should have one half-day in the week, *throughout the year*, in the fields. There are few towns where country of some sort is not accessible, and every child should have the opportunity of watching, from week to week, the procession of the seasons.

Geography, geology, the course of the sun, the behaviour of the clouds, weather signs, all that the 'open' has to offer, are made use of in these walks; but all is incidental, easy, and things are noticed as they occur. It is probable that in most neighbourhoods there are naturalists who would be willing to give their help in the 'nature walks' of a given school.

We supplement this direct 'nature walk' by

occasional object-lessons, as, on the hairs of plants, on diversity of wings, on the sorts of matters taken up in Professor Miall's capital books; but our main dependence is on *books* as an adjunct to out-of-door work—Mrs Fisher's, Mrs Brightwen's, Professor Lloyd Morgan's, Professor Geikie's, Professors Geddes' and Thomson's (the two last for children over fourteen), etc., etc. In the books of these and some other authors the children are put in the position of the original observer of biological and other phenomena. They learn what to observe, and make discoveries for themselves, original so far as they are concerned. They are put in the right attitude of mind for scientific observations and deductions, and their keen interest is awakened. We are extremely careful not to burden the verbal memory with scientific nomenclature. Children learn of pollen, antennæ, and what not, incidentally, when the thing is present and they require a name for it. The children who are curious about it, and they only, should have the opportunity of seeing with the microscope any minute wonder of structure that has come up in their reading or their walks; but a good lens is a capital and almost an indispensable companion in field work. I think there is danger in giving *too* prominent a place to education by Things, enormous as is its value ; a certain want of atmosphere is apt to result, and a deplorable absence of a standard of comparison and of the principle of veneration. ' We are the people ! ' seems to be the note of an education which is not largely sustained on *books* as well as on *things*.

Drawing.—In pictorial art we eschew mechanical aids such as chequers, lines of direction, etc., nor do we use the blacklead pencil, which lends itself rather to the copying of linear work than to the free rendering of objects. The children work always from the round, whether in charcoal or brushwork. They produce, also, illustrations of tales or poems, which leave much to seek in the matter of drawing, and are of little value as art instruction, but are useful imaginative exercises.

**Picture Talks.**—We attach a good deal of value to what we call picture talks, that is :—a reproduction of a suitable picture, by Millet, for example, is put into the children's hands, and they study it by themselves. Then, children of from six to nine describe the picture, giving all the details and showing by a few lines on the blackboard where is such a tree or such a house; judging if they can the time of day ; discovering the story if there be one. The older children add to this some study of the lines of composition, light and shade, the particular style of the master ; and reproduce from memory certain details. The object of these lessons is that the pupils should learn how to appreciate rather than how to produce.

But there is no space for further details of a curriculum which is more fully illustrated in an appendix.

# CHAPTER XXII

## SUGGESTIONS TOWARDS A CURRICULUM

### PART III.—*THE LOVE OF KNOWLEDGE*

**The Use of Books makes for Short Hours.**—
Considering that under the head of 'Education by
Books' some half-dozen groups of subjects are included,
with several subjects in each group, the practical
teacher will be inclined to laugh at what will seem to
him Education in Utopia. In practice, however, we
find that the use of books makes for short hours. No
book-work or writing, no preparation or report, is
done in the *Parents' Review* School, except between
the hours of 9 and 11.30 for the lowest class, to
9 and 1 for the highest, with half an hour's interval
for drill, etc.

From one to two hours, according to age and class,
are given in the afternoons to handicrafts, field-work,
drawing, etc. ; and the evenings are absolutely free,
so that the children have leisure for hobbies, family
reading, and the like. We are able to get through a
greater variety of subjects, and through more work in
each subject, in a shorter time than is usually allowed,
because children taught in this way get the habit of
close attention and are carried on by steady interest.

'**Utilitarian**' **Education.**—I should be inclined
to say of education, as Mr Lecky says of morals,

THE LOVE OF KNOWLEDGE

that "the Utilitarian theory is profoundly immoral."
To educate children for any immediate end—towards
commercial or manufacturing aptitude, for example
—is to put a premium upon general ignorance with
a view to such special aptitude. The greater includes the less, but the less does not include the
greater. Excellent work of whatever kind is produced by a person of character and intelligence,
and we who teach cannot do better for the nation
than to prepare such persons for its uses. He who
has intelligent relations with life will produce good
work.

Relations and Interests. — I have throughout
spoken of '*Relations*,' and not of '*Interests*,' because
interests may be casual, unworthy, and passing. Everyone, even the most ignorant, has interests of a sort ;
while to make valid any one relation, implies that
knowledge has begun in, at any rate, that one direction.
But the defect in our educational thought is that we
have ceased to realise that knowledge is vital ; and,
as children and adults, we suffer from underfed minds.
This intellectual inanition is, no doubt, partly due
to the fact that educational theorists systematically
depreciate knowledge. Such theorists are, I think,
inclined to attach more importance to the working of
the intellectual machinery than to the output of the
product; that is, they feel it to be more important
that a child should *think* than that he should *know*.
My contention is rather that he cannot *know* without
having *thought* ; and also that he cannot think without
an abundant, varied, and regular supply of the material
of knowledge. We all know how the reading of a
passage may stimulate in us thought, inquiry, inference,
and thus get for us in the end some added knowledge.

The depreciation of which I speak is by no means of set purpose, nor is it even realised ; but the more education presents itself as a series of psychological problems, the greater will be the tendency to doctor, modify, and practically eliminate *knowledge* ; — that knowledge, which is as the air, and the food, and the exercise, the whole life of the mind of man.   In giving ' education ' without abundant knowledge, we are as persons who should aim at physical development by giving the maximum of exercise with the minimum of food. The getting of knowledge and the getting of delight in knowledge are the ends of a child's education ; and well has said one of our prophets, "that there should one man die ignorant who had capacity for knowledge, this I call a tragedy."

To sum up, I believe that our efforts at intellectual education commonly fail from six causes :—

**Causes of Failure.**—(*a*) The oral lesson, which at its worst is very poor twaddle, and at its best is far below the ordered treatment of the same subject by an original mind in the right book.   (The right books exist, old and new, in countless numbers, but very great care is necessary in the choice, as well as much experience of the rather whimsical tastes and distastes of children.)

(*b*) The lecture, commonly gathered from various books in rapid notes by the teacher ; and issuing in hasty notes, afterwards written out, and finally crammed up by the pupils.   The lecture is often careful, thorough, and well-illustrated ; but is it ever equal in educational value to direct contact with the original mind of one able thinker who has written his book on the subject ?   Arnold, Thring, Bowen, we know, lectured with great effect, but then each of them lectured on only a few subjects, and each lecture was as the breaking out of a spring of slowly gathered knowledge. We are not all Arnolds or even Bowens.

(c) The text-book, compressed and re-compressed from one or many big books. These handbooks are of two kinds—the frankly dry and uninteresting, which enumerate facts and details ; and the easy and beguiling. I think we are safe in saying that there is *no educational value* in either sort of text-book.

(d) The debauchery of the mind which comes of exciting other desires to do the work of the inherent and fully adequate desire of knowledge.

(e) In elementary schools, the dependence upon apparatus and illustrative appliances which have a paralysing effect on the mind.

(f) Again in elementary schools, the use of 'Readers,' which, however well selected, cannot have the value of consecutive works.

**Education by Books.**—For the last twelve years we have tried the plan of bringing children up on *Books* and *Things*, and, on the whole, the results are pleasing. The *average* child studies with 'delight.' We do not say he will remember all he knows, but, to use a phrase of Jane Austen's, he will have had his 'imagination warmed' in many regions of knowledge.

**Blind Alleys.**—May I digress for a moment to raise a warning note against the following of blind alleys, whether in our educational thought or our methods. We do not, in the sphere of education, find hidden treasure by casual digging in the common roadways. Believing in evolution, we perceive that ideas also have their pedigree and their progeny and follow their own laws of generation. A learned and thoughtful Chinese will abstract himself from the outer world, separate himself from the ideas of others, and, when he has arrived at a due state of vacuity, take his writing-brushes and produce out of his inner consciousness—not anything that he has ever seen or heard of, or even imagined—but some hieroglyph of curves, rather pleasing and presentable if he happen to be an artist.    This disconnected production he arbitrarily invests with the character of a symbol, and his fellows are willing to receive it as such, and it is duly hung in his Hall of Tablets.[1]    Some of us perhaps know the flowing curves which stand for 'happiness' in this language of symbols.

Now, all this is very engaging, and the Western mind is ready enough to succumb to the charm of such fancies.    But does it not offer a key to that baffling problem we call China?    Here we have a vast people with some high moral qualities, of astute and sometimes profound intelligence, whose civilisation has for thousands of years remained to all appearance *stationary*.    Is the cause, perhaps, a tendency to follow intellectual futilities, blind alleys, in every direction?    These people do not realise that method implies an end perceived, a way to that end, and step by step progress in the way; nor do they perceive that a notion becomes a fruitful idea only upon the impact of an idea from without.    A fine Celestial arrogance assures them of their right to casual finds ; hence, they do not progress, but remain in all things as they were.

Now, here is the danger that besets us in education. We seize upon ambidexterity, upon figures drawn with the compasses without intention, upon 'child study' as applied to mind, upon terrible agglutinations which

---

[1] See *Through Hidden Shensi*, by F. Nichols.

we call 'apperception masses,' upon intellectual futilities in a hundred directions, each of which will, we hope, give us the key to education. We may perceive the futility of such notions by applying the test of progress. Are they the way to anything, and, if so, to what ? Let us, out of reverence for the children, be modest ; let us not stake their interests on the hope that this or that new way would lead to great results if people had only the courage to follow it. It is exciting to become a pioneer ; but, for the children's sake, it may be well to constrain ourselves to follow those roads only by which we know that persons have arrived, or those newer roads which offer evident and assured means of *progress towards a desired end.* Self-will is not permitted to the educationalist ; and he may not take up fads.

**An Educated Child.**—Knowledge is, no doubt, a comparative term, and the knowledge of a subject possessed by a child would be the ignorance of a student. All the same, there is such a thing as an educated child—a child who possesses a sound and fairly wide knowledge of a number of subjects, all of which serve to interest him ; such a child studies with ' delight.'

**Children delight in School, but not for Love of Knowledge.**—It will be said with truth that most children delight in school ; they delight in the stimulus of school life, in the social stir of companionship ; they are emulous, eager for reward and praise; they enjoy the thousand lawful interests of school life, including the attractive personality of such and such a teacher ; but it seems doubtful whether the love of knowledge, in itself and for itself, is usually a powerful motive with the young scholar. The matter is important, because, of all the joyous motives of school life, the love of knowledge is the only abiding one; the only one which determines the scale, so to speak, upon which the person will hereafter live. My contention is, to repeat what has been said, that all children have a capacity for and a latent love of knowledge; and, that knowledge concerning persons and States can best be derived from books, and should be got by the children out of their own books.

In a hundred biographies there are hints of boys and girls who have grown up on books; and there is no doubt that in many schools the study of books is the staple of the work. This probably is the principle which keeps our great public schools perennially alive; they live, so far as they do live, upon books. The best public schoolboy is a fine product; and perhaps the worst has had his imagination touched by ideas; yet most of us recognise that the public school often fails, in that it launches the average and dull boy ignorant upon the world because the curriculum has been too narrow to make any appeal to him. And we must remember, that if a young person leave school at seventeen or eighteen without having become a diligent and delighted reader, it is tolerably certain that he will never become a reader. It may be, however, that the essential step in any reform of public schools should come in the shape of due *preparation* upon a wide curriculum, dealt with intelligently, between the ages of six and twelve.

**An Educational Revolution.**—I add appendices to show, (*a*) how a wide curriculum and the use of many books work in the *Parents' Review* School; (*b*) what progress a pupil of twelve should have made under such conditions; and (c) what use is made of oral lessons. Should the reader consider that the children in question prove their right of entry to several fields of knowledge, that they show a distinct appetite for such knowledge, that thought and power of mind develop upon the books we read, as they do not and cannot upon the lectures we hear; should he indeed be convinced of the truth of what I have advanced, I think he will see that, not an educational reform here and there, but an EDUCATIONAL REVOLUTION is before us to which every one of us is bound to put his hand.

The Children's Magna Carta.—My plea is, and I think I have justified it by experience, that many doors shall be opened to boys and girls until they are at least twelve or fourteen, and always the doors of good houses, ('Education,' says Taine, 'is but a card of invitation to noble and privileged salons'); that they shall be introduced to no subject whatever through compendiums, abstracts, or selections; that the young people shall learn what history is, what literature is, what life is, from the living books of those who know. I know it can be done, because it is being done on a considerable scale.

If conviction has indeed reached us, the Magna Carta of children's intellectual liberty is before us. The need is immediate, the means are evident. This, at least, I think we ought to claim, that, up to the age of twelve, all boys and girls shall be educated on some such curriculum, with some such *habit* of *Books* as we have been considering.[1]

[1] It is highly encouraging that the new regulations of the Board of Education both for primary and secondary schools lend themselves to the lines of work advocated in these pages.

# Appendices

———•———

## APPENDIX I

*Questions for the Use of Readers* [1]

### CHAPTER I

DOCILITY AND AUTHORITY IN THE HOME AND SCHOOL

1. In what points are there better relations between children and their elders than there were a generation or two ago?

2. Characterise the elder generation of parents.

3. What of 'ill-guided' homes?

4. Give an example of martinet rule. Name some notable men who grew up under such rule.

5. Compare the arbitrary parent now with the arbitrary parent of the past.

6. Was arbitrary rule a failure?

7. What thought should encourage our own efforts?

8. Show that arbitrariness arose from limitations.

9. That it is one cause of the reticence of children.

10. In what way has the direction of philosophic thought altered the relations of parents and children?

11. What effect has the doctrine of the 'Infallible Reason' upon authority?

12. Show that English thought again proclaims the apotheosis of Reason.

———

[1] See note at the end of the volume.

13. What is the final justification of the idea of authority?

14. Why is the enthronement of the human reason the dethronement of the highest authority?

15. Show that the spread of an idea is 'quick as thought.'

16. Why has the notion of the finality of human reason become intolerable?

17. On what grounds would you say that authority and docility are fundamental principles?

18. Show that self-interest does not account for the response of docility to authority.

19. Show that the work of the rationalistic philosophers was necessary.

20. Show that they hold a brief for human freedom.

21. Describe the way in which the education of the world seems to be carried on.

22. Show the danger of the notion that authority is vested in persons.

23. Show that a person in authority is under authority.


## CHAPTER II

### DOCILITY AND AUTHORITY IN THE HOME AND SCHOOL

#### *Part II.—How Authority Behaves*

1. Show, by example, that it is easy to go wrong on principle.

2. Distinguish between authority and autocracy.

3. How does autocracy behave?

4. Show that it is the autocrat who remits duties and grants indulgences.

5. How does authority behave?

6. Give half-a-dozen features by which we may distinguish the rule of authority.

7. What are the qualities proper to a ruler?

8. Distinguish between mechanical and reasonable obedience.

9. Show the use of the former.

10. Show how acts of mechanical obedience help a child to the masterly use of his body.

11. How is the man, who can make himself do what he wills, trained?

12. Why is the effort of decision the greatest effort of life?

13. Show how habit spares us much of this labour.

14. Show how the habit of obedience eases the lives of children.

15. How does authority avoid cause of offence?

16. Show that alert authority in the home is a preventive force.

17. Show how important the changing of the thoughts, diverting, is in the formation of habit.

18. Show that children, too, exercise authority.

19. What question might parents put to themselves daily as an aid to the maintenance of authority?

## CHAPTER III

### 'MASTERLY INACTIVITY

1. Contrast our sense of responsibility with that held in the fifties and sixties.

2. Show that the change in our point of view indicates moral progress.

3. What kind of responsibility presses heavily at present upon thoughtful people?

4. Show that anxiety is the note of a transition stage.

5. Why does a sense of responsibility produce a fussy and restless habit?

6. Why should we do well to admit the idea of 'masterly inactivity' as a factor in education?

7. What four or five ideas are contained in this of 'masterly inactivity'?

8. What is Wordsworth's phrase?

9. What is the first element in this attitude of mind?

10. Show that good-humour is the second element.

11. That self-confidence also is necessary.

12. What may mothers learn from the fine, easy, way of some fathers?

13. Show that confidence in children, also, is an element of 'masterly inactivity.'

14. Why must parents and teachers be omniscient?

15. Show why 'masterly inactivity' is necessary to the bringing up of a child whose life is conditioned by 'fate and free-will.'

16. What delicate poise between fate and free-will is to be aimed at for the child?

17. Show the importance of a sound mind in a sound body to the parent.

18. What may we learn from the quality which all the early painters have bestowed upon the pattern Mother?

19. Give one or two practical hints for tired mothers.

20. Why is leisure necessary to children's well-being?

21. What is the foundation of the 'masterly inactivity' we have in view?

## CHAPTER IV

### SOME OF THE RIGHTS OF CHILDREN AS PERSONS

1. Why should children be free in their play?

2. In what respect are organised games not play?

3. Why should we beware of interfering with children's work?

4. Show that children must stand or fall by their own efforts.

5. Show the danger of a system of prodding.

6. How far may we count upon the dutifulness of boys and girls?

7. How far should children be free to choose their friends?

8. To spend their pocket-money?

9. To form their opinions?

10. Show that spontaneity is not an indigenous wild-flower.

## CHAPTER V

### Psychology in Relation to Current Thought

1. Characterise the educational thought of the eighteenth century.

2. Show that we, too, have had a period of certainty.

3. Account for the general dissatisfaction we labour under now.

4. By what tests may we discern a working psychology for our own age?

5. Illustrate the fact that the sacredness of the person is among the living thoughts of the age upon which we are being brought up.

6. On what grounds do we demand of education that it should make the most of the person?

7. How is 'the solidarity of the race' to be reckoned with in education?

8. Show that the best thought of any age is common thought.

9. Discuss Locke's *States of Consciousness*.

10. Show that this theory does not provide for the evolution of the person.

11. How does modern physiological-psychology compare with Locke's theory?

12. How does Professor James define this psychology?

13. Show that this definition makes the production of thought, etc., purely mechanical.

14. How far is this assumption 'unjustifiable materialism'?

15. What is Professor James' pronouncement about what is called the 'new psychology'?

16. Illustrate the fact that a psychology which eliminates personality is dreary and devitalising.

17. By what signs may we recognise the fact when the 'new psychology' becomes part of our faith?

18. Show that this system is inadequate, unnecessary, and inharmonious.

19. At what point does it check the evolution of the individual?

## CHAPTER VI

### SOME EDUCATIONAL THEORIES EXAMINED

1. What do we owe to the Schools of Pestalozzi and Froebel?

2. What is the source of weakness in their conceptions?

3. Compare 'make children happy and they will be good' with 'be good and you will be happy.'

4. Show the fundamental error of regarding man merely as part of the *Cosmos*.

5. Show that the struggle for existence is a part of life even to a child.

6. That any sort of transition violates the principles of unity and continuity.

7. Why is the Herbartian theory tempting?

8. Show that this theory treats the person as an effect and not a cause.

9. Show that the functions of education are overrated by it.

10. Show that this system of psychology is not in harmony with current thought in three particulars.

11. Show that educational truth is a common possession.

12. What are the characteristics of a child who is being adequately educated?

13. What, roughly speaking, is expressed in the word *person*?

14. Show how a person is like Wordsworth's ' cloud.'

15. Describe an adequate doctrine of education.

16. Show how it is in touch with the three great ideas which are now moving in men's minds.

17. What would you say of personal influence in education?

18. What is implied in saying, *Education is the science of relations*?

19. Why must teaching not be obtrusive?

20. What attitude on the teacher's part arises from the recognition of a child as a person?


## CHAPTER VII

### AN ADEQUATE THEORY OF EDUCATION

1. Give, roughly, a definition of a human being.

2. What would you say of his capacities?

3. What of his limitations?

4. What are the two functions of a human being under education?

5. Upon what physical process does education depend?

6. What do we know, or guess, of the behaviour of ideas?

7. What appears to be the law of the generation of ideas?

8. Why do different ideas appeal to different minds? Illustrate by a figure.

9. Have we any reason for believing that an idea is able to make an impression upon matter?

10. Mention some of the reflex actions by which we respond to an idea which strikes us.

11. How does spirit correspond with spirit, human or divine?

12. Is a child born equipped with ideas?

13. What is the field open to the educationalist?

14. What may we learn from the fairly well accredited story of the ' Child of Nuremberg '?

15. What does nature, unassisted, do for a child?

16. Show that the normal child has every power that will serve him.

17. In how far does fulness of living depend on the establishment of relations?

18. Show that in our common way of treating science, for instance, we maim a natural affinity.

19. Why should a child be taught to recognise the natural things about him?

20. How may he be helped to appreciate beauty?

21. Why should he begin with a first-hand knowledge of science?

22. Show that appreciation and exact knowledge each has its season.

## CHAPTER VIII

### CERTAIN RELATIONS PROPER TO A CHILD

1. How long would you give a child to initiate the range of relationships proper to him?

2. What dynamic relations should he have?

3. What power over material?

4. Show that he should have intimacy with animals.

5. What range of studies belong to the human relationships?

6. Give example of the awakening idea and its outcome.

7. Show that intelligence is limited by interests.

8. What should be the effect if children were fully realised as persons?

9. What effect has the psychology of the hour had upon the sense of duty?

10. Show that children used to get a fairly sound ethical training.

11. What is the case now?

12. Show that 'my duty towards my neighbour' is the only sound basis for moral relations.

13. Does the sense of what is due from us come by nature?

14. Why should a child be taught something of self-management?

15. Why should children have intimacy with persons of all classes?

16. How may their fitness as citizens be promoted?

17. What are the three great groups of relations a child has to establish?

18. Which is the most important of these?

19. Show that religious sentiments or emotions do not fulfil '*duty* towards God.'

20. Distinguish between sentiment and duty.


## CHAPTER IX

### A GREAT EDUCATIONALIST

1. Illustrate the fact that Herbartian thought has more influence than any other on the Continent.

2. Show that we, like Herbart, discard the 'faculties.'

3. What does Herbart say of the pervasiveness of dominant ideas?

4. In what ways do we, too, recognise the influence of the *Zeitgeist*?

5. How does Herbart enumerate the child's school-masters?

6. Show that we are one with him in realising the place of the family.

7. What does Herbart say of the child in the family?

8. Show that we, too, hold that all education springs from and rests upon our relation to Almighty God.

9. Why should we not divide education into religious and secular?

10. What doctrine of the mediæval Church do we hold with regard to 'secular subjects'?

11. Upon what, according to Herbart, does the welfare, civilisation, and culture of a people depend?

12. Discuss the vast uncertainty that exists as to the purpose of education.

13. Shall we follow Rousseau, Basedow, Locke, Pestalozzi, Froebel, in our attempts to fix the purpose of education?

14. Show, according to Dr Rein, why not, in each case?

15. Show that Herbart's theory is ethical, as is ours.

16. Quote this author on the obscurity of psychology.

17. But we have two luminous principles. What are they?

18. What is probably the root defect of the educational philosophy of this great thinker?

## CHAPTER X

### SOME UNCONSIDERED ASPECTS OF PHYSICAL TRAINING

1. Why does not our physical culture tend to make heroes?

2. What is the end of physical culture?

3. Show that this implies the idea of vocation.

4. What principle should check excess, whether in labour or pleasure?

5. Should parents bring up their children with rigour? Why not?

6. Write a short theme on each of the points suggested for consideration.

7. Show how large a part habit plays in physical training.

8. Prove that self-restraint is a habit.

9. Show the evil of the excessive exercises that lead to after-indulgence.

10. How may self-control in emergencies become a trained habit?

11. What have you to say of the physical signs of mental states?

12. Show that discipline must become self-discipline.

13. What is the part of parents in the holidays as regards school discipline?

14. How do 'local habits' point to the necessity for self-discipline in even a young child?

15. Show how alertness must be trained as a physical habit.

16. That 'quick perception' is less a gift than a habit.

17. Write short themes on each of the subjects here suggested for consideration.

18. Show the value of inspiring ideas in initiating habits.

19. How could you use the idea of 'fortitude' in education?

20. Of 'service'?

21. Of 'courage'?

22. Of 'prudence' as concerned with the *duty* of health?

23. What is the highest impulse towards chastity we can have?

24. Write short themes on the subjects suggested.

## CHAPTER XI

### SOME UNCONSIDERED ASPECTS OF INTELLECTUAL TRAINING

1. Show that we are somewhat law-abiding in matters physical and moral.

2. That we are not so in matters intellectual.

3. What are the three ultimate facts which are not open to question?

4. Show that one or other of the three is always matter of debate.

5. What three fixed points of thought do we attain when we realise that God is, self is, and the world is?

6. Why is it necessary to recognise the limitations of reason?

7. Describe the involuntary action of reason.

8. Show, by examples, (*a*) what the function of reason is, and (*b*) what the function of reason is not.

9. Show, by examples, that wars, persecutions, and family feuds are due to the notion that, what reason demonstrates is right and true.

10. Why should a child be taught the limitations of his own reason?

11. What mistake is commonly made regarding intellect and knowledge?

12. Show that the world is educated by knowledge given 'in repasts.'

13. How would you characterise our own era as regards the knowledge given to us?

14. How did the mediæval Church recognise the divine origin of knowledge?

15. Why is nothing so practical as a great idea?

16. Show the importance of forming intellectual habits.

17. Show that we trust blindly to disciplinary studies for the formation of such habits.

18. Name and describe half-a-dozen intellectual habits in which a child should be trained.

19. Show that progress in the intellectual as in the Christian life depends upon meditation.

20. Show that a child must have daily sustenance of living ideas. How do we err in this respect?

21. Make some remarks upon the literature proper for children.

22. Illustrate the fact that the intellectual development of children is independent.

23. By what law do children appropriate nourishing ideas?

24. What, then, is the part of parents and teachers?

25. What failing on the part of parents is often fatal to intellectual growth?

26. Write a few remarks on each of the subjects

suggested in connection with the intellectual life of children.

27. What was the educational aim of Plato?

## CHAPTER XII

### SOME UNCONSIDERED ASPECTS OF MORAL TRAINING

1. What are the three principles which underlie the educational thought proposed in these volumes?

2. What principle is universally acknowledged as the basis of moral teaching?

3. How does authority work?

4. 'A man can but act up to his lights'—discuss this fallacy.

5. Define the limits of authority.

6. What is the consequence of arbitrary action?

7. What old contention as to the sanctions of morality is exercising men now?

8. Show that Socrates had to contend with the popular doctrine of to-day in other forms.

9. What is the necessary issue of this teaching?

10. How should children be taught that duty can exist only as that which we owe to God?

11. Show that morals do not come by nature.

12. That a certain rough and ready morality does come by heredity and environment.

13. How do we get an educated conscience?

14. Show that children are born neither moral nor immoral.

15. Show the danger of spasmodic moral efforts.

16. Where shall we look for the basis of our moral teaching?

17. What do we owe to the poets in this regard?

18. How did the mediæval Church provide moral object lessons?

19 Illustrate our failure in this respect.

20. Why should children have the inspiration of high ideals?

21. Show the value of biography in this connection.

22. Name any virtues with which the poets inspire us.

23. Make a suggestion with regard to the culling of mottoes.

24. How may parents and teachers help children to the habit of sweet thoughts?

25. Enumerate and discuss some of the virtues which children should be trained to develop.

26. Distinguish between 'being good' and loving God.

## CHAPTER XIII

### SOME UNCONSIDERED ASPECTS OF RELIGIOUS EDUCATION

1. Show how the principle of authority bears on religious teaching.

2. In what ideas do the children of our day need especially to be brought up?

3. How do certain questions 'in the air' militate against the sense of authority?

4. In what respects does authority work like a good and just national government?

5. Discuss authority in connection with punishment.

6. Discuss each of the various themes suggested in connection with the subject of authority in the religious life.

7. Show that lines of habit are as important for the religious as for the physical, moral, and intellectual life.

8. How would you endeavour to keep a child in the habit of the thought of God?

9. Discuss the question of reverent attitudes.

10. How would you use 'because of the angels' in this connection?

11. Show the importance of regularity in time and place in children's prayers.

12. Why should not their evening prayers be left till bed-time?

13. What is to be said of little text-books?

14. Show the danger of losing the narrative teaching of the Scriptures.

15. Why should not children be encouraged in long readings or long prayers?

16. How should the habit of praise be fostered?

17. Show the value of the habit of Sunday-keeping, and describe a child's Sunday.

18. Write your reflections on each of the themes suggested in connection with the habits of the religious life.

19. Show the importance of selecting the inspiring ideas we propose to give children in the things of the Divine life.

20. What other point demands our care?

21. What vitalising idea is of first importance in the teaching of children?

22. How should children be taught that the essence of Christianity is devotion to a Person?

23. Why is it necessary to teach children that there is a Saviour of the world?

24. What teaching would you give them about the work of the Holy Spirit?

## CHAPTER XIV

### A MASTER-THOUGHT

1. What is the motto of the Parents' Union?

2. Show that this motto is a master-thought.

3. Why is 'education is an atmosphere' the clause of the motto that pleases us most?

4. What is the result if this *part* be taken for the *whole*?

5. What defect in education leads to *ennui* and the desire to be amused by shows.

6. What was the unconscious formula of the eighteenth century?

7. What was the result of this one-sided view of education?

8. Show that the idea of the development of the faculties also rests upon a one-sided notion.

9. What is the tendency of an education grounded upon the development of faculties?

10. Should it be our aim to produce specialists? Why not?

11. Show what manner of education results in a sound and well-balanced mind.

12. Show that the mediæval Church understood, better than we, that 'education is a life.'

13. Sketch the scheme of educational philosophy to be found on the walls of the 'Spanish Chapel' of S. Maria Novella.

14. Show how this educational creed unifies life.

15. What does Coleridge say of the origin of great ideas of nature?

16. What does Michael Angelo write to his friend of the need for a diet of great ideas?

17. What is the special teaching vouchsafed to men to-day?

18. What views are people apt to take with regard to this teaching?

19. What does Huxley say about ideas in science?

20. How does the teaching of Simone Memmi and Coleridge relieve us from anxiety and make clear our perplexities?

21. How does Coleridge describe Botany, as that science existed in his day?

22. What has evolution, the key-word of our age, done for this and other perplexities?

23. But what has been the object of pursuit among philosophers for three thousand years?

24. How did Heraklitos attempt to solve the problem?

25. How did Demokritos?

26. Show that some knowledge of history and philosophy should give us pause in using the key of evolution.

27. Show that personality remains, and is not resolvable by this key.

28. Why is it necessary for parents and teachers to consider their attitude towards this question?

29. What are the four attitudes which it is possible to take up?

30. What gains will the children derive if their teachers adopt the last-mentioned of these?

31. What two things are incumbent upon us with regard to the great ideas by which the world is being taught?

32. Show the danger of making too personal a matter of education.

33. If education is a world-business, show that we must have a guiding idea about it.

34. What ideas should regulate the curriculum of a boy or girl under fourteen?

35. Show the importance of good books and many books for the use of children.

36. Why may we not choose or reject certain 'subjects' arbitrarily?

## CHAPTER XV

### SCHOOL-BOOKS, AND HOW THEY MAKE FOR EDUCATION

1. What ideas do we get from the incident quoted from *The Neighbours*?

2. What manner of books sustains the life of thought?

3. What have you to say of the 'school-books' of the publishers?

4. Why do intelligent teachers fall back upon oral lessons?

5. Mention some of the disadvantages of these.

6. What questions should we ask about a youth who has finished his education?

7. Wherein lies the error of our educational system ?

8. Show that we undervalue children, and therefore educate them amiss.

9. What was the note of home-life in the last generation ?

10. How would you describe children as they are ?

11. Show that our great work is to give them vitalising ideas.


## CHAPTER XVI

### How to Use School-Books

1. What question must we ask concerning a subject of instruction ?

2. What do you understand by disciplinary subjects ?

3. What danger attends the blind use of these ?

4. What idea should prove an 'open sesame' to many vitalising studies ?

5. Illustrate the fact that the Bible is the great source of moral impressions.

6. What impressions were made on De Quincey by his nursery Bible readings ?

7. In what ways did the liturgy appeal to him ?

8. Why should a child *dig* for his own knowledge ?

9. What are the uses of the oral lesson and the lecture ?

10. Why should children use living books for themselves ?

11. What is the mark of a fit book ?

12. How shall we know if children enjoy a book ?

13. What should the teacher do towards the teaching given by the book ?

14. In what ways must children labour over their books ?

15. What is the simplest way of dealing with a paragraph or chapter ?

16. Why should preparation consist of a single careful reading ?

17. Mention some other ways of using books.

18. What mechanical devices might children use in their studies?

19. What does the teacher do towards the preparation of a lesson?

20. What is the danger of too many disciplinary devices?

21. Why are we in some danger of neglecting books?

## CHAPTER XVII

### EDUCATION IS THE SCIENCE OF RELATIONS: WE ARE EDUCATED BY OUR INTIMACIES

1. What are our three educational instruments, and why are we confined to these?

2. Why may we not encroach upon the personality of children?

3. In what ways may we temper life too much for children?

4. What example of fairy-lore serving as a screen and shelter does Wordsworth give us in *The Prelude*?

5. What have you to say of the spontaneous living of children?

6. On what does fulness of living depend?

7. Distinguish between the relation of ideas to ideas and the relation of persons to the ideas proper for them.

8. Show that the object of education is not to make something of the child, but to put the child in touch with all that concerns him.

9. Describe the self-education of an infant. What does Wordsworth tell us on this point?

10. What is our part in his education?

11. What is our common error; what are its results?

12. Distinguish between business and desire.

13. What attempts were made to teach Ruskin to ride, and what does he think of those attempts?

14. What indictment does he bring against the limitations of his condition?

15. Why should those parents especially who are villa-dwellers learn much from *Præterita*?

16. Enumerate Wordsworth's opportunities for forming dynamic relations.

17. Show that these came naturally in the course of things.

## CHAPTER XVIII

### WE ARE EDUCATED BY OUR INTIMACIES

#### *Part II.—Further Affinities*

1. What chances had Ruskin to learn the use of material?

2. What do we hear of the intimacy of either boy with natural objects?

3. Describe Ruskin's flower studies.

4. His pebble studies.

5. Show that these became a life-shaping intimacy.

6. Upon what books did Ruskin grow up?

7. What is the first mention we get of his insatiate delight in a book?

8. What qualities in Byron delighted him?

9. Describe Wordsworth's delight in the *Arabian Nights*.

10. What is Wordsworth's plea for 'romance' in education?

11. What does he say in favour of liberty to range among books?

12. Describe his first enthralment by poetry.

13. Show that Ruskin's historic sense appears to be always connected with places.

14. How does he betray some want of living touch with the past?

15. Show that Wordsworth, too, was aloof

16. Show that the knowledge 'learned in schools' laid little hold of either boy.

17. Compare the experiences of the two boys with regard to chances of comradeship.

## CHAPTER XIX

### WE ARE EDUCATED BY OUR INTIMACIES

#### *Part III.— Vocation*

1. Describe Turner's 'call' to Ruskin.

2. What does Ruskin consider his first sincere drawing?

3. What account does he give of his true initiation?

4. What is the first hint we get of nature as a passion?

5. How does Wordsworth trace the beginnings of this passion?

6. Describe the 'calling' of the poet.

7. How does Wordsworth describe the education of the little prig of his day?

8. Show that the child prig is the child who is the end and aim of his own education.

9. Mention a few of the directions in which children have affinities.

10. Show from the example of *Waverley* the danger of a desultory education.

11. How does Mr Ruskin express that 'the child is father to the man'?

12. Show that strenuous effort and reverence are conditions of education.

13. Show that comradeship has its duties.

14. Why should children have a steady, unruffled course of work?

15. Describe from *Brother Lawrence* one way in which the highest relationship may be initiated.

16. What does Browning say about this relation?

## CHAPTER XX

### SUGGESTIONS TOWARDS A CURRICULUM

1. Give a short summary of the preceding chapters.

2. Comment upon the educational methods of the day.

3. What two conditions are necessary to any sound reform?

4. Why do many boys and girls leave school intellectually devitalised?

5. How does Mr Benson characterise the aims of Masters of public schools?

6. How may we characterise the minds of children?

7. Show the practical working of this view.

8. Distinguish between knowledge and information.

9. In what ways will the child show power in dealing with knowledge?

10. To what do stereotyped phrases and mangled notes in children's work point?

11. Work out an analogy between knowledge and food.

12. Why may we call 'mark-hunger' a debauchery of the mind?

13. Why should not epitomes and compilations be allowed for children's use?

14. What are the advantages of working through a considerable book?

## CHAPTER XXI

### SUGGESTIONS TOWARDS A CURRICULUM

#### *Part II.—School-Books*

1. Who must, in the end, decide upon the right school-books?

2. What are the relative places of lecture and book?

3. Show the danger of elaborate appliances.

4. Upon what principle should studies be co-ordinated?

5. What results of education should we look for in a young person leaving school?

6. Show that the worth of education by *things* is now fully recognised.

7. What habit should we look for as a chief acquirement of school-life?

8. Give a rough classification of the subjects in which knowledge is due to children.

9. Show the importance of the Bible as a means of education.

10. What knowledge of history should boys and girls of twelve to fourteen have?

11. What mistake is commonly made in teaching this subject?

12. What knowledge of languages should they have?

13. What should we aim at in the early teaching of science?

14. What least amount of time in the open is a *sine quâ non* of a living education?

15. What is the use of books in nature-teaching?

16. Name a few useful books.

17. What do you understand by 'picture-talks'?


## CHAPTER XXII

### SUGGESTIONS TOWARDS A CURRICULUM

#### Part III.—The Love of Knowledge

1. Why does the use of books make for short hours?

2. What is the evil of a utilitarian education?

3. Distinguish between relations and interests.

4. Show that the tendency of present-day education is to depreciate knowledge.

5. Enumerate some causes of the failure of our efforts at intellectual education.

6. Show the danger, which besets teachers, of pursuing intellectual futilities.

7. By what test may we distinguish a fad from an educational method?

8. Our end is to produce an educated child. How is he to be recognised?

9. Children delight in school for many reasons. Which of these is the only abiding motive?

10. What change in our educational methods should secure the children's educational Magna Carta?

---

## APPENDIX II

### SOME SPECIMENS OF EXAMINATION WORK DONE IN THE 'PARENTS' REVIEW' SCHOOL, IN WHICH THE PUPILS ARE EDUCATED UPON BOOKS AND THINGS

THE *Parents' Review* School, an output of the Parents Union, was, in the first place, designed to bring home schools, taught by governesses, up to the standard of other schools. A Training College for governesses, with Practising School, etc., was established later. Children may not enter the School under six; because we think the first six years of life are wanted for physical growth and the self-education which children carry on with little ordered aid. The *Parents' Review* School is conducted by means of programmes of work, in five classes, sent out, term by term, to each of the home schools (and to some other schools); and the same programmes are used in the Practising School. Examination papers are set at the end of each term.

The work is arranged on the principles which have been set forth in this volume; a wide curriculum, a considerable number of books for each child in the several classes, and, besides, a couple of hours' work daily, not with *Books* but with *Things*. Many of the pupils in the school have absorbed, in a way, the culture of their parents; but the children of uncultured parents take with equal readiness and comparable results to this sort of work, which is, I think, fitted, not only for the clever, but for the average and even the dull child.

**Class Ia.**—The child of six goes into Class Ia.; he works for $2\frac{1}{2}$ hours a day, but half an hour of this time is spent in drill and games. Including drill, he has thirteen 'subjects' of study, for which about sixteen books are used. He recites hymns, poems, and Bible verses; works from Messrs Sonnenschein and Nesbitt's *A B C Arithmetic*; sings French and English songs; begins Mrs Curwen's *Child Pianist*, learns to write and to print, learns to read, learns French orally, does brush-drawing and various handicrafts. All these things are done with joy, but cannot be illustrated here. Bible lessons, read from the Bible; tales, natural history, and geography are taught from appointed books, helped by the child's own observation.

Our plan in each of these subjects is to read him the passage for the lesson (a good long passage), talk about it a little, avoiding much explanation, and then let him narrate what has been read. This he does very well and with pleasure, and is often happy in catching the style as well as the words of the author.

Certain pages, say 40 or 50, from each of the children's books are appointed for a term's reading. At the end of the term an examination paper is sent out containing one or two questions on each book. Here are a few of the answers. The children in the first two classes narrate their answers, which someone writes from their dictation.

*Q.* Tell the story of Naaman.

*A.* (aged $6\frac{3}{4}$):—

"Naaman had something the matter with him, and his master sent a letter to the King of Israel, and the king was very unhappy and did not know what to do because he thought that he wanted to come and fight against him, and he rent his clothes. And he said, ' I can't cure him,' so he sent him to Elisha, and he told him to take a lot of presents and a lot of things with him. And when Naaman came to Elisha's door, Elisha sent Gehazi to tell him to dip himself seven times in the waters of Jordan, and he said to himself, 'I surely thought he would have come out, and I thought a lot of people would come out and make a fuss'; and he went back in a rage. And his servant said to him, 'Why didn't you go?' And he said, 'My rivers are much the best.' So his servants said, 'If he had asked you to do some great thing, wouldst thou have done it?' So he went and dipped himself seven times in the water, and when he came out he was quite all right again. And when he was coming home they saw Gehazi coming, so Naaman told them to stop the horses, and so they stopped, and Gehazi said, 'There are some people come to see me, please give me some money and some cloaks,' and they were very heavy, so Naaman sent some of his men to carry them, and when he came near the house he said to his servants, 'You can go now.' Elisha said, 'Because you have done this you shall have the leprosy that Naaman had.'"

*Q.* Tell a fairy story.
*B.* (aged 6¾):—

"When Ulysses was coming back from Troy he passed the Sirens. He could hear them, but he couldn't get to them, because he was bound. He wanted to get to them so as he could listen to them a long time, because a lot of people had come and listened to them, and they found it so beautiful that they wanted to stay there, and they stayed till they died. His companions couldn't hear them because they stopped up their ears with wax and cotton-wool. And this was the song they sang:—

> 'Hither, come hither and hearken awhile,
>    Odysseus far-famed king,
> No sailor has ever passed this way
>    But has paused to hear us sing.
> Our song is sweeter than honey,
>    And he that hears it knows
> What he never learnt from another,
>    And his joy before he goes.
> We know what the heroes bore at Troy
>    In the ten long years of strife,
> We know what happened in all the world,
>    And the secret things of life.'

And then they rowed on till at last the song faded away, and they rowed on and on for a long time, and then when they could not hear them nor see them, the wax was taken out of their ears, and then they unbound Ulysses."

*Q.* What have you noticed (yourself) about a spider ?

C. (aged 7¾) :—

"We have found out the name of one spider, and often have seen spiders under the microscope—they were all very hairy. We have often noticed a lot of spiders running about the ground —quantities.  Last term we saw a spider's web up in the corner of the window with a spider sucking out the juice of a fly ; and we have often touched a web to try and make the spider come out, and we never could, because she saw it wasn't a fly, before she came out.

"I saw the claw of a spider under the microscope, with its little teeth ; we saw her spinnerets and her great eyes.  There were the two big eyes in one row, four little ones in the next row, and two little ones in the next row.  We have often found eggs of the spiders ; we have some now that we have got in a little box, and we want to hatch them out, so we have put them on the mantelpiece to force them.

"Once we saw a spider on a leaf, and we tried to catch it, but we couldn't ; he immediately let himself down on to the ground with a thread.

"We saw the circulation in the leg of another spider under the microscope ; it looked like a little line going up and down."

*Q.* Gather three sorts of tree leaf-buds and two sorts of catkin, and tell all you can about them.

D. (aged 6):—

(1) "The chestnut bud is brown and sticky, it is a sort of cotton-woolly with the leaves inside.  It splits open and sends out two leaves, and the leaves split open.

(2) "The oak twig has always a lot of buds on the top, and one bud always dies.  Where the bud starts there is a little bit of knot-wood.  The oak-bud is very tiny.

(3) "The lime bud has a green side and a red side, and then it bursts open and several little leaves come out and all the little things that shut up the leaves die away.

(4) "Golden catkins and silver pussy palms of a willow tree. The golden catkins have stamens with all the pollen on them. They grow upwards, and two never grow opposite to each other. The silver pussy palms have seed boxes, with a little tube growing out, and a little sticky knob on the top.  The bees rub the pollen off their backs on to the sticky knob."

*Q.* Tell about the North-West Passage.  (Book studied, *The World at Home.*)

E. (aged 7) :—

"People in England are very fond of finding things out, and they wanted to find out the North-West Passage. If people wanted to go to the Pacific Ocean, they had to go round Africa by the Cape of Good Hope, or else round South America by Cape Horn. This was a very long way. They thought they might find out a shorter way by going along the North Coast by America, and they would come out in the Pacific Ocean. They would call this way the North-West Passage. First one man and then another tried to find a way. They found a lot of straits and bays which they called after themselves. The enemy they met which made them turn back was the cold. It was in the frozen zone, and the sea was all ice, and the ice lumps were as big as mountains, and when they came against a ship they crashed it to pieces. Once a man named Captain Franklin tried over and over again to find the North-West Passage, and once he went and never came back again, for he got stuck fast in the ice, and the ice did not break, and he had not much food with him, and what he had was soon eaten up, and he could not get any more, for all the animals in that country had gone away, for it was winter, and he could not wait for the summer, when they would return. A ship went out from England called the *Fox* to look for him, but all they found was a boat, a Bible, a watch, and a pair of slippers near each other. After looking a lot they found the North-West Passage, but because there is so much ice there the ships can't use it."

Class Ib.—In Class Ib., the children are usually between seven and eight, but may be nine. They have fifteen 'subjects' (perhaps twenty-three books). The subjects which do not lend themselves to illustration are a continuation of the work in Class Ia. But by this time the children can usually read, and read for themselves some, at any rate, of their books for *History, Geography, and Tales.* In Class Ib. the children narrate their lessons as in Ia., and, also, their answers to the examination questions. They appear to enjoy doing this; indeed, the examinations which come at the end of each term are a pleasure; the only difficulty is that small children want to go on 'telling.' Their words are taken down literally. One is struck by the correctness and copiousness of the language used; but young children delight in words, and often surprise their elders by their

free and correct use of ' dictionary words.' One notices
the verve with which the children tell the tale, the orderly
sequence of events, the correctness and fulness of detail,
the accuracy of names. These things are natural to children
until they are schooled out of them.

*Q.* Tell all you know about St Patrick. (Book studied,
*Old Tales from British History.*)

A. (aged 7) :—

" St Patrick was the son of a Scotch farming clergyman, and
one day some Irish pirates came and took Patrick with them to
make him a slave ; and they sold him to an Irish nobleman.
And the Irish nobleman made him a shepherd to take care of his
flocks, and shepherds have a lot of time to think when they are
out guarding their flocks by night. And Patrick was very sorry
that the poor Irish were heathens. One day he slipped off and
got into a boat with some sailors, and after a great adventure,
for their food ran short, they arrived safely in Scotland. And
Patrick was still thinking about the Irish, so he went off in a boat
of his own, with a few followers, to Ireland. A shepherd saw
them coming, and told his master the pirates were coming. So he
armed his servants and went down to meet the pirates, but when
he heard the errand they were on, he offered them to come into
his house. Now Patrick settled in Ireland, but some heathen
priests rose up against him, and a wise man said, ' What is the
good of killing him ? Other Irish people are now Christians, and
they will teach too.' So he saved his life. And Patrick gave
him the book of Psalms written by his own hand. One day Patrick
asked a rich man if he might have a little plot of land on the top
of a hill, but the rich man refused him, but gave him a little plot
of land at the bottom of the hill. And there Patrick built a
church, and a house for himself and servants to live in. Then
the rich man got ill, and was just about to die, but got better,
but as he thought Patrick was like a wizard, who could foretell
his fortune, he thought he'd better try to please him. So he sent
him a brass cauldron, enough to hold one whole sheep, and Patrick
said ' I thank you, master.' The rich man was angry, and sent
for the cauldron back again, and Patrick said, ' I thank you,
master.' So the rich man was ashamed, and brought back the
cauldron, and said he could have the little plot of land on the top
of the hill. So they went up to measure it. Then a roe-deer
dashed out of the thicket, but left her fawn behind her, and the
men were going to kill the fawn, but Patrick took it up and
carried it down the hill ; the mother followed, for she saw he
was doing no harm to it. On that place he built a fine church,

which is still standing. And Patrick died on a journey, and was buried at a place called Downpatrick after him."

*Q.* Tell what you know about Alfred Tennyson. (Book studied, Mrs Frewen Lord's *Tales from Westminster Abbey*.)

B. (aged $7\frac{1}{2}$) :—

"Alfred Tennyson was born in 1809, and he loved the country very much. One Sunday when they were going out to chapel, except Lord Tennyson as he was very young, his brother Charles gave him his slate to write about birds and flowers, and when they came back he had filled his slate with his first poem. He and his brother used to make up stories that sometimes lasted a month. He was very shortsighted, and when he was looking at anything it looked as if he were smelling it. He had good ears, for he could hear the shriek of a bat. Alfred Tennyson wrote *The Revenge* and *The Siege of Lucknow*, and Sir John Franklin's poem :—

> ' Not here ; the white North hath thy bones,
>    And thou, heroic sailor soul,
> Art passing on thy happier voyage now,
>    Toward no earthly pole.'

And he also wrote the *May Queen* and *Cradle Song*. Because his poetry was so good the Queen gave him a name and knighted him. He says that if you tread on a daisy it will turn up and get red. He was 83 years old when he died—the year he died in was 1892. He was buried in Westminster Abbey, in Poets' Corner."

*Q.* What is a hero? What heroes have you heard of? Tell about one.

C. (aged 7) :—

"(1) A hero is a brave man. (2) Count Roland, Huon ot Bordeaux, the Horatii and Curatii. (3) Once there was a brave Emperor called Charlemagne, and he was fighting with the heathen King of Saragossa. Just a wee bit of land was left to the heathen king, so he sent a messenger to speak about peace. They pretended that they would have peace, so they went back to Charlemagne and asked him to leave Roland behind to take charge of the mountain passes. So Charlemagne said that he would leave Roland behind because there was none so brave as him, so that when Charlemagne had turned his army they should come in great numbers to fight against Roland. And Roland stayed behind with twenty thousand men, and Oliver heard a great noise by the side of Spain, and then Oliver climbed on a pine tree, and he saw the arms glimmering and the spears shining, and then he said to Roland that there were a full hundred thousand, and that they just had so few, and that it was much better to sound his horn and Charlemagne will turn his army. Roland said he would be mad if he did that. Oliver said again to sound his horn, and Roland said he would lose his fame in France if he did it. Then Oliver said again, 'Friend Roland, sound thy horn and Charles will hear it, and turn his army.' Then all the mountain passes were full of the enemies, and when they came nearer they fought, and they fought, and they fought, and at last the Christians were falling too, and when there were only sixty left he blew his horn. Charlemagne heard it and said he must go, and Ganelon said he was just pretending, but then Charlemagne heard it fainter, and knew that it was true that he must go, and then fainter again, but Charlemagne was nearer and so heard it better. And Roland said, 'Ride as fast as you can for many men have been killed, and there are few left.' Then Charlemagne bade his men sound their horns, so that they knew that help was near and then the heathen fled away. There were just the two left, Roland and the Archbishop, and Roland said to the Archbishop that he would try to fetch the dead bodies of the braver soldiers. Then the Archbishop said to Roland, 'Quick, before I die.' Then Roland went and brought them before the Archbishop and laid them down there. Then he went and searched the field again, and under a pine tree he found Oliver's body, then he brought it too and laid it in front of the Archbishop. Then Roland fainted to the ground, then the Archbishop tried to bring some water for Roland, and he fell down and died. Then Roland put the hands over the chest of the Archbishop, then he prayed to God to give him a place in Paradise, and then he said that the field was his. Before he died he put his sword and his ivory horn under him, and laid himself down on the ground, so that Charlemagne, when he came, would know that he was the conqueror. And God sent St Michael and another saint to fetch his soul up to heaven."

*Q*. Gather three sorts of tree leaf-bud and two sorts of catkin and tell all you can about them.

E. (a cottage child aged 9) :—

" *Beech Twig.*—It has rather a woody stalk, and it is a very light grey-browny stalk, and it is very thin, and the little branches that grow out are light brown and it is thicker where the buds are and it is a lighter brown up at the top than it is at the bottom, and the buds are a light reddy-brown and very pointed, and they are scaly. The bark is rather rough and there is a lot of little kind of brown spots on it.

"*Lime Twig.*--It is called Ruby-budded Lime because the buds are red, and they are fat rather, and they have got some green in as well, and they come rather to a point at the top, they grow alternately and the little stalk that they grow out of is reddy-green, and the top part of the stalk is green, and it is woody, and it is rough, and it is a reddy-green at the bottom. Where the buds come out it is swelled out, the bark has come off and it has left it white and woody. At the top of one of the stalks the bud has come off.

"*Sycamore Twig.*—Well, the back is *very* woody, and it is a brown stalk and it is rough and there is a little weeny bud growing out of the side, and the buds grow out two and two, and there are a lot of little buds.

"*Willow.*—Well, the stalk is a dark brown, and is very smooth and it will bend very easily, and the buds when they first come on the stalk are little brown ones, and then a silvery-green comes out and there is a scale at the bottom, and then they get greyer and bigger with little green leaves at the bottom, and then it comes yellow, and there is a lot of pollen on it. If you touch it the pollen comes on your finger.

"*Hazel.*—Well, the stalk is a dark brown, something the colour of the willow, and it bends easily, and the buds are green and there is little scales, and then the catkins come and they grow very long, and there is a lot of little flowers in one, and there is pollen in that, and the stalk is rather rough, and there are some big buds at the top just bursting, and the leaves are coming out, and the buds are very soft and glossy, and the scales are at the bottom."

*Q.* What have you noticed about a thrush? Tell all you know about it.

F. (aged 8) :—

"Thrushes are browny birds. They eat snails, and they take the snail in their mouths and knock it against a stone to break the shell and eat the snail. I found a stone with a lot of bits of shell round it, so knew that a thrush had been there. Where we used to live a thrush used to sing every morning on the same tree. The song of the thrush is like a nightingale. We often see a lot of thrushes on the lawn before breakfast or after a shower. They have yellow beaks and their breasts are specked with lovely yellow and brown. Once we found a thrush asleep on a sponge in a bedroom and we carried it out and put it on a tree. Thrushes eat worms as well as snails, and on the lawn they listen with their heads on one side and go along as the worm gets under the ground, and presently, perhaps, the worm comes up and they gobble it up, or they put their beaks in and get it. Thrushes build their nests with sticks at the bottom and line them with little bits of wool they pick up, or feathers, and they like to get down very much."

**Class II.**—In Class II. the children are between nine and twelve, occasionally over twelve. They have twenty-one 'subjects,' and about twenty-five books are used. They work from 9 to 12 each day, with half an hour's interval for games and drill. Some Latin and German (optional) are added to the curriculum. In music we continue Mrs Curwen's (*Child Pianist*) method and Tonic Sol-fa, and learn French, German (optional), and English songs. But I cannot here give details of our work, and must confine myself to illustrations from seven of the subjects on the programme. Children in Class II. write or dictate, or write a part and dictate a part of their examination answers according to their age. The examination lasts a week, and to write the whole of their work would be fatiguing at this stage. The plan followed is, that the examination in each subject shall be done in the time for that subject on the time-table.

I should like to say a word about the Greek and Roman History. Plutarch's *Lives* are read in Classes II. and III., and as children are usually five years in these two classes, they may read some fifteen of these *Lives*, which I think stand alone in literature as teaching that a man is part of the State, that his business is to be of service to the State, but that the value of his service depends upon his personal character. The *Lives* are read to the children almost without comment, but *with necessary omissions*. Proper names are written on the blackboard; and, at the end, children narrate the substance of the lesson. The English History book used in Classes II. and III. is extremely popular; it is Mr Arnold-Forster's (of about 800 pages), and is well known as a serious, manly, and statesmanlike treatment of English History; in no case is there any writing down to the children. Mrs Creighton's *First History of France* is also a favourite, though I should have thought there was hardly enough detail to make it so. Contemporary periods of English and French History are studied term by term. For Natural History, Miss Arabella Buckley's *Fairyland of Science* and *Life and Her Children*, Mrs Brightwen's books, etc., give scientific information and excite intelligent curiosity, while out-of-door nature-study lays the foundation for science. The handiworks of Class II. are such as cardboard Sloyd, clay modelling, needlework, gardening, etc. These, field-work, piano practice, etc., are done in the afternoons or after tea.

*Q.* "Ah! Pericles, those that have need of a lamp, take care to supply it with oil." Who said this? Tell the story. (Book studied, Plutarch's *Lives : Pericles.*)

D. (aged $11\frac{1}{2}$), answer dictated :—

"Anaxagoras, the philosopher, said these words to Pericles.
"Pericles was the ruler of Athens, and Anaxagoras had taught him when a boy. Being ruler of Athens, he led a very busy life, attending to the affairs of State, and so was not able to give much time to his household affairs. Once a year he collected his money, and could only manage his income by giving out an allowance to each member of his family and household every day : this was done by Evangelus, his steward. Anaxagoras thought this a very wrong way of arranging matters, and said that Pericles paid too much heed to bodily affairs, because he thought you ought to mind only about philosophy and spiritual doings, and not about the affairs of the world. To give an example to Pericles he gave up all his household and tried to live entirely on philosophy. But he soon found his mistake when he found himself starving and penniless, with no house. So he covered his head up and prepared to die. Pericles, hearing of this, went immediately to his rescue and begged him to live ; not because he thought death a misfortune, but that he said, 'What shall I do without your help in the affairs of State?' And then Anaxagoras uttered the words which are above, meaning, of course (though putting it in a clever way), that Pericles was to keep him. On the other hand, he might have meant that he had been mistaken in his philosophy."

*Q.* Tell the history of ' F.D.' on a penny. (Book studied, Arnold-Forster's *History of England.*)

C. (aged 10), answer written by child:—

"The letters ' F.D.' stand for the Latin words *Fidei Defensor*, meaning 'The Defender of the Faith.' Henry VIII. had a little while ago written a book on the Pope (who was Clement VII.) saying that the Pope was the true head of the Church, and everyone ought to obey him. The Pope was so pleased that he made Henry *Fidei Defensor*. It must be remembered that the king had married his brother Arthur's [1] widow, a Spanish princess, namely, Catherine of Aragon (*sic*), and as they had no son Henry wished to divorce her, but the Pope would not allow him to, as he had given Henry special leaf (*sic*) to marry her. At this Henry was furious, and began to think about the Pope's words, ' Defender of the Faith.' He would not act as he thought till someone suggested it. So two men, called Cromwell and Cranmer, came forward, telling the king to take the Pope's words, not as he meant them, but as they really were, as they stood. The king was delighted, and made Cranmer a bishop and Cromwell his wisest counsellor.[1] In 1534 Parliament[1] was called upon to declare Henry head of the Church. All said he was, except two men, Sir Thomas More and Fisher, bishop of Rochester ; these would not agree, and were executed in 1535. If we look on a penny we see the letters ' F.D.,' which shows from the reign of Henry VIII. till now the Pope has not been allowed to interfere with England. In order to spite the Pope, Henry allowed the Lutherans and learned men to come into England."

*Q*. What did you see in the *Seagull* sailing up the Firth of Forth ? (Book studied, *Geographical Reader*, Book II.)

G. (aged 9), answer dictated :—

"In sailing up the Forth we first of all see Leith, which is the seaport town of Edinburgh. Then we come to Edinburgh. The old and new Edinburghs are built on opposite hills, the valley in between is laid out in lovely gardens. One thing very odd about Edinburgh is that the streets look as if they are built one on top of the other. At one end of the town there is a castle which looks so like the rocks and mountains it is built on, one can hardly distinguish it. At the other end of the town there is Holyrood, where the ancient kings used to live. We do not see many merchantmen because there are no good harbours, there are a good many fishing smacks and pleasure boats. As we go along we see women with big baskets with a strap across their foreheads, and they are calling out ' caller herrings.'"

[1] The writers have been in two minds about the spelling of words marked ([1]).

APPENDICES 283

*Q.* "And Jonathan loved him as his own soul." Of whom was this said? Tell a story of Jonathan's love.

E. (aged 9), answer dictated:—

"This was said of David. Saul's anger was kindled against David; and Jonathan and David were talking together, and Jonathan had been telling David that he would do anything for him, and David said, 'To-morrow is the feast of a new moon, and Saul will expect me to sit with him at the table; therefore say, 'David earnestly asked leave of me to go to Bethlehem, his city, where there is a sacrifice of his family.' If Saul is angry, then I shall know that he would kill me, but if he is not angry, it will be all right.' Jonathan said, 'So shall it be, but it will not be safe for anybody to know anything about it; come into the field, and I will tell you what to do. Thou shalt remain hidden by the stone, and I will bring a lad and my arrows and bow, and I will shoot an arrow as if firing at a target; and if I say 'Run,' to the lad, ' is not the arrow beyond thee? go fetch it,' then thou shalt know that thou must flee from Saul.' David's seat was empty at the feast that night, but Saul said nothing. But the next day his seat was empty, and when Saul asked why, Jonathan told him what David had asked him to say. And Saul's anger was kindled, so much so that Jonathan feasted not that day, for he was grieved; and next morning he went out with his bow and arrows, and the lad, and shot an arrow as if at a mark. Then Jonathan said to the lad, 'Run, is not the arrow beyond thee? haste.' Then Jonathan gave his artillery unto the lad and sent him back to the city; and David came out of his hiding-place, and they made a covenant together, for Jonathan loved him as his own soul. Then David had to flee to Naioth in Ramah and Jonathan went back to the city."

*Q.* What do you know of Richelieu? (Book studied, Mrs Creighton's *First History of France*.)

E. (aged 10), answer partly written, partly dictated:—

"Cardinal Richeleu (*sic*) was brought to the French Court by the Queen mother, who thought he would do as she wished, but she was mistaken, for he no sooner was there than he turned against her, for Louse (*sic*) took him into his favour and made him Prime Minister after he had been there a few weeks. Richeleu (*sic*) was a devoted Catholic, and was determined to put down the Hugenots (*sic*), or Protestants as we call them, so he laid siege to La Rochelle, the chief town of the Hugenots (*sic*), who applied to the English for help. Charles sent a fleet to La Rochelle under pretence of helping the Hugenots (*sic*)[1]

[1] After this the answer was dictated.

but Admiral Pennington, who was in command of the ships, received orders when half way down the channel to take in French soldiers and sailors at Calais and to go to the French side. When Admiral Pennington ordered the ships to take in the soldiers, his men mutinied and he had to go back. Richelieu had thrown up earthworks across the harbour so that it was impossible to get in. Now Rochelle held out bravely, but at last it had to surrender, and out of 40,000, 140 crawled out, too weak to bury the dead in the streets. La Rochelle was razed to the ground, and never recovered its prosperity. One by one the Huguenot towns surrendered, and thus the Huguenots were destroyed. When Richelieu was made Prime Minister, the nobles did not like him, because they thought he had too much power, and now when Louis was ill, the Queen mother came to him, and in a stormy passion of tears begged Louis to send away his ungrateful servant. Louis promised he would do so, and Richelieu's fall seemed certain. Now all the nobles crowded to the Queen mother to pay their respects to her, as they thought she would now be the most important person in the Government. But one noble, who was wiser than the rest, went to Richelieu and begged to plead his cause before the King. The King promised he would keep him if he would serve him as he had done before. The Queen mother was foiled, and returned to Brussels, where she died."

*Q*. What towns, rivers, and castles would you see in travelling about Warwickshire ? (Book studied, *Geographical Reader*, Book III.)

B. (aged 9½), answer dictated:—

"Warwick, Kenilworth, Coventry, Stratford, Leamington, and Birmingham are all towns which you would see if you travelled through Warwick.

"The Avon stretches from north to south of Warwickshire. It has its tributary the Leam, upon which Leamington is situated.

"There is a castle of Warwick and Coventry and Kenilworth.

"Warwick is the capital of the county. It has a famous castle, whose high and lofty towers stand upon the bank of the river Avon.

"Coventry is a very old town. It also has a beautiful castle, where the fair Lady Godiva and her father used to live, about whom I suppose you have read.

"Stratford is called 'The Swan on the Avon,' because that is where Shakespeare, the great poet, was born and died, and this is a little piece of poetry about him :—

> 'Where his first infant lays, sweet Shakespeare sung,
> Where the last accents faltered on his tongue.'

"The river Avon takes its rise in the vale of Evesham, then winds through pleasant fields and meadows till it comes to the south of Warwickshire, and then it becomes broad and stately and flows on up to Coventry, where the Leam branches off from it (!), and then it becomes narrower and narrower until it gets out of Warwickshire and stops altogether at Naseby (!)"

*Q.* How many kinds of bees are there in a hive? What work does each do? Tell how they build the comb. (Book studied, *Fairyland of Science.*)

F. (aged 10), answer dictated :—

"Three kinds. The *drones* or males, the *workers* or females, and the *queen* bee. The drone is fat, the queen is long and thin, the workers are small and slim. The queen bee lays the eggs, the worker bee brings the honey in and makes the cell, and the drones wait to be fed. On a summer's day you see something hanging on a tree like a plum pudding, this is a swarm of bees. You will soon see someone come up with a hive, turn it upside down, shake the bough gently, and they will fall in. They will put some clean calico quickly over the bottom of the hive, and turn it back over on a bench. The bees first close up every little hole in the hive with wax, then they hang on to the roof, clinging on to one another by their legs. Then one comes away and scrapes some wax from under its body, and bites it in its mouth until it is pulled out like ribbon, this she plasters on the roof of the hive, then she flies out to get honey, and comes home to digest it, hanging from the roof, and in 24 hours this digested honey turns to wax, then she goes through the same process again. Next, the nursing bees come and poke their heads into this wax, bite the wax away (20 bees do this before one hole is ready to make a cell). Other bees are working on the other side at the same time. Each cell is made six-sided, so as to take up the least wax and the smallest space. When the cells are made the bees come in with honey in their honey-bag or first stomach ; they can easily pass the honey back though their mouths into the cells. It takes many bees to fill one cell, so they are hard at work."

G. (aged 9), written by child :—
Composition on *'The Opening of Parliament.'*

"The opening of Parliament by King Edward VII and Queen Alexander (*sic*) was rather grand. First, they drove to the

Houses of Parliament in a grand state carriage which had been used by George III, and then when they got there they had to robe in a certain room in great big robes, all edged with ermine fur, and with huge trains.    Queen Alexandra had an evening dress on, and King Edward a very nice kingly sort of suit (which was nearly covered up by his robes), and then they walked along to the real Houses of Parliament, where the members really sit. Then the king made a speech to open Parliment (*sic*), and other people made speeches too, and everything was done with grandeur and stateliness such as would befit a king.    May Parliament long be his! "

Class III.—In Class III. the range of age is from eleven or twelve to fifteen. The 'subjects': Bible Lessons and Recitations (Poetry and Bible passages); English Grammar, French, German, and Latin; Italian (optional); English, French, and Ancient History (Plutarch's *Lives*); Singing (French, English, and German Songs); Writing, Dictation, Drill; Drawing in Brush and Charcoal; Natural History, Botany, Physiology, Geography; Arithmetic; Geometry, and Reading. About thirty-five books are used. Time, $3\frac{1}{2}$ hours a day; half an hour out of this time, as before, for drill and games. There is no preparation or home work in any of the classes. The reader will notice from the subjoined specimens that the papers are still written *con amore*, and show an intelligent grasp of the several subjects. Though there are errors in many of the papers, they are not often the mistakes of ignorance or stupidity, nor are they those of a person who has never understood what he is writing about. 'Composition' is never taught as a subject; well-taught children compose as well-bred children behave—by the light of nature. It is probable that no considerable writer was ever taught the art of 'composition.' The same remark may be made about spelling: excepting for an occasional 'inveterate' case, the habit of reading teaches spelling. All the pupils of the *Parents' Review* School do not take all the subjects set in the programmes of the several classes. Sometimes, parents have the mistaken notion that the greater the number of subjects the heavier the work; though, in reality, the contrary is the case, unless the hours of study are increased. Sometimes, outside lessons in languages, music, etc., interfere ; sometimes, health will not allow of more than an hour or two of work in the day. The children in the practising school do all the work set, and their work compares satisfactorily with the rest, though the classes have the disadvantage of changing teachers every week. Children in Class III. write the whole of their examination work.

*Q.* Describe the founding of Christ's Kingdom. What are the laws of His Kingdom ?

A. (aged 13) :—

" Christ came to found His kingdom. He preached the laws to His people. He taught them to pray for it : 'Thy kingdom come.' And He told His chosen few to 'go and preach the Gospel of the kingdom.' He founded His kingdom in their hearts, and He reigned there. He will still found His kingdom in our hearts. He will come and reign as King. The kingdom was first founded by the sea of Galilee. 'Follow Me,' said our Lord to Andrew, and from that moment the kingdom was founded in Andrew's heart. Then there were Peter, James, John, Phillip (*sic*), Nathaniel (*sic*), and the kingdom grew. From that moment Christ never stopped His work for the kingdom— preaching and teaching, healing and comforting, proclaiming the laws of the kingdom. 'Think not that I am come to destroy the law or the prophets. I am not come to destroy, but to fulfil.' 'One jot or one tittle shall in no wise pass from the law.' 'Whosoever shall break one of these least commandments, and shall teach men so, the same shall be called the least in the kingdom.' No commandment was to pass from the law, but there was a new commandment, a new law, and that was 'love.' 'Love your enemies.' The Pharisees could not understand it. 'Love your friends, and hate your enemies,' was their law. But Jesus said, 'Bless them that curse you, and pray for them that despitefully use you.' 'Give, hoping for nothing in return' ; and, 'Whosoever shall smite thee on one cheek turn to him the other also.' Christ's law is the love which 'suffereth long and is kind . . . . seeketh not her own . . . . never faileth  . . . hopeth all things, endureth all things' ; and 'now abideth faith, hope, and charity, these three, but the greatest of these is— love.'"

*Q.* Explain 'English Funds, Consols 2¾ per cent., 113.

And give an account of the South Sea Bubble. (Book studied, Arnold-Forster's *History of England*.)

B. (aged 14½) :—

"This means that when the South Sea Company first appeared, the Government gave them £113 on condition that the Company should give 2¾ per cent., which means £2 15s. on every £100 lent, for a certain number of years. In the reign of George I. the money matters of the country were in a very bad state. The Government was very much in debt, especially to those people who had purchased annuities, and had a right to receive a certain sum of money from the Government every year as long as they lived. Sir Robert Walpole, who was then Prime Minister, was most anxious to pay off part of this debt. He heard of a Company which had just been started, called the South Sea Company, whose object was to trade in the South Seas. This was what Walpole wished for. He suggested to them that they should pay off the debt due to the people who had bought annuities, and in return the Government would give them some priveleges (*sic*) and charts which would be useful to them. This the Company agreed to do, but instead of paying the people in money they gave them what were called 'shares' in the South Sea Company. These shares were supposed to be very valuable, and it was thought that the South Sea Company was really prosperous, and that those who had shares in it would have most enormous profit in the end. Thousands of people came to buy shares, and some of them were so anxious to get them that they spent enormous sums of money on these worthless pieces of paper. All was well for a time, but at last the people began to wish for their money instead of the shares, and claimed it loudly from the Company. It was then that the bubble burst. It was discovered then that the Company was quite unable to pay what was due, and that all this time they had been deluding the nation by promises and giving them shares, and that they had never been the rich and prosperous Company they made themselves out to be. Naturally, the most dreadful distress prevailed everywhere, and many were absolutely ruined, so that the Government had to help those who were most distressed. At this point Sir Robert Walpole came to the rescue. He made the Bank of England pay some of the debts, and behaved with such cleverness that he saved the country almost from ruin."

*Q.* What do you know of the States General? (Book studied, Mrs Creighton's *First History of France*.)

C. (aged 12) :—

"The States General met in May, 1789. The people had long wanted reforms, and been talking about them, and now on the 5th of May, 1789, the States General met again for the first time since 1614. If the nobles sat in one house, and the people in another, as was the custom, they could never get the changes made. So the people with their leader, the Marquis of Mirabeau, declared that they would not leave the tennis court on which they were standing till it was agreed that they could sit together with the nobles. When Louis XVI. came down in State, and told them they were to sit apart, they said they would not leave their place except at the bayonets (*sic*) point. When he heard this he said, 'Very well, leave them alone.' So they sat together."

*Q.* Show fully how Aristides acquired the title of 'The Just.' Why was it a strange title for a man in those days? (Book studied, Plutarch's *Lives : Aristides.*)

D. (aged 13¼) :—

"Aristides acquired the title of 'The Just' by his justice, and because he never did anything unjust in order to become rich or powerful. While many of the judges and chief men in Athens took bribes, he alone always refused to do so, and he also never spent the public money on himself. When, after having defeated the Persians, at Platae, the Greek States decided to have a standing army, it was Aristides who was sent round to settle how much each town should contribute. And he did this so fairly and well, that all the Greek States blessed and praised his arrangement. It is said that Aristides could not only resiste (*sic*) the unjust claims of those whom he loved, but also those of his enemies. Once when he was judging a quarrel between two men, one of them remarked that the other had often injured Aristides. 'Tell me not that,' was the reply of Aristides, 'but what he has done to thee, for it is thy cause I am judging, not my own.' Another time when he had gone to law himself, and when, after having heard what he had to say, his judges were going to pass sentence on his adversary without having heard him, Aristides rose and entreated his judges to hear what his enemy could say in his own defence. In all that he did Aristides was inflexibly just, and many stories were told of his justice. Though he loved his country well, he would never do anything wrong to gain for Athens some advantage, and in all he did his one aim was justice, and his only ambition to be called 'The Just.' He was so just and good, that he was called the 'most just man in Greece.' In the times in which Aristides lived, men used to care more to be called great, rich, or powerful than just. Themistocles, the great rival of Aristides, used to do all he could to become the first man in Athens, and rich as well as powerful. He did not hesitate to take bribes, and all he did for the Athenians was done with a view to making himself the head of the people, and the first man in the State. He used often to do unjust as well as cruel things in order to get his own ends. It was the same with most other men who lived at this time, they prefered (*sic*) being rich, powerful, or great, to being distinguished by the title of ' The Just.' "

*Q.* Describe a journey in Northern Italy. (Book studied, *Geographical Reader*, Book IV.).

E. (aged 12) :—

" I am about to go for a tour round the northern part of Italy, and after I have taken a train to Savoy, which is about the south-east of France, I enter into Italy by the Cenis pass, which is very lofty, about 7,000 feet above sea level.

"On arriving in Italy, I come into the province of Piedmont, which has three mountain torrents or streams running through it. These streams join at Turin, the capital of Piedmont, and form the Po river, which flows out on the east coast of France into the Gulf of Venice. On the banks of the three mountain streams are some Protestants by the name of Waldenses, who say they are followers of the disciples, but if you ask any outsider, they will say, ' Oh ! the Waldenses are followers of a good man, by the name of Waldo, who fled out of France in the 12th century.'

" We will now go and see Turin, and the first thing we say is, ' What a clean town,' and so it certainly is, for it is quite the cleanest town in Italy, as the people have only to turn on the fountain taps to clean their paved streets. And after we have looked at Alessandria, where Napoleon gained his great victory, we leave Piedmont and follow up the river Po, until we come to its next tributary, the river Ticino, which runs up north into the Lake Maggiore, which is five to six miles wide and about sixty miles in length. This lake has four islands, which are named after Count Borromeo and so called the Borromean Islands, which are cultivated like gardens with terrases (*sic*) for resting places.

" Now let us go to Milan, which is so well known by its beautiful cathedral of white and black marble which have (*sic*) no less than 4000 sculptures of white marble, with pillars of Egyptian granite. Milan is famous for silks and lace to provide for the numerous palaces.

" We will now go back to the next lake, Lake Como, which is surrounded by mountains, and supposed to be the most beautiful of all lakes. At the south it goes out in a fork, and between the fork is a beautiful piece of land called Bellagia (*sic*).

" The next lake we come to is the Garda, the largest of all the lakes, and then we go on to the smallest of lakes called Lugano.

" We now having visited all the lakes, take a look at Lodi, the famous cheese market in Italy; after which we visit Verona, where Pliny the naturalist was born, also Paul Veronese. Shakespeare lays the scene of his play 'Romeo and Juliet' in Verona. The short time we have we spend at Venice, the queen of the Italian citys (*sic*) with its wonderful canals and the marvellous cathedral of St Mark's, also the dark, gloomy palace of the Doge."

*Q.* How are the following seeds dispersed :—Birch, Pine, Dandelion, Balsam, Broom ? Give diagrams and observations. (Book studied, Mrs Brightwen's *Glimpses into Plant Life.*)

F. (aged 13) :—

"The seeds of the Birch are very small, with two wings, one on each side, so that in a high wind numbers of them are blown on to high places, such as crevises (*sic*) on the face of a rock, or crevises (*sic*) on a church tower, or the tower of an old ruin. They are so light that they are carried a long way.

"The seeds of the Pine are very small, and the veins in the seed are wriggly, so that the seed is curly, which makes it whirl rapidly in the air, and the whirling motion carries it along a little way before it rests on the ground. It has two small wings.

"The seeds of the Dandilion (*sic*) are large, with a kind of silky parashute (*sic*) attached, so that when they fall off they do not fall to the ground, but are carried a little way because the wind catches the under part of the parashute (*sic*). The seed has a little hook at the top of it which prevents it from being pulled out of the ground by the parashute (*sic*) after it is once in.

"The Balsam seed case splits when the seeds are ripe and sends them flying in all directions, so they are far enough dispersed, and need no wings or parashutes (*sic*) to help them.

"The Broom seed case is a carpel, more like that of the sweet pea. When the seeds are ripe the two sides of the carpel split open and curl up like springs and send the seeds flying out, so they are dispersed without needing wings or parachutes."

*Q.* Describe the tissue of a potato and of a piece of rhubarb. (Book studied, Oliver's *Elementary Botany.*)

G. (aged 13) :—

"The tissue of *Rhubarb* is *very* fibrous indeed. In fact, it is almost entirely made up of vessels. These are cells which have become tubes by the dividing cell-wall being absorbed. These vessels are very beautiful when seen under a microscope, for their walls are all thickened in some way, in order to make them strong enough to bear the weight of the leaf.   Some are thickened by a spiral cord, which goes round and round the wall of the vessel.   In some vessels this is quite tightly twisted round the wall, that is to say, the rings do not come far apart ; in others it is quite loose and far apart.   Another kind of thickening is by rings, which just go round the tube and are not joined to each other.   Other vessels, again, have little knots in them like what there are in birch bark.

"The *Potato* tissue is mainly made up of starch, as it is one of the plant's storehouses, and starch is one of the plant's principal foods."

*Q.* Give a diagram of the eye, and explain how we see everything.   (Book studied, Dr Schofield's *Physiology for Schools.*)

H. (aged 13) :—

"The eye can be likened to a camera, and the brain to the man behind the camera.   The image enters at the hole, passes through the lens, is reflected on the plate, but the camera does not see, it is the man behind the camera who sees.    In the same way, the image passes in at the pupil and through the lens, both sides of which are curved, and can be tightened or slackened according to the distance of the image.    Then the image passes along the nerve of sight to the two bulbs in the brain which see. If you hold a rounded glass between a sheet of paper and the image at the right distance (for the glass cannot tighten or slacken like our lens), you will see the image reflected upside-down on the paper.   This is the way the lens acts.   There is a small yellow spot a little below the middle of the back of the eye ; here the sight is more acute, and so, though we can see lots of things at one time, we can only look at one thing at a time. There is a blind spot where the nerve enters the eye (which shows that the nerve of sight itself is blind) so that some part of every image is lost, like a black dot punched in it.   But we are so used to it that we cannot see it.

*Q.* Describe your favourite scene in *Waverley*.

I. (aged 12½) :—

"*A Highland Stag Hunt.*—The Highland Cheifs (*sic*) were in various postures : some reclining lazily on their plaids, others stalking up and down conversing with one another, and a few were already seated in position for the sport.   MacIvor was talking with another Cheif (*sic*) as to what the sport would be ; but as they talked in Gaelic, Edward had no part in the conversation, but sat looking at the scene before him.   They were seated on a low hill at the head of a broad valley which narrowed into a small opening or cleft in the hills at the extreme end. It was hemmed in on all sides by hills of various heights. It was through this opening that the beaters were to drive the deer. Already Waverly (*sic*) could hear the distant shouts of the men calling to each other coming nearer and nearer. Soon he could distinguish the antlers of the deer moving towards the opening like a forest of trees stiped (*sic*) of their leaves. The sportsmen prepared themselves to give them a warm reception, and all were ready as the deer entered the valley.

"They looked very ferocious, as they advanced towards where Edward and the cheifs (*sic*) were standing and seemed as if they were determined to fight ; the roes and weaker ones in the centre, and the bulls standing as if on defence. As soon as they came within range, some of the cheifs (*sic*) fired, and two or three deer came down. Waverly (*sic*) also had the good fortune (and also the skill) to bring down a couple and gain the aplause (*sic*) of the other sportsmen. But the herd was now charging furiously up the valley towards them. The order was given to lie down, as it was impossible to stem the coming wave of deer ; but as it was given in Gaelic it conveyed no meaning to Edward's mind, and he remained standing.

"The heard (*sic*) was now not fifty yards from him ; and in another minute he would have been trampled to death ; but MacIvor at his own risk, jumped up and literaly (*sic*) dragged him to the ground just as the deer reached them. Edward had a sensation as if he was out in a severe hail storm, but this did not last long.

"When they had passed, and Edward attempted to rise, he found that besides a number of bruises he had also severely sprained his ancle (*sic*), and was unable to walk, or even stand. A shelter was soon made for him out of a plaid in which he was laid ; and then MacIvor called the Highland doctor or herbalist, to attend him. The doctor approached Edward with every sign of humiliation, but before attending to his ancle (*sic*), he insisted upon walking slowly round him several times, in the direction in which the sun goes, muttering at the same time a spell over him as he went, and though Waverly (*sic*) was in great pain he had to submit to his foolery. Waverly (*sic*) saw to his great astonishment that MacIvor believed or seemed to believe in the old man's cantations (*sic*). At last, when he had finished his spells, which he seemed to think more necessary than the dressing, he drew from his pocket a little packet of herbs, some of which he applied to the sprained ancle (*sic*) and after it had been bound up, Edward felt much relieved. He rewarded the doctor with some money, the value of which seemed to exceed his wildest imaginations, for he heaped so many blessings upon the head of Waverly (*sic*) that MacIvor said, ' A hundred thousand curses on you,' whereupon he stopped."

Class IV.—Girls are usually in Class IV. for two or three years, from fourteen or fifteen to seventeen, after which they are ready to specialise and usually do well. The programme for Class IV. is especially interesting ; it adds Geology and Astronomy to the sciences studied, more advanced Algebra to the Mathematics, and sets the history of Modern Europe instead of French history. The literature, to illustrate the history, includes the reading of a good many books, and the German and French books when possible illustrate the history studied. All the books (about forty) are of a different calibre from those used in the lower classes ; they are books for intelligent students.

I think the reader will observe that due growth has taken place in the minds of the girls, both as regards judgment and power of appreciation. Not, I think, in intelligence,—

> " Love has no nonage, nor the mind."

But as our concern is with boys and girls under twelve, it will be enough to show by two or three papers that this sort of education by books results in intelligence.

*Q.* For what purpose were priests instituted ? (Book studied, Dr Abbot's *Bible Lessons*.)

A. (aged 15½) :—

"The system of the Jewish priesthood was almost entirely symbolical. God ordained it, we believe, to lead the primitive mind of his chosen people onwards and upwards, to the true belief and earthly comprehension of that great sacrifice, by the grace of which we are all now honoured to become 'kings and priests unto God.' In the earliest times of the patriarchs, there was in every holy and honourable Jewish family some voluntary priest to offer up the burnt offerings and yearly sacrifices. We have an example of this in Job the patriarch, who, we read, ministered to his family in the capacity of priest of their offerings. In the wilderness, however, God commanded through Moses the foundation of a separate and holy priesthood to minister in His

Tabernacle and offer His appointed sacrifices. The tribe of Levi and the family of Aaron were set apart for this purpose, and in the building of the tabernacle, and the annointing (*sic*) of Aaron and his four sons, the cornerstone was laid to that great building which became a fit dwelling for the presence of God and the heart of Israel, until Christ came to change and lighten the world ; and the symbol and the shadow became the truth."

*Q*. "His power was to assert itself in deeds, not words." Write a short sketch of the character of Cromwell, discussing the above statement. (Book studied, Green's *Shorter History of the English People.*)

B. (aged 15) :—

"Cromwell was no orator. It has been said that if all his speeches were taken and made into a book, it would seem simply a pack of nonsense. In Parliament though, the earnestness with which he spoke attracted attention. His deeds proved his innate power, which could not express itself in words. He may be called the inarticulate man. In his mind, everything was clear, and his various actions proved his purposes and determinations, but in speaking, he simply brought out a hurried volume of words, in the mazes of which one entirely lost the point meant to be implied. Cromwell also was more of an administrator than a statesman, unspeculative and conservative. He was subject to fits of hypocondria (*sic*), which naturally had some effect on his character. He considered himself a servant of God, and acted accordingly. Undoubtedly he was under the conviction that he was carrying out the Lord's will in all he did. He was not in calm moods a bloody man, but when his anger was kindled he would spare no one. At times he would be filled with remorse for the part he had taken in the martyrdom of the king ; then, again he would say it was the just punishment of heaven on Charles. In giving orders his words were curt and to the point, but in making speeches he adopted the phraseology of the Bible, which added to their ambiguity. One would think he was ambitious, for at one time he asked Whitelock : ' What if a man should take upon himself to be king ? ' evidently having in view the regal power, and yet according to his own assertion he would rather have returned to his occupation as a farmer, than have undertaken the government of Britain. But in this, as in other acts, he recognised the call of God, (as he thought) and obeyed it."

*Q*. What do you know of the Girondins ? (Book studied, Lord's *Modern Europe.*)

C. (aged 17) :—

"The Girondins were the perhaps most tolerant and reasonable of the revolutionary parties. They were a body of men who found the government of France under the king more than they could stand, and who were the first to welcome any changes, but were shocked and horrified at the dreadful riots and massacres which followed the fall of the throne. Such a party, representing justice and reform, could not be popular with the more violent Jacobins and like clubs. The day came when these latter were in power, and all the Girondins were thrown into prison.

"They were all taken from prison before the Court of Justice for trial, and placed before the judge, where they sat quite silently ; they were one by one condemned to execution, receiving the sentence of death with perfect calmness. Only their leader was seen to fall down ; one of his companions leant over him and said : ' What, are *you* afraid ? ' ' Non,' was the answer, ' Je mours,' he had stabbed himself with his dagger.

"As the Girondins marched back to their cells, condemned to die the next morning, they all sang the ' Marseillaise,' as they had arranged, to tell their fellow-prisoners what the sentence had been. When they reached the prison a splendid supper was placed for them, and they all sat down with great cheerfulness to eat it, none of them showing the least signs of breaking down. Towards morning priests were sent to them, and very early in the day they all marched to the foot of the guillotine, singing as they went. They kept on singing a solemn chant when the executions commenced, which became fainter and fainter as one by one they were beheaded, until all were gone."

*Q.* Distinguish between *arrogant* and *presumptuous, interference* and *interposition, genuine* and *authentic, hate* and *detest, loathe* and *abhor, education* and *instruction, apprehend* and *comprehend*, using each word in a sentence. (Book studied, Trench's *Study of Words*.)

E. (aged 15) :—

"A man who is ' arrogant ' is a man who has right to what he wants, but who is harsh and exacting in taking it. A ' presumptuous ' man is a man who expects more than is due and takes it. ' Judge Jeffries was an *arrogant* old man.' ' Charles II. was a *presumptuous* king, he thought he could have absolute power.'

" ' Interference,' is not minding your own business, and meddling with other people's when we are not wanted. ' Interposition ' is more the ' doing good by interfering ' as protecting a little boy from a bully. ' But for the *interference* of James all would have gone well.' 'Thanks to the *interposition* of Mary a quarrel was averted.'

"'Genuine' means real, true, what it seems to be as—'a real *genuine* ruby.' 'Authentic,' in speaking of a book, means really written by the author to which it is ascribed. 'Dickens' *Oliver Twist* is certainly *authentic.*'

"You would 'hate' a man who killed your father. 'Charles II. hated Cromwell.' You would 'detest' a man who had not done you any personal injury, but who (*sic*) you knew to be a murderer. 'Yeo *detested* the Spaniards.'

"You would 'loathe' a poisonous snake or a hypocrite. 'David Copperfield *loathed* Uriah Heep.' You would abhor a man inferior to you in intellect or principles, as a great king would 'abhor' a cringing coward, leave him behind, go on without him, refuse to listen to him. 'Napoleon *abhorred* the traitor.'

"'Education' is the lessons you receive as a matter of course, as French, writing, grammar. 'Instruction' is this, but more also, it includes moral teaching, the teaching of honesty, and the teaching of gentleness. 'Henry had a good *education.*' 'No well-*instructed* Britain (*sic*) is a coward.'

"'Apprehend' is to see, or hear, and notice. 'Comprehend' is to understand, without seeing or hearing perhaps. 'Phillip *apprehended* that danger was near, but he did not *comprehend* it.'"

*Q.* Give shortly Carlyle's estimate of Burns, showing what he did for Scotland, and what was the cause of his personal failure in life. (Book studied, Carlyle's *Essay on Burns.*)

*F.* (aged 17):—

"Carlyle looked upon Burns as one of the nicest of men and greatest of poets ; rather a weak man, perhaps, but covering all his faults with his genius and kindness of heart, clever and persevering, and basely neglected and shunned by his contemporaries. It is quite extraordinary to read the world-famous poems of this poet, and to remember that he was a ploughman, and surrounded only by the most uneducated peasants and fellow-labourers, though, of course, the life of a ploughman in the hills of Scotland is far more likely to encourage poetry and reflection than the life of many a London dentist or hair-dresser far higher in rank ; but it is easy to believe in fact, that Burns would have found inspirations for his genius in a flat sandy waste or a grocer's shop, and, as Carlyle says, a man or woman is not a genius unless they are extraordinary, not really inspired if such a person could have been imagined before. Robert Burns has provided Scotland for centuries at least, with plenty of national poetry, his poems are such as can be enjoyed, like flowers and trees and all things really beautiful, by old and young, stupid and clever, fishermen and prime ministers—surely that is a work of which any man would be proud !

"Burns (*sic*) chief fault, if fault it can be called, and the cause of his failure in life, seems to have been a sort of bitterness against people more fortunate than himself without the art of hiding it. This, real or affected, seems very common in poets, and such an inspired man, a man with a mind greater than kings, must have felt very deeply, almost without knowing it, the 'unrefinedness' of the people he loved best, and his own distance from the admirers who clustered round him later in life.

"All his life, it seems, he was in a place by himself, now spending his time with his own family, acting a part all day, trying to make his relations feel him an equal, pretending to take a great interest in what he did not care for—the pigs, and cows, and porridge, seeing his own dearest friends looking at him with awe, and feeling him something above them, thinking of his 'great' friends, and feeling embarrassed when he came, and more at ease without his presence.

"Now, on the other hand, associating with people, high in rank and education, enjoying their friendship and praise, but feeling, be they ever so kind and familiar, that he was not their equal by birth, and that they could not treat him quite as such, however hard they might try, turning familiarity in his mind into slights, and kindness into condescension. This to a proud man must have been misery, and Burns must have been very lonely in a crowd of companions, thronged with admirers, but without a friend.

"Nobody understood Burns ; he shared his opinions with no one he knew. When, at the beginning of the French Revolution he expressed his delight and approval, the people who admired him were shocked, refused to speak to him, and regarded him either as mad or terribly wicked. His poems were not admired as much as they deserved to be, he had hardly any money, was never likely to get on in the world, was shunned and disgraced, and began, as a last resource,[1] to drink too much. Ill-health was one of his misfortunes, and this intemperance killed him.

"Thus died at the age of thirty-seven, poor, friendless, despised, the man who has given pleasure to thousands, and an undying collection of poems and songs to his country."

*Q.* Give some account, as far as you can in the *style* of Carlyle, of the Procession of May 4th. (Book studied, Carlyle's *French Revolution.*)

[1] The writers have been in two minds about the spelling of words marked ([1]).

G. (aged $14\frac{1}{2}$) :—

"See the doors of Notre Dame open wide, the Procession issuing[1] forth, a sea of human faces that are to reform France. First come the nobles in their gayly (*sic*) tinted robes, next the clergy, and then the commons, the Tiers Etats in their slouched hats firm and resolute, and lastly the king, and the Œuil-de-bœuf, these are greeted by a tremendous storm of vivats. Vive le roi ! Vive la nation ! Let us suppose we can take up some coigne (*sic*) of vantage from which we can watch the procession, but with eyes different from other eyes, namely with prophetic eyes. See a man coming, striding at the head of the Tiers Etats, tall and with thick lips and black hair, whose father and brother walk among the nobles. Close beside walks Doctor Guillotin,[1] learned Doctor Guillotin,[1] who said, 'My friends (*mes amis*), I have a machine that will whisk off your heads in a second, and cause you no pain,' now doomed for two years to see and hear nothing but guillotin, and for more than two centuries after yonder a desolate ghost on this (*sic*) of the Styx. Mark, too, a small mean man, a sea-green man with sea-green eyes, Robespierre by name, a small underhand secretary walking beside one Dantun (*sic*) tall and massive, cruelty and vengeance on their faces. We may not linger longer, but one other we must note, one tall and active with a cunning air, namely, Camille Desmouellins (*sic*), one day to rise to fame and the next to be forgotten.

"Many more walk in that procession one day to become famous, Bailli, future president of a New Republick (*sic*), and Marat, with Broglie the War-God and others.

"The Tiers Etats with Mayor Bailli march to the rooms where they are to sit, but the doors are shut : there is sound of hammering within.

"Mayor Bailli knocks, and wants to know why they are shut out ? It is the king's orders. He wants his papers. He may come in and get them, and with this they must be content.

"They swarm to Versailles, the king steps out on the balconny (*sic*) and speaks. He says the room is being prepared for his own august presence ; a platform is being erected, he says he is sorry to inconvience (*sic*) them ; but he is afraid they must wait, and with that he retires. Meanwhile patriotism consults as to what had best be done. Shall they meet on the palace steps ? or even in the streets ? At length they adjourn to the tennis court, and there patriotism swears one by one to be faithful to the New National Assembly, as they now name themselves This is known as the Oath of the Tennis Court."

[1] The writers have been in two minds about the spelling of words marked ([1]).

I have placed before the reader examples of a portion of some thirty pupils' work to illustrate their education by books. It is not necessary to speak of their education by Things: that is thorough and systematic; but may I point out that what has been cited is average work. I do not know if the reader considers that I have proved my point, that is, that 'studies' — schoolroom studies — 'are for delight, for ornament, and for ability.'

---

# APPENDIX III

## What a Child should Know at Twelve

In order to induce the heads of schools (private schools, preparatory schools, girls' schools, and 'Lower' schools) to consider seriously whether it is not possible to introduce some such method of *Education by Books*, let me put forward a few considerations:—

1. The cost of the books per pupil for the six years—from six to twelve—does not average more than £1 a year. A scheme of work for elementary schools might be arranged at a much less annual cost for books.

2. Two and a half, for Class I., to three and a half hours a day, for Class III., is ample time for this book education.

3. Much writing is unnecessary, because the pupils have the matter in their books and know where to find it.

4. Classes II. and III. are able to occupy themselves in study with pleasure and profit.

5. Teachers are relieved of the exhausting drudgery of many corrections.

6. The pupils have the afternoons for handicrafts, nature-work, walks, games, etc.

7. The evenings are free, whether at school or at home, for reading aloud, choral singing, hobbies, etc.

8. The pupils get many intelligent interests, beget hobbies, and have leisure for them.

9. There is no distressing cramming for the term's examination. The pupils know their work, and find it easy to answer questions set to find out what they know, rather than what they do not know.

10. Children of any age, however taught hitherto, take up this sort of work with avidity.

11. Boys and girls taught in this way take up ordinary school work, preparation for examinations, etc., with intelligence, zeal, and success.

The six years' work—from six to twelve—which I suggest, should and does result in the power of the pupils—

(a) To grasp the sense of a passage of some length at a single reading : and to narrate the substance of what they have read or heard.

(b) To spell, and express themselves in writing with ease and fair correctness.

(c) To give an orderly and detailed account of any subject they have studied.

(d) To describe in writing what they have seen, or heard from the newspapers.

(e) They should have a familiar acquaintance with the common objects of the country, with power to reproduce some of these in brushwork.

(f) Should have skill in various handicrafts, as cardboard Sloyd, basket-making, clay-modelling, etc.

(g) In Arithmetic, they should have some knowledge of vulgar and decimal fractions, percentage, household accounts, etc.

(h) Should have a knowledge of Elementary Algebra, and should have done practical exercises in Geometry.

(i) Of Elementary Latin Grammar ; should read fables and easy tales, and, say, one or two books of ' Cæsar.'

(j) They should have some power of understanding spoken French, and be able to speak a little ; and to read an easy French book without a dictionary.

(k) In German, much the same as in French, but less progress.

(l) In History, they will have gone through a rather detailed study of English, French, and Classical (Plutarch) History.

(m) In Geography they will have studied in detail the map of the world, and have been at one time able to fill in the landscape, industries, etc., from their studies, of each division of the map.

(n) They will have learned the elements of Physical Geography, Botany, Human Physiology, and Natural History, and will have read interesting books on some of these subjects.

(o) They should have some knowledge of English Grammar.

(p) They should have a considerable knowledge of Scripture History and the Bible text.

(*q*) They should have learned a good deal of Scripture and of Poetry, and should have read some Literature.

(*r*) They should have learned to sing on the Tonic Sol-fa method, and should know a number of English, French, and German Songs.

(*s*) They should have learned Swedish Drill and various drills and calisthenic exercises.

(*t*) In Drawing they should be able to represent common objects of the house and field with brush or charcoal; should be able to give rudimentary expression to ideas; and should be acquainted with the works of some artists through reproductions.

(*u*) In Music their knowledge of theory and their ear-training should keep pace with their powers of execution.

This is the degree of progress an average pupil of twelve should have made under a teacher of knowledge and ability. Progress in the *disciplinary* subjects, languages and mathematics, for example, must depend entirely on the knowledge and ability of the teacher.

---

# APPENDIX IV

## EXAMINATION OF A CHILD OF TWELVE, IN THE 'PARENTS' REVIEW' SCHOOL, ON THE WORK OF A TERM

POSSIBLY a complete set of answers to an examination paper may be of use as showing the all-round standing of a scholar educated on the principles I have advanced. This paper is not exceptional,[1] and some weakness will be noticed in what I have called the disciplinary subjects.

*Programme of the Term's Work on which the Examination Questions are set.*

*Bible Lessons.*

*The Bible for the Young,* by the Rev. J. Paterson Smyth (Sampson, Low, 2s.), *Genesis,* Lessons xvii.-xxiv.,

---

[1] A large number of complete sets of examination answers may be seen at the office, and further information can be had from the Secretary, P.N.E.U., 26 Victoria Street, London, S.W.

*S. Matthew*, Lessons xvi.-xxiv., and the Lesson on Christmas. Teacher to prepare lesson beforehand, and to use the Bible passages in teaching. Answers to Catechism with explanations from the beginning to the *Lord's Prayer* (optional).

*Recitations.*

Learn two passages of 20 verses each from chapters in Bible Lessons. Learn *The Death of the Duke of Wellington*; *The Charge of the Light Brigade*; *You ask me Why*.

*French.*[1]

The Gouin *Series*; *A Study of French*, by Eugène & Duriaux (Edition 1898, Macmillan & Co., 3s. 6d.), pages 184, 194, 196, 198; teacher study preface. *Première Année Grammaire*, par P. Larousse, Rules 61, 63, 64, 66, 70, 74, Exercises 55, 58, 61, 63. Read the first half of *Le Général Dourakine*, par Mdme. de Ségur (Hachette, 1s.), parse two pages. Learn a poem from *Recueil de Poésies*, par Mdme. de Witt (Hachette, 2s.).

*German.*[1]

Eight sections of the Gouin *Series*; (or, translate into English and retranslate into German pages 1-8 from Niebuhr's *Heroengeschichten* (Clarendon Press, 1s. 6d.). *Book of Ballads on German History* (University Press, 2s.); two ballads to be learnt by heart. *First German Book*, by A. L. Becker (Hachette, 1s.), Lessons xxvii.-xxxv. Use the words, from the lists of useful words, in sentences. Beginners read from Part II., reading lessons, §§ 16-23. Practise letters on pages xiii.-xvi.

[1] Where the Gouin *Series* are not taken, French, German, and Italian should be taught *orally*, teacher repeating aloud, pupil reciting after her.

*Italian.*

Ex-Students of House of Education, six of the Gouin *Series.* Twelve grammar rules exemplified in *Series.* Teachers use Perini's *Italian Conversation Grammar* (Hachette, 4s.).

*Latin.*

*Young Beginners' Third Latin Book* (Murray, 2s.), pages 9–15. Revise back work by means of exercises. *Young Beginners' Second Latin Book* (Murray, 2s.), pages 60–71.

BEGINNERS.—Hall's *Child's First Latin Book* (Murray, 2s.), 15–32 ; or, better, *A First Latin Book*, by E. H. Scott and F. Jones (Blackie, 1s. 6d.), pages 1–32.

*English History.*

*A History of England*, by H. O. Arnold-Forster (Cassell, 5s.), pages 719–758 (1820–1897). Read Scott's *Lady of the Lake*, and, if possible, Henry Kingsley's *Valentin* (Ward, Lock & Co.).

*French History.*

Creighton's *First History of France* (Longmans, 3s. 6d.), pages 279–293, to be contemporary with English history.

*Roman History.*

Plutarch's *Romulus*, teacher omitting unsuitable parts (Cassell's National Library, 3d.).

*Geography.*

Geikie's *Physical Geography* (Macmillan, 1s.), pages 108–131, §§ 224–270. *London Geographical Readers* (Stanford), Book V. (2s. 6d.), pages 238–267, with special reference to recent events ; map questions to be answered from map and then from memory, and then in filling up blank map from memory before each lesson. Know something about foreign places coming into notice in the current newspapers. Ten minutes' exercise on the map of the world every week. *The School Atlas*, edited by H. O. Arnold-Forster (37 Bedford Street, London, 1s. 6d. or 3s.). Read also Arnold-Forster's *History of England*, chapters lxxv. and lxxvi.

*English Grammar.*

Morris's *English Grammar* (Macmillan, 1s.), pages 100–108, 98–99 (inclusive). Parse and analyse, using pages 109–125. Work from Morris's *English Grammar Exercises* (Macmillan, 1s.).

*Singing.*

Three French songs, *La Lyre des Écoles* (Curwen & Son). Three German songs, Erk's *Deutscher Liederschatz* (Peters, Leipsic). Three English songs, Novello's *School Songs*, Vol. XX. (8d.). Stainer's *Primer of Tonic Sol-fa* (Curwen & Son).

*Writing.*

Choose and transcribe ten poems or passages from Wordsworth. German Copybook, No. I. (Nutt, 4d.). *A New Handwriting for Teachers*, by M. M. Bridges (Mrs Bridges, Yattenden, Newbury, 2s. 9d.); work to page 6, following instructions.

*Drill.*

Grecian Exercises and Marching Drills from *Musical Drills for the Standards* (Philip & Son, 2s. 6d.). Ex-Students, House of Education Drills.

*Dictation.*

*Growth and Greatness of our World-wide Empire*, pages 32–77 (four or five pages a week) to be prepared, a passage dictated, or, occasionally, written from memory.

*Drawing.*

> *Pour Dessiner Simplement*, par V. Jacquot et P. Ravoux
> (3s. 6d.), cahier ii., iii., for occasional use. Twelve
> wild fruits on their branches, with background, in
> brushwork ; illustrations in brush-drawing from *The
> Lady of the Lake.* Study and be able to describe
> the pictures in *The Holy Gospels*, Part II. (S.P.C.K.,
> 1s. 8d.) (optional) ;
>
> or, Join the Portfolio of Paintings (see *The Children's
> Quarterly*) ;
>
> or, Follow the *Fésole Club Papers.*

*Natural History.*

> Keep a Nature Note-Book. Geikie's *Geology* (Mac-
> millan, 1s.), pages 125–144 (mountains), with questions.
> Refer to in holidays, and study in term, *Lowly Water
> Animals*, Lessons 1–21, inclusive.

*Botany.*

> Oliver's *Elementary Botany* (Macmillan, 4s. 6d.), chapter
> vii., pages 63–87. *Glimpses into Plant Life*, Brightwen
> (Fisher Unwin, 2s.), chapters v. and ix. Record the
> finding of and describe twenty wild fruits (see Oliver).
> Specimens must be used in all botanical work. Ob-
> serve all you can about the structure of various fruits
> (not edible), and about the dispersion of seeds. *Plant
> Life in Field and Garden*, by A. Buckley, pages 40–80.

*Physiology.*

> Schofield's *Physiology for Schools* (Cassell, 1s. 9d.), pages
> 43–64.

*Arithmetic.*

> Mair's *Mental Arithmetic* (Sonnenschein, 9d.). Long-
> man's *Junior School Arithmetic* (1s.), chapters xxi.
> and xxii., *Practice* and *Bills*. Miscellaneous examples
> from pages 192 and 193.
>
> BEGINNERS, chapters xvii., xviii., and xix., §§ 74–81.

*Euclid.*

*A First Step in Euclid*, by J. G. Bradshaw (Macmillan, 1s. 6d.), pages 63-81.

BEGINNERS.—*Inductive Geometry*, by H. A. Nesbitt, M.A. (Sonnenschein, 1s. 6d.), chapters iv., v., vi.

Members who have Hamblin Smith's Euclid may continue to use it. The books now set are more modern and lead to more intelligent work.

*Reading.*

Geography, English history, French history, and tales should afford exercise in careful reading. Poetry should be read daily.

*Composition.*

Read on Thursdays and write from memory on Tuesdays (a) a passage from *Ecce Homo, Ecce Rex*, Part II., chapters ii. and iii., by Mrs R. Charles (S.P.C.K., 3s. 6d.); (b) Arnold-Forster's *History of England*, chapter lxxvii.

*Work.*

Attend to garden. *Bent Iron Work*, by F. J. Erskine (Upcott Gill, 1s.). Make six models. *Self-Teaching Needlework Manual*, edited by S. Loch (Longmans, 1s.), pages 25-54. Make a baby's crochet petticoat with body part. Make a linen book cover, with design drawn and worked by yourself.

*N.B.*—For illustrations for History, Geography, etc., see the catalogue of the Perry Pictures (Art for Schools Association, 46 Great Ormond Street, London, 3d.).

Children who are beginners or who have just been moved up from Class II., or who find the work difficult, may omit three subjects.

*Questions on Preceding Programme.*

*Bible Lessons.*

I. 1. Show how God trained Joseph for his work. What lessons may we learn from Joseph (*a*) in prison, (*b*) in a palace?

2. (*a*) "I am Joseph," (*b*) "Bless the lads," (*c*) "Until Shiloh come." Give the context in each case, and describe the occasions on which these words were used.

II. 1. Tell the parable (*a*) of the Fig-tree, (*b*) of the Two Sons. What lessons may we learn from each?

2. (*a*) "Shall I crucify your King?" (*b*) "He . . . . wept bitterly," (*c*) "He is risen." Give the context (in the Bible words if possible) of each of these quotations.

*Recitations.*

Father to choose two passages, of ten verses each, from the Bible Lessons, and a poem.

*French.*

1. Write down in French the names of things that a huntsman uses for the chase.

2. Recite the poem learned.

3. Write in French a short *résumé* of the chapters read in *Le Général Dourakine*.

4. Make sentences to show the use of *cette, ces, ce, cet, leurs, ses, tel, chaque, même, nul.*

*German.*

1. Say three sections of a Gouin *Series,* and translate into English and retranslate into German page 6, lines 14–24, from *Heroengeschichten.*

2. Translate into German :—(*a*) Which of these flowers is the finest? (*b*) I have been once in Berlin and three times in Paris.

3. Make sentences with other adjectives, using the German for 6, 15, 17, 9, 4, 18.

*Italian.*

Recite two *Series*, and give two rules exemplified.

*Latin.*

1. Translate into English and retranslate into Latin Fable V., page 61, and parse each word in the first sentence.

2. Translate into Latin :—(*a*) We dream whole nights ; (*b*) I will teach you music ; (*c*) The Roman people elected Numa king ; (*d*) The Gauls dwell on this side the Rhine ; (*e*) The master sees that many boys play. What rule is illustrated in each sentence?

BEGINNERS—

1. Translate into Latin :—(*a*) Where is the shield? (*b*) A narrow shield is bad; (*c*) The hen is small.

2. Make sentences using the words *hic, porta, augusta, duo, capita, dux, quattuor, qui, sumus, murum, vident.*

*English History.*

1. What do you know of the Anti-Corn Law League, and what have you heard or read about a similar agitation in this country to-day?

2. What reasons induced each of the five countries engaged to enter on the Crimean War? Give some account of the war.

3. "It was felt by all . . . . that the government of India . . . . could not be left in the hands of the East India Company." Why? Give some account of the events which led up to this.

*French History.*

1. Write shortly the history of the war with Prussia.

2. Describe the new constitution of 1875.

*Roman History.*

1. "Sardians to be sold." Who said this? Tell the story.
2. How did Romulus unite the Romans and the Sabines?

*Geography.*

1. Describe, with a map, a visit to the West Indies. What recent event in these islands do you know of?
2. Write a short description of (*a*) Mexico, and (*b*) a Brazilian forest.
3. What is meant by saying, "The gates of the pathways of the sea are in the hands of the British race"? Illustrate with a map.
4. How are coral reefs formed? Give a diagram of one. Describe, with diagrams, a volcano.

*English Grammar.*

1. Analyse, parsing the words in italics:—

    *One by* one the flowers *close*,
    Lily and dewy rose
    *Shutting their* tender petals *from* the moon.
    The grasshoppers are *still*; but not *so soon*
    Are still the *noisy* crows.

2. Make sentences, showing the different ways in which the following may be used:—*dying, making, t tell, but.*
3. Give some words with each of the following prefixes:—*epi, hypo, cata, di, syn.*

*Singing.*[1]

Father to choose an English, a French, and a German song, and three Tonic Sol-fa exercises.

*Writing.*

Write ten lines of Tennyson's from memory.

[1] Subjects thus indicated to be marked by the parents according to *Regulations.*

*Drill.*[1]

Drill, before parents.

*Dictation.*

> *Growth and Greatness of our World-Wide Empire*, page 43, "Not . . . . home."

*Reading.*[1]

Father to choose unseen poem.

*Drawing.*

(*a*) Paint a carrot, an onion, and a potato grouped together, (*b*) an illustration in brushdrawing of a scene from *The Lady of the Lake*, (*c*) a glove, a trowel, and a rake in charcoal.

*Natural History.*

1. Describe (*a*) six sea (or pond) creatures you found this last summer, (*b*) the *Foraminiferæ*. How do sponges grow? Give a diagram.

2. What do we know of the origin of mountains? Describe any formation you have examined this term—in cliff, river basin, or quarry.

*Botany.*

1. Give rough diagrams showing the manner of growth, with leaf buds, of the twigs of the following trees: —oak, ash, horse-chestnut, beech, sycamore.

2. Compare the fruits of the raspberry, strawberry, and blackberry, with diagrams.

3. What are some of the ways in which plants store food? Give examples.

*Physiology.*

1. What are the functions of the skin? Give a diagram of the skin cells.

[1] See Note, p. 310.

*Arithmetic.*

1. Find, by Practice, the cost of 1 ton 2 cwt. 2 qrs. and 20 lbs. at £1, 13s. 10d. per cwt.
2. Find the cost of 4959 balls at 11¾d. each.
3. How much property tax should I pay on £5238, 10s. 0d. at 8½d. in the £?
4. Make out an invoice for 5 pairs of stockings at 1s. 3½d. per pair; 40 needles at 13½d. per score; 96 buttons at 6½d. a dozen; 6¾ yds. silk at 5s. 1d. a yard.

BEGINNERS—

1. Find the G.C.M. of 12321 and 54345, and the L.C.M. of 12, 18, 30, 48, and 60.
2. Reduce: $\dfrac{11385}{16335}, \dfrac{96679}{119427}$.
3. Find the sum of the quotient and remainder when 36789241 is divided by 365.

*Euclid.*

1. To bisect a given finite straight line.
2. To draw a straight line perpendicular to a given straight line of unlimited length from a given point without it.
3. Divide a given angle into four equal parts.

or, 1. Prove that the two angles of a triangle are always less than two right angles.
2. Draw a kite consisting of an equilateral triangle and an isosceles triangle twice the height.
3. The latitude of London is 51½° N. How far is it from the South Pole?

*Composition.*

Write some account of—

(a) Recent events with regard to Korea and Macedonia;
or, (b) (a) Scott, or (b) Burns, and his work.

(c) Write twenty lines on " An Autumn Evening " in the metre of *The Lady of the Lake.*

*Work.*[1]

Outside friend to examine.

## P. Q., aged 12. CLASS III.

*List of Subjects taken.*

| | |
|---|---|
| Bible Lessons. | Writing. |
| French. | Dictation. |
| German. | Natural History. |
| Latin. | Botany. |
| English History. | Physiology. |
| French do. | Arithmetic. |
| Roman do. | Euclid. |
| Geography. | Composition. |
| English Grammar. | |

All the answers, in the subjects taken, have been attempted; a few of these are omitted here for reasons of space. The maps and diagrams are rather well done, but cannot be reproduced. The writer's spelling, pointing, etc. have been carefully preserved.

### *Bible Lessons.*

I. 2. (a) "I am Joseph, your brother, whom ye sold into Egypt." These words were spoken by Joseph when he was revealing himself to his brethren. His brothers had come down into Egypt a second time to buy food, and had persuaded their father Jacob to let them take Benjamin down with them, because Joseph had told them that they must. So Jacob reluctantly let Benjamin go. And now they had bought their corn, and actually been asked to dine with Joseph, and were on their homeward way, when some

[1] See Note, p. 310.

officers of Joseph's household come galloping after them, and angrily ask whether the way to return hospitality is to steal Joseph's cup, his favourite silver cup. Then when the cup is found in Benjamin's sack, Judah, who has promised to be surety for him, begs that he may be a slave to Joseph instead of Benjamin, as he promised Jacob his father to bring him back safe. Then they are all taken in to see Joseph, and he cannot stand it any longer, and bursts into tears, and says "I am Joseph; doth my father yet live?" ' And his brethren could not answer him for they were troubled at his presence. And Joseph said unto his brethren "Come near to me, I pray you." And they came near. And he said "I am Joseph your brother whom ye sold into Egypt."' So then of course they believed him, and everything was made all right.

(*c*) Jacob lay on his death-bed with his sons around him, listening to his words which seemed to come straight from God. But instead of Reuben, as the first-born getting the best or most wonderful blessing, he seems to have been put below Judah, who is told that he shall be "a fruitful bough," and shall remain "Until Shiloh come." This seems to be a wonderful inspiration in Jacob that someone should come from the descendants of his son Judah who "should save His people from their sins." Of course, *now*, we see in it a prophecy of the coming of our Lord Jesus Christ, though then it was most likely an undefined thought.

II. 1. (*b*) "There was a man that had two sons; and he went to one, and said "Son, go to work to-day in my vineyard." And he answered and said "I will not"; but afterwards he repented, and went. And the father went to the other son and said "Son, go to work to-day in my vineyard." And he answered and said "I go, sir," but went not at all to the work. Whether of the twain did the will of their father?" They (the priests) say unto him "the first." "From this we see that the parable was aimed at the chief priests, scribes, and Pharisees, who had been trying to trap him in his talk. The man was God, the two sons, those that did his will, and those that did not, and the vineyard was the world. The scribes and Pharisees were those who made a lot of show, and were very particular about all the little outside observances of religion, but did not really work, like the son in the parable who said "I go, sir" and did not go at all. Thus they were made to condemn themselves by saying that the first did the will of God, and not the second.

2. (a) Pilate had been cross-examining Jesus, and had "found no fault in him." When he asked the people what he should do with him, they cried out, saying "Crucify him, crucify him." But Pilate answered and said "Shall I crucify your King?" But they cried out yet the more, saying "Crucify him, crucify him." Then Pilate took a bason, and washed his hands before the multitude saying "I have nothing to do with this righteous man; see ye to it." And the people cried out, saying "His blood be upon us and upon our children." Then Jesus was led away.

## *French.*

1. Un fusil, une bandoulière, des cartouches, une gibecière, un permis de chasse, et une meute de chiens.

2 (*recited*).

> " Savez-vous son nom ? "—La nature
> Réunit en vain ces cent voix.
> L'étoile à l'étoile murmure
> " Quel Dieu nous imposa nos lois ? "
> La vague à la vague demande
> "Quel est celui qui nous gourmande ? "
> La foudre dit à l'aquilon
> "Sais-tu comment ton Dieu se nomme ? "
> Et les astres, la terre, et l'homme
> Ne peuvent achever son nom.

Que tes temples, Seigneur, sont étroits pour mon âme !
Tombez, murs impuissants, tombez !
Laissez-moi voir ce ciel que vous me derobez !
Architecte divin, tes domes sont de flammes !
Que tes temples, Seigneur, sont étroits pour mon âme !
Tombez, murs impuissants, tombez !

4. Cette aiguille est très aigue. Ces animaux sont de trois
familles. Ce mouvement est très facile ; un pas avec ce
pied, et il faut qu'un bras faire ce tour. Cet homme était
bien fait de sa personne. Ils étaient très sages ; ils mettaient
leurs livres dans l'armoire, pas sur la table. Ses filles
étaient très méchantes. Il fit un tel pas, que je pensais
qu'il tomberait. Chaque personne fit une grande revérence,
quand le roi venait.

### German.

1. (*Heroengeschichten* has not been taken, so "Kaiser
Karl am Luther's Grab" is recited, from page 24 of *A
Book of German Ballads*, Cambridge University Press.)

In Wittenberg, der starken Luther's Feste
Ist Kaiser Karl, der Sieger, eingedrungen ;
Wohl ist den Stamm, zu fällen, ihm gelungen
Doch neue Wurzeln schlagen rings die Aeste.
In Luther's Feste hausen fremde Geste
Doch Luthers Geist der bleibet unbezwungen
Da, wo des Geistes Schwert er hat geschwungen
Da ruhen billig auch des Leibes Reste.
Am Grabe steht der Kaiser, tief gerühret.
"Auf denn, und räche dich an dem Gebeinen
Den Flammen gib sie preis, wie sich's gebühret."
So hört man aus der Diener Tross den Einen.
Der Kaiser spricht "Den Krieg hab' ich geführet
Mit Lebenden ; um Todte lasst uns weinen."

2. Welche dieses Blümen ist den schönsten ? Ich war
einmal in Berlin und dreimal in Paris.

3. Ich habe sechs gute Bücher. Er ist fünfzehnmal gestraft worden. Wir sind siebzehn edle Knaben. Neun Knaben sind in dieses Spiel. Vier Bücher wären gross-Achtzehn-hundert schlecht Knaben.

*Arithmetic.*

1. 2 qrs. = ½ of 1 cwt.    ½ of

|  | £ | s. | d. |  | tons. | cwts. | qrs. | lbs. |
|---|---|---|---|---|---|---|---|---|
|  | 1 | 13 | 10 | value of | 0 | 1 | 0 | 0 |
|  |  |  | 1 1 |  |  |  |  |  |
|  | 18 | 12 | 2 | ,, | 0 | 11 | 0 | 0 |
|  |  |  | 2 |  |  |  |  |  |
|  | 37 | 4 | 4 | ,, | 1 | 2 | 0 | 0 |
| 8 lbs. = 1/7 of 2 qrs.   1/7 of | 0 | 16 | 11 | ,, | 0 | 0 | 2 | 0 |
| 8 lbs. =   ,,       ,, | 0 | 2 | 5 | ,, | 0 | 0 | 0 | 8 |
| 4 lbs. = ½ of 8 lbs.    ½ of | 0 | 2 | 5 | ,, | 0 | 0 | 0 | 8 |
|  | 0 | 1 | 2½ | ,, | 0 | 0 | 0 | 4 |
| Answer :— £38 | | 5 | 3½ | ,, | 1 | 2 | 2 | 20 |

2. 4959 balls @ 11¾d. each = 4959 balls @ 1s. ea. − 4959 farthings.

4959 farthings = 1239¾d. = 103s. 3¾d. = £5   3   3¾.

4959 shillings = £247   19   0.

$$\begin{array}{rrr} £ & s. & d. \\ 247 & 19 & 0 \\ - \quad 5 & 3 & 3¾ \\ \hline = 242 & 15 & 8¼ \end{array}$$ the cost of 4959 balls @ 11¾d. ea.

3. 8d. = 1/30 of £1.    1/30 of

|  | £ | s. | d. |
|---|---|---|---|
|  | 5238 | 10 | 0 |
| ½ = 1/16 of 8d.    1/16 of | 171 | 5 | 7¾ (nearest ¼d.) |
|  |  | 10 14 | 1¼ |
| Ans. :— £181 | | 19 | 9 |

LONDON,
*May 21st* 1906.

4.　　JONES, BROWN & Co.
Bought of D. H. EVANS & Co.,
Oxford St., W.

|  | £ | s. | d. |
|---|---|---|---|
| 5 pairs stockings @ 1s. 3½d. per pair . | 0 | 6 | 5½ |
| 40 needles @ 1s. 1½d. per score . . | 0 | 2 | 3 |
| 96 buttons @ 6½d. per doz. . . . | 0 | 4 | 4 |
| 6¾ yds. of silk @ 5s. 1d. per yd. . . | 1 | 13 | 3¾ |
| Total . . | £2 | 6 | 4¼ |

## *Composition.*

(*a*) Sir Walter Scott was a well-known writer in the
early part of the 19th century. His novels are read by
almost everyone; and though, perhaps, his poetry is not
quite so well-known, still, at most places one finds people
who have read or heard of the "Lady of the Lake" or
"Marmion." The first of his novels was "Waverly" (*sic*),
and so they are often called the "Waverley Novels." The
historical tales are very good, giving the reader a splendid
idea of life in the 12th or 13th centuries; "Ivanhoe,"
"Betrothed," "The Talisman" and "Kenilworth" (this
latter is about the 16th century, in Queen Elizabeth's
reign). "The Heart of Midlothian" is also very interesting,
and "Peveril of the Peak" tells about the fighting between
the Cavaliers and Roundheads in the time of Charles I.,
and Oliver Cromwell. The "Lady of the Lake" is about
the longest poem Sir Walter Scott ever wrote; it is very
beautiful, and many pieces in it are most interesting.
"Marmion" tell (*sic*) of a battle, and how a Lord Marmion
was killed there.

## *Latin.*

1. Alexander once upon a time asked a pirate whom he
had taken by what right he infested the seas? At that,

"The same," said he "by which you do (infest) the world.
But because I do it with a small ship, I am called a robber;
you, because you do it with a great fleet and army are called
a general." Alexander dismissed the man unhurt. Did he
do rightly?

Alexander olim comprehensum pirātam interrogavit, quo
jure maria infestaret? Ille "Eodem," inquit "quo tu orbem
terrarum. Sed quia ego parvo navigio facio, latro vocor;
tu, quia magna classe et exercitu, imperator." Alexander
inviolatum hominem dimisit. Num juste fecit?

> *Alexander*, noun proper, masc., sing., nominative case.
> *Olim*, adv. modifies verb "interrogavit."
> *Comprehensum*, participle used as adj., modifying
> "piratam."
> *Piratam*, n. common, masc., sing., objective case, governed
> by "interrogavit."
> *Interrogavit*, verb, transitive, 3rd pers. sing. Past Tense.
> *Quo*, relative pron., ablative case, antecedent "jure."
> *Jure*, n. common, neuter, sing., ablative case.
> *Maria*, n. common, neuter singular, objective case to
> "infestaret."
> *Infestaret*, intransitive verb, 3rd person singular Present
> Subjunctive Tense.

2. (*a*) Somnimus totus noctes. (*b*) Docebo te musicam.
(*c*) Romani Numam regem elexerunt. (*d*) Galli cis Rhenum
habitaverunt. (*e*) Magister videt multos pueros ludere.

> (*a*) illustrates that the object is in the accusative in Latin.
> (*b*)  „  „ the double object is in the accusative.
> (*c*)  „  „ the double object is in the accusative.
> (*d*) illustrates that all prepositions as "cis" take the acc.
> case.
> (*e*)  „  „ with a sentence like "The master sees
> that many boys play" you prefix with "Master sees" leave
> out "that" turn "many boys" into accusative, and turn
> "play" into the infinitive.

*English History.*

1. The Anti-Corn-law League was formed early in the reign of Queen Victoria. Its name shews that its object was to get the Corn Laws repealed or rather to have the taxes on corn taken off, as they were causing distress in the country. Eloquent men went about the country, speaking to the people, and telling them how much better it would be not to have them, until they were convinced that it was so, and made rather a fuss over it, so that one Prime Minister, Lord Russell, resigned, and Lord Melbourne came in, and took off some of the taxes. People now seem to be thinking that it would be a good thing to put on some of these corn taxes again, and the country is again rather agitated about it, and Mr Chamberlain, Mr Balfour, and many other gentlemen go about making speeches either for, or against it, according to their different views, just as people did then, when Sir Robert Peel did take them off.

2. England joined in the Crimean war, because they were afraid that if Russia got hold of Turkey, they might prevent the English going to and from India, and that thus the command we had over India might be loosened and India might once more become an independent country. France entered because Napoleon III. wished to show that he had some power, and was not afraid of war. Sardinia entered in because the King of Sardinia's minister, Count Cavour, wished to shew that Sardinia had some power, and he also thought that by making powerful friends such as England and France, his master, King Victor Emmanuel might one day become king of Italy. Russia wanted to put down Turkey, and Turkey of course went against Russia. It was a very sad war, mostly because of the bad management. The charges of the Light and Heavy Brigades, the battles of Inkerman, Balaclava, and last of all, the long siege of Sebastopol, which might have been prevented, had we charged the day before at the Russians, so as to prevent

them get (*sic*) hold of, and fortifying the chief tower, all tells (*sic*) of suffering from the intense cold, and death of the soldiers by scores.

### French History.

1. The Prussians advanced into France, meeting with resistance everywhere, but still they went steadily on, till at last they reached Paris, which they besieged for a long time, so that the people were obliged to eats cats dogs, horses and even rats and mice, so that they had to give in. Then there was a treaty made, and Prussia made France give up the two provinces of Alsace and Lorraine, and also made them pay an immense sum of money, which was only paid off about 10 years ago. France cannot rest with Alsace and Lorraine in the hands of the Emperor of Germany, and keeps up large armies in the hopes of winning them back some day. Germany also keeps up large armies, in readiness for resistance, and these two countries make Europe like an armed camp.

2. In 1875 people thought that they would like a king again, but after all a new Constitution was made and passed by the Assembly. This government still lasts. There is a Chamber of Deputies, something like our English Parliament. There is also another Chamber called the Senate, like the House of Lords in England. A President is chosen, and after seven years, gives up his post, and someone else is chosen. Ministers carry on the government so as to please the National Assembly. New people must be chosen if they are not liked by the Assembly.

### Roman History.

1. The Veintes, one of the Tuscan nations, declared that Romulus ill-treated the Fidenæ, who belonged to them. This was absurd, as the Veintes had not tried to help the Fidenæ when Romulus took them, and therefore they had

a war, in which Romulus was victorious and on the anniversary for some years after the Romans celebrated their victory by having a herald who called through the town "Sardians to be sold" (the Veientes were called Sardians, because the Tuscans were descended from the Sardians) and several young boys in ropes represent (*sic*) the Veientes.

2. The Romans imagined that there were not enough women for them all to have a wife, so they attacked the Sabines and carried off several women. These were treated with courtesy and respect, but the Sabine men did not like it, and declared war. But while they were fighting the women ran in between, and beseeching, on one side their fathers, and on the other their husbands, to stop, they did stop, and made up the quarrel.

## *Geography.*

1. The West Indies are a set of islands enclosing the Gulf of Mexico and the Caribbean Sea. They form two large groups, the Greater Antilles and the Lesser Antilles. The largest island in the Greater Antilles is Cuba, which belongs to Spain. It is a lovely place, with palm-trees cocoa and coffee plantations, and sugar and tobacco are largely exported. The capital is Havana, where the best cigars in the world are made; and it also has a good harbour from whence is exported the sugar, coffee, cocoa and rum made in the island. The island next in size in our first group is Hayti, or St Domingo. Part of this island belongs to Spain, and the other part once belonged to France, but is now a little negro kingdom. Its capital is Port au Prince. Jamaica is the next island; this belongs to Britain, and is the chief place from which we get our sugar, cocoa and coffee. The capital is Kingston, a nice bright town, with churches and a Town Hall, and a governor's residence. Porto Rico is a Spanish island of not very much importance.

Its capital is Don Juan, named after the Spanish sailor who first discovered it. Then comes a little group of islands called the Virgin Islands, of which the most important is Santa Cruz, which belongs to Denmark. They are between the Greater and Lesser Antilles. The largest island in the Lesser Antilles is Guadeloupe, which belongs to France. It is a pleasant island, with a lovely bay on which stands the capital, Grande Terre. Dominica (British), Barbuda, Anguilla, Antigua, and St John's (also British) are some of the most important British islands. The other French islands are Martinique, and Marie Galante. St Vincent, and Barbadoes (capital Bridgetown) are also important British islands. After passing the Lesser Antilles, we come to the beautiful island of Trinidad, with its capital, Port of Spain, on the lovely blue Gulf of Paria, which separates it from Venezuela.

[*Map.*]

4. Coral reefs are formed by tiny animals called "coral polypes" which, almost as soon as they are born, begin to separate part of their food to build up their houses. They often stick to one another and build in companies. We will imagine 10 of these little animals have started building at the bottom of the sea. Two or three of them may have stuck to each other, and soon a little pillar appears of red, white or (very rarely) black coral. New little polypes are born, and they build on and round their parents' work. So it get (*sic*) broader and higher, and more and more little ones come to enlarge the work, till one day a point of red or white coral appears above the surface of the sea. More and more of it appears, till there is quite a little island. Then the wind often blows seeds, and the birds bring them, and the sea washes up sand into the nooks and crannies, till palm-trees grow, and other plants, and birds build their nests there, and maybe have tiny birds themselves, and so there is an island fit for man's use, and it all started

from two or three little coral polypes about $\frac{1}{8}$ of an inch long.

Volcanos are apparently openings in the earth's crust down to (*sic*) very centre of the earth, where many people believe that there is a great fire, the remains of the days when the earth was a seething mass of fiery vapour. When eruptions break forth, flames and smoke reaching to an enormous height come out of the crater, and fiery lava runs in streams down the sides of the mountain, burning everything in its course, and stones and ashes are thrown out ever so far. In the sad eruption of Mont Pélée in 1901 ashes fell on steamers more than 100 miles away, and the noise of the eruption was heard for miles, and the city of St Pierre (the capital of Martinique) was entirely buried in ashes and lava ; only a few church walls or street corners are remaining now to show that St Pierre was once a flourishing city. This shews that volcanoes are evidently openings through which the inside of the earth seems sometimes to "let off steam."

[*Diagrams.*]

*English Grammar.*

| Subject. | Attrib. of Subj. | Predicate. | Dir. Obj. | Averbial Adjunts. |
|---|---|---|---|---|
| 1. Flowers | The, lily and dewy rose | close | | one by one |
| Shutting | | | their tender petals | from the moon |
| Grasshoppers | The | are still | | |
| Crows | The noisy | are still | | but not so soon |

*One*, numeral adj., modifying "flowers." *By*, preposition, joining "one" to "one." *Close*, transitive verb, 3rd pers. plur., Present Tense. *Shutting*, present participle, governing "petals." *Their*, pers. poss. pron., 3rd pers. plur. *From*, preposition, governing "moon." *Still*, adj., modifying "grasshoppers." *So*, adv., modifying "soon." *Soon*, adv. of time, modifying "are still." *Noisy*, adj., qualifying "crows."

2. Go quickly; he is dying. A dying man lies there. Making a dress is difficult. I am making a box. To tell tales is mean. I was to tell you that. But for him, I should not be here. Had you but a knife, we should be safe. Yes, but he is stupid, so I cannot make him hear.

3. Episode, epi-tome. Hypo-crite, hypo-thesis. Cataract, cat-astrophe, cat-hedral. Di-phong (*sic*). Syn-tax, syllable, sym-pathy.

*Natural History.*

1. (*b*) Foraminiferæ are in the Rhizopoda, or root-footed family. They have a little opening in their shells, through which they send out hairs to catch very tiny water creatures and suck them in. Their shells are made from something they swallow. They are all sorts of shapes, and can be seen without a microscope, though their lovely coloured shells and tiny bodies can be seen better with it. They increase by self-division, but they generally grow from tiny buds on the bodies of their mothers.

[*Diagrams.*]

Sponges are cousins to the Foraminiferæ, but are slightly higher up in the Rhizopoda family. They are full of tiny holes, with sometimes a bigger opening. These little holes lead into little passages, which are continually leading into one another, and the bigger holes lead into bigger passages. They are made of some sort of fine tissue, which the sponge animal makes out of some part of its food after it has been digested. In these passages tiny, soft slimy creatures live, which are able to throw out hairs from themselves, with which they sweep water in and out of their house. Their children are born from buds, by self-division, and also from eggs. Some sponges increase in all these different ways at once, so that one sponge often becomes the father of several families. Little hard things called Sponge spicules grow round the eggs to protect them. They are made from the lime the Sponge finds in the water, and often have beautiful shapes.

[*Diagram.*]

2. It has been found, that though people speak of the "everlasting hills" yet they cannot have been always where they are now. Mountains that are formed of rocks of any kind, either sedimentary, or organic, must have been laid down at the sea-bottom and something must have pushed them up; either earthquakes, or volcanic eruptions. If, for example, several different kinds of Sedimentary Rocks were laid down flat at the sea-bottom (fig. 1) till they were

[*Diagram.*]

hundreds, perhaps thousands of feet thick, and they also happened to lie on some weak part of the earth's crust, where earthquakes sometimes happen, they may be squeezed or pushed up above the surface of the sea, and round them may be deposited more rocks, and they may be pushed up, and so land may be formed, with some parts higher than the rest, and these parts are called mountains.

*Botany.*

[*Diagrams.*]

2. The raspberry, strawberry and blackberry are all of the Rose family. But there are little differences between them; they are not all alike. The raspberry is like the strawberry in that its seedboxes grow on a mound. But when you look at the ripe fruit, you will see that the seedboxes themselves grow bigger, softer and rounder, and also they shrink away from the white mound, so that a ripe raspberry comes off without a little stalk, etc., hanging on. The Blackberry is just the same as the raspberry, only it is black, and the round juicy seed boxes do not shrink away from the mound quite so much. The construction of the strawberry fruit, however, is slightly different. Here it is the little mound that swells,

and becomes a bright red, and the seed boxes (generally wrongly called "seeds") remain hard and small, looking something like little yellow apple pips.

*Euclid* (first set).

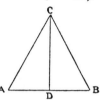

1. Let AB be a given st. line.
It is reqd. to bisect AB.
On AB describe an equilateral △ ACB.      I. 1.
Bisect ∠ ACB by the st. line CD,      I. 9.
meeting AB in D; then shall AB be bisected in D.
In △s ACD, DCB the side AC = side CB, and CD is common and ∠ ACD = ∠ DCB.      Hyp.
∴ △s are equal in all respects      I. 4.
and side AD = side DB.      Q.E.F.

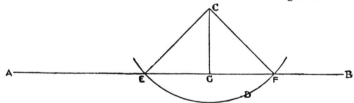

2. Let AB be the given st. line of unlimited length and C the given pt. outside it.
It is reqd. to draw from C a st. line perpendicular to AB.
Take a pt. D on the other side of AB; and with centre C and radius CD describe a ⊙ FE cutting AB in E and F.
Bisect EF in G, and join CE, CG, CF.      I. 10.
Then shall CG be at right angles to AB.
In the △s ECG, CGF, EC = CF, and EG = GF (Const.) and CG is common.

∴ △s are equal in all respects.                    I. 7.
and ∠ EGC = ∠ CGF.
and ∴ CG is perpendicular to AB.                   Def.
                                                   Q.E.F.

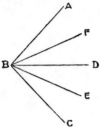

3. Let ABC be the given ∠.
It is reqd. to divide ∠ ABC into four equal parts.
Bisect ∠ ABC by the st. line BD.                   I. 9.
Bisect the ∠ ABD by the st. line BF.               I. 9.
Bisect the ∠ DBC by the st. line BE.               I. 9.
Then ∠ ABF, FBD, DBE, EBC are all equal.  Ax. 7.
∴ ∠ ABD has been divided into four equal parts.
                                                   Q.E.F.

-------

# APPENDIX V

## How Oral Lessons are Used

THOUGH the part of the teacher should, in a general way,
be that of the University tutor who "reads with" his men,
the oral lesson, also, is indispensable, whether in introducing
a course of reading or as bringing certain readings to a point.
Oral lessons, too, give the teacher opportunities for the
reading of passages from various books bearing on the
subject in hand, a sure way to increase the desire of the
children for extended knowledge. Some subjects, again,

as Languages, Mathematics, Science, depend very largely upon oral teaching and demonstrations. It might be well if the lecture, with its accompaniments of note-taking and reports, were cut out of the ordinary curriculum, and the oral lesson made a channel for free intellectual sympathy between teacher and taught, and a means of widening the intellectual horizon of children. I add a few sets of notes of criticism lessons which have been given by various students of the House of Education to the children in the Practising School. These lessons are always expansions or illustrations or summaries of some part of the scholars' current book-work.

## ORAL LESSONS

### SOME NOTES OF BIBLE LESSONS

*Subject: Old Testament History.*

Group: History.   Class Ib.   Average age: 8.
Time: 20 minutes.

#### OBJECTS.

1. To so interest the children in the story of Jacob's death, that they may not forget it.
2. To give a new idea of God as drawn from the story of Jacob's deathbed:—God's abiding presence.
3. To give them an admiration for Joseph as one who honoured his father and mother.

#### LESSON.

*Step* 1.—Recapitulate the former lesson, and follow Jacob's journeying with his family from Canaan to Egypt, on a map.

*Step* 2.—Show the children how Joseph was the first of Jacob's sons to visit him when he was ill. Draw their attention to the particular trait of Joseph's character shown in this story.

*Step* 3.—Describe in a few words the surroundings in which the events of the story take place.

*Step* 4.—Read carefully to the children suitable parts of Genesis xlviii., reminding them to pay special attention to the words of the Bible, as they so beautifully express the scene.

*Step* 5.—While the children are narrating in the words of the Bible, help them by questions to bring out the important points of the story.

*Step* 6.—Help the children to realise how Joseph's love of his father affected his life, and how they should let their parents feel their love.

*Step* 7.—Let the children see that this family realised God's abiding presence, and show them how any family can realise it in the same way, if it will.

*Subject: New Testament Story—The Stilling of the Tempest.*

Group: History.      Class II.      Average age of children: 10.
                    Time: 30 minutes.

#### OBJECTS.

1. To try to give to the children some new spiritual thought and a practical idea of faith.
2. To bring the story of the Stilling of the Tempest vividly before their minds.
3. To interest them in the geography of the Holy Land.
4. By means of careful, graphic reading, to help them to feel the wonderful directness, beauty, and simplicity of the Bible language: in short, to make them feel the poetry of the Bible.

#### APPARATUS REQUIRED.

1. Bibles for the children.
2. A map of Palestine.
3. Thomson's *Land and Book.*
4. Pictures of (1) A storm on a lake; (2) Galilean boats; (3) The Sea of Galilee.

## LESSON.

*Step* 1.—Ask the children to find St Matt. viii. 23 in their Bibles. Tell the story of the Stilling of the Tempest, keeping as closely as possible to the language of the Bible.

(*a*) Let the children find the Sea of Galilee on the map, gathering *from the map* some notion of the surrounding country; compare with Lake Windermere.

Show course of journey by reference to verses 5 and 28 in the same chapter.

Show pictures of ships used in the East and on the Sea of Galilee.

(*b*) Describe the tempest graphically, drawing from the children the reason for the sudden storms (caused by the ravines, down which the winds rush); get from them their idea of a storm at sea or on a lake.

Show photograph of a storm on Lake Windermere.

(*c*) Try to make the children understand the twofold nature of our Lord :—

　　(1) His Humanity—He was evidently weary.

　　(2) His Divinity—His power over Nature

(*d*) Try to make the children feel the simplicity of the Bible language and the forceful way in which it brings pictures before the mind.

There arose a great tempest—His disciples came to Him —He arose—there was a great calm—Refer to Psalm cvii.

(*e*) "The men marvelled." Try to show the children that faith is just another word for understanding, knowing : how, the better we know a person, the more we can trust him. Draw from the children how faith is shown in nearly every verse of this story, but, as far as the disciples were concerned, it did not go far enough.

Draw from them that it is not necessary to be with a person *always* in order to have faith in him. Ask them how people show faith in all the actions of their daily lives.

*Step* 2.—Read the story from the Bible ; read it carefully, so that the children will appreciate its literary value and see the vivid pictures which it brings before the mind.

*Step* 3.—Let the children narrate the story, keeping as much as possible to the Bible words.

## *Subject : Reading.*

Group : English.  Class III.  Average age : 13.
Time : 25 minutes.

### OBJECTS.

1. To try to improve the children's reading by drilling them in clear and pure pronunciation.
2. To show them that by their reading a series of mental pictures should be presented to the listener.

### LESSON.

*Step* 1.—Breathing exercises.  Ask reason for the same.

*Step* 2.—Practise the children in consonant and vowel sounds, by giving them sentences in which difficulties in pronunciation occur.

*m*, *en*, *n*.  A stricken maiden musing on a mountain was given from heaven man in mortal form.

*final t.*  A just knight felt a weight on his heart, and yet a sweet quiet rest was present when he went to meet the light.

*p*, *b*.  A path of prickly brambles, bordered by pure pale poppies, breathed peace between the broken beams.

*d.*  Touched by the hand that appeared from the cloud under which nodded the dead leaves.  (Notice final *d* is sometimes pronounced like *t*.)

*Step* 3.—Read the passage chosen, from Tennyson's 'Sir Galahad,' asking the girls afterwards to describe the mental pictures they have drawn.

"A maiden knight—to me is given
Such hope, I know not fear ;
I yearn to breathe the airs of heaven
That often meet me here.
I muse on joy that will not cease,
Pure spaces clothed in living beams,
Pure lilies of eternal peace,
Whose odours haunt my dreams ;
And, stricken by an angel's hand,
This mortal armour that I wear,
This weight and size, this heart and eyes
Are touched, are turned to finest air.
The clouds are broken in the sky,
And through the mountain walls
A rolling organ-harmony
Swells up, and shakes and falls.
Then move the trees, the copses nod,
Wings flutter, voices hover clear :
' O just and faithful knight of God !
Ride on ! the prize is near.'
So pass I hostel, hall and grange ;
By bridge and ford, by park and pale,
All-armed I ride, whate'er betide,
Until I find the Holy Grail."

*Step* 4.—Show the girls a reproduction of Watts' conception of the idea, asking them in what points the poet's and artist's ideas coincide.

*Step* 5.—Let the children read the passage.

*Subject : Narration* (Plutarch's life of Alexander—part of the term's work).

Group : Language. Class II. Average age : 10.
Time : 20 minutes.

### OBJECTS.

1. To improve the children's power of narration by impressing on them Plutarch's style (as translated by North), and making them narrate as much as possible in his words.

2 To rouse in the children admiration of Alexander's love of simplicity, generosity, and kindness to his men.

### LESSON.

*Step* 1.—Connect with the last lesson by questioning the children. They read last time stories illustrating Alexander's graciousness and tact.

*Step* 2.—Tell the children shortly the substance of what I am going to read to them, letting them find any places mentioned, in their maps.

*Step* 3.—Read to the children about three pages, dealing with the luxury of the Macedonians, Alexander's march to Bactria, and the death of Darius. Read this slowly and distinctly, and *into* the children as much as possible.

*Step* 4.—Ask the children in turn to narrate, each narrating a part of what was read.

---

*Subject: From Plutarch's ' Greek Lives.'*

### ALEXANDER THE GREAT.

*(An Introductory Lesson.)*

Group : History.    Class II.    Age : 8 and 9.
Time : 30 minutes.

### OBJECTS.

1. To establish relations with the past.
2. To introduce the boys to a fresh hero.
3. To stir them to admiration of the wisdom, valour, and self-reliance of Alexander the Great.
4. To increase the boys' power of narration.

### LESSON.

*Step* 1.—Begin by connecting Alexander the Great with the time of Demosthenes, of whom the boys have been learning recently.

*Step* 2.—Draw from them some account of the times in which Alexander lived and of Philip of Macedon.

*Step* 3.—Arouse the boys' interest in Alexander by the story of the taming of Bucephalus, which must be read, discussed, and then narrated by the boys.

*Step* 4.—Ask the boys what they mean by a hero. The old meaning was demi-god, the Anglo-Saxon meaning, a man. Both really meant a man who was brave and true in every circumstance.

Ask them, 'What are the qualities which go to make a hero?' Draw from them how far we can trace these qualities in Alexander. We notice :—

*Wisdom.*—'What a horse are they losing for want of skill to manage him!'

*Perseverance.*—He kept repeating the same expression

*Self-reliance.*—'And I certainly could.' This was justified by the fact that he *could*.

*Observation.*—He noticed that the horse was afraid of its shadow.

*Courage.*—Seeing his opportunity, he leaped upon its back.

*Prudence.*—He went very gently till he could feel that he had perfect control of the animal.

These are not all the qualities one looks for in a hero, but as the boys will be learning all about Alexander next term, they will be able to find out for themselves what others he had. They will see, for instance, how he never imagined a defeat, but went on, conquering as he went (*Hope*).

The name of Alexander has never been forgotten, because he was so great a hero. Owing to him, the language and civilisation of Greece were carried over a great part of Asia.

Show map illustrating his campaigns. He tried to improve the land wherever he went. Owing to his travels, people began to know more than they had ever known of geography and natural history.

Himself a hero, Alexander reverenced heroes, keeping 'the casket copy' of *The Iliad*.

*Step* 5.—Recapitulate Step 4 by means of questions.

### *Subject: The Godwins.*

Group : History.    Class III.    Average age : 13.
Time : 30 minutes.

#### OBJECTS.

1. To recapitulate and enlarge on the period of history taken during the term (A.D. 871–1066).
2. To increase the children's interest in it by giving as much as possible in detail the history of one of the prominent families of the period.
3. To exemplify patriotism in the character of the Godwins.

#### LESSON.

*Step* 1.—Recapitulate what the girls know of the period briefly by questioning about the Saxon and the Danish kings and leading men, making a chart on the blackboard.

*Step* 2.—Begin with the reign of Canute. Enlarge upon their present knowledge as to his character and deeds whilst king of England, and let a girl read the account of his pilgrimage to Rome (Freeman's *Old English History*, p. 242).

*Step* 3.—Give an account of the early history of Earl Godwin—his apparently humble origin—his love of his country—his character. He rose by his valour and wisdom —was loved by both Saxons and Danes—was merciful to his foes. He married Gytha, sister of Earl Ulf—was made Earl by King Canute—and had Wessex given him as his kingdom. Put on the blackboard the names of the three divisions of England, with their earls or rulers.

*Step* 4.—The period between the death of Canute and

Edward the Confessor's coming to the throne. Under Harold and Hartha-Canute Danish rule became distasteful, and the English longed for an English king. Let a girl read the account of Hartha-Canute's treatment of the people of Worcester and the conduct of Godwin and the other earls on that occasion (p. 250).

*Step* 5.—Edward the Confessor. Ask them questions about his early life and education, and how these affected his character and ideas. Was he a suitable man for a king? Not powerful enough to rule—Godwin became his supporter and adviser. Marriage of Godwin's daughter, Edith, to the king. Godwin's eloquence and influence over the people. (Read from Knight's *History*, p. 162.)

*Step* 6.—Godwin's patriotism is put to the test. Speak of his banishment with his wife and six sons, and its consequences. William of Normandy invited over to England—great dissatisfaction at misrule in England— the people resent the Normans being put in office. Let G—— read (p. 262).

*Step* 7.—Godwin's return—he and his family again received into favour—his death—the crime which had been laid to his charge—Harold a worthy successor. Show from a map the divisions of England at the death of the 'Confessor.' Read from Lord Lytton's *Harold* (p. 63).

*Subject : History.*

Group : History.      Class IV.      Age : 16.      Time : 40 minutes.

## THE STATE OF FRANCE IN 1789.

### OBJECTS.

1. To establish relations with the past.
2. To show how closely literature and history are linked together and how the one influences the other.

3. To try to give yet a clearer idea of the social and political state of France before the Revolution than the girls have now, and to draw from them the causes which brought about the Revolution in *France* and at *this time* (1789).

### LESSON.

*Step* 1.—Begin by noticing the state of France generally. *Feudalism* was still in existence, without its usefulness and with most of its abuses, and it led to the great *division of Classes*—the Privileged and the Unprivileged. In both Army and Church it was impossible for the unprivileged to rise by merit; all offices were filled by the privileged classes. These were exempt from many taxes. Draw from G—— and S—— the chief taxes—*Taille*, levied on property, and the *Gabelle*, which forced everyone to buy a certain amount of salt from the Government at an enormous rate.

*Step* 2.—Speak of the state of France in the country, showing what was the relation of the peasant to his lord. The land he lived on generally belonged to him; in return for which he had to grind his corn at his lord's mill, etc., had to give his work free on certain days in the year, and help to make the roads in his lord's land (*corvée*). Tell them something of the Game Laws and the 'Intendants.'

*Step* 3.—Notice the state of France in the towns, showing how impossible it was for a poor man to set up in a trade, owing to the guilds and monopolies. The merchants, together with men who held certain offices under Government, formed a separate class, far removed from both the peasants and the nobles.

*Step* 4.—The state of the Church. For the most part the higher ecclesiastics were hated and despised. This was not the case with the 'curés,' for they were of the peasantry, and shared their troubles. But the higher ecclesiastics were generally younger sons of nobles, who drew the salaries of their offices and lived a gay life at Court. The Church also imposed heavy dues.

*Step* 5.—Show that these evils might have been remedied gradually (as in England) had there been a representative assembly regularly called, or any true justice. But as justice could be bought and sold, the poor man always lost his cause, and the pleadings of the peasants could in no way make themselves heard. They had risen just before this time, but unsuccessfully.

*Step* 6.—Draw from G—— and S—— the reason why the Revolution broke out in France rather than in any other Continental country. Because, though the evils in France were no worse than those borne by the German peasants, the French people had been awakened to the knowledge of their misery and of their right to liberty by many great writers. Such were Voltaire, Rousseau, Diderot, d'Alembert, and Montesquieu. Get from G—— and S—— all I can about these men and their influence on history.

*Step* 7.—Draw from G—— and S—— why the Revolution broke out just in 1789. Rousseau had written his works since about 1730, and Voltaire since 1718.

The French had borne their lot under Louis XIV.'s strong government. Louis XV. was very different. The evils of a despotic government were clearly shown by him. He it was who said, 'Après nous le déluge!' Then came Louis XVI., conscientious and full of good intentions. Get from the girls something of Louis' character. But the great opportunity of the people came in the calling of the States General, in order to raise money.

*Step* 8.—A short recapitulation of the principal points.

*Subject : Literature.*

Group : English.　Class IV.　Age : 16.　Time : 45 minutes.

## CHARLES LAMB.

### OBJECTS.

1. To give some main principles to guide the choice of reading.

2. To give a short sketch of the life of Charles Lamb.

3. To show how the writer's character is reflected in *The Essays of Elia.*

4. To emphasise the fact that very thoughtful reading is necessary in order to get full pleasure and benefit from a book.

### LESSON.

*Step* 1.—Decide with the pupils as to some principles which should guide us in the choice of books, such as the following :—

Never waste time on valueless books.

Have respect for the books themselves.

Try to cultivate taste by noticing the best passages in any book that is being read.

Time is too short to read much ; there is a necessity, therefore, for judicious selection.

The best literature can only be appreciated by those who have fitted themselves for it.

It is more important to read well than to read much.

The gain of reading some of the most beautiful literature while we are young is that we shall then have beautiful thoughts and images to carry with us through life.

To get at the full significance of a book it is necessary to dig for it.

Thus *The Essays of Elia* are not only pleasant reading, but they are the reflection of the writer's character.　All that Lamb was can be gathered from his works, and to rightly understand these one must know something of the grand though obscure life of Charles Lamb.

*Step* 2.—Try to draw from the girls, who are already familiar with some of the essays, what they tell us of Charles Lamb.

Charles Lamb was born 1775. His father was in the service of Mr Salt, whose portrait is found in *The Old Bencher of the Inner Temple.* 1782, Charles received a presentation from Mr Salt to Christ's Hospital (see *Essay*). The result of his education is summed up in *The Schoolmaster.* From fifteen to twenty he was a clerk in the South Sea House (*Essay*).

In 1795 he was transferred to the India House. He lived near Holborn with his parents and his sister Mary. Here took place the calamity occasioned by Mary's insanity.

Charles' heroic resolution. One learns something of the dream he renounced in *Dream Children.* His work at the India House was uninteresting, but such as left him leisure for intellectual pursuits. This distribution of occupation was a means of conserving his mental balance. His literary work was all done in the evening : 'Candle Light' in *Popular Fallacies.*

The girls will then read Talfourd's estimate of Lamb.

Letters to Robert Lloyd show Lamb's persistent cheerfulness. This cheerful tone is also noticeable in many of his essays : *Mrs Battle, All Fools' Day, My Relations* (portrait of John Lamb), *Mackery End* (portrait of Mary Lamb) *Poor Relations,* and *Captain Jackson.* C. Lamb died 1834.

*Step* 3.—Summarise by questions.

*Subject : English Grammar.*

Group : Language.    Class II.    Average age : 10.
Time : 20 minutes.

## OBJECTS.

1. To increase the children's power of reasoning and attention.
2. To increase their knowledge of English Grammar.
3. To introduce a new part of speech—preposition.

## LESSON.

*Step* 1.—Draw from the children the names of the two kinds of verbs and the difference between them, by putting up sentences on the board. Thus in the sentence 'Father slept,' 'slept,' as they know, is intransitive; therefore he could not 'slept' anything, as 'slept' cannot have an object.

*Step* 2.—Put on the board the sentence 'Mary went,' and ask the children to try and make it more complete by adding an object. 'Mary went school' would not be sense, but 'Mary went *to* school' would. Ask for other phrases saying where Mary went, as, *for* a walk, *into* the town, *with* mother, *on* her bicycle, *by* train, etc.

*Step* 3.—Tell the children that these little words, on, in, by, for, with, etc., belong to a class of words which are very much used with intransitive verbs; they have not much meaning when used alone, yet in a sentence they cannot stand without an object. You cannot say 'Mary went in,' without saying what she went in.

*Step* 4.—Introduce the word 'preposition,' giving its derivation. Because these little words always take objects after them, and because their place is before the object, they are called prepositions, 'pre' being the Latin word for 'before,' and 'position' another word for 'place.'

*Step* 5.—Write on the board the definition :—'A pre position always has an object after it.'

*Step* 6.—Let the children work through the following exercises :—

(1) Put three objects after each of the following prepositions :—in, on, over, by, with, and from.

(2) Put three prepositions and their objects after the following :—Mary plays, Mother sits, John runs.

(3) Supply three prepositions in each of the following sentences :—The book is —— the table. The chair is —— the door. I stood —— the window.

(4) Supply three subjects and verbs to each of the following prepositions and objects :— —— —— in the garden, —— —— on the floor, —— —— by the fire.

(5) Make three sentences about each of the following, each sentence to contain an intransitive verb, a preposition and its object :—The white pony, My little brother, That pretty flower.

*Subject : German Grammar.*

Group : Languages. Class III. Average age : 13.
Time : 30 minutes.

#### OBJECTS.

1. To show the pupil that although the German construction of sentences may seem very much complicated, yet with the help of a few simple rules it can be made much clearer.
2. To draw these rules from the pupil by means of examples.
3. To teach two or three of these elementary rules.
4. To strengthen the relationship with the foreign language.

#### LESSON.

*Step* 1.—Begin by finding out what the pupils know of compound sentences in English, *i.e.* that they consist of two or more clauses depending on each other, etc., and let them give one or two examples. Connect this lesson with a former one on the arrangement of words in German sentences by letting the pupils put one or two compound clauses on the board in German, and then giving the rule they illustrate.

*Rule.*—Dependent clauses take the verb at the end of the clause.

These sentences the pupils can probably give themselves.

*Step* 2.—Get the old rule that the past participle comes at the end of the sentence, with a few examples, one or two of which the pupils may write upon the board to compare with those illustrating the new rule.

Let the pupils put several sentences on the board illustrating the new rule.

*Rule.*—In dependent clauses the auxiliary follows the past participle.

*Sentences.*—' Ich kehre zurück, wenn sie angekommen ist.'
' Das Kind, welches verloren war, ist gefunden.'

Let the pupils translate these literally into English, and with the simple German clauses already on the board and the translation let them find the rule. Let them translate a few sentences into German to show that they thoroughly understand the rule.

*Step* 3.—Treat the next rule almost in the same way, but have each sentence put on the board twice in different order, and find the rule by comparing these.

*Rule.*—If the subordinate clause comes first the principal clause takes its verb at the beginning.

*Sentences.*—(1) ' Sie gab den Armen viel, weil sie gut war.'
(2) ' Wiel sie gut war, gab sie den Armen viel.'
(1) ' Er ging immer fort, obwohl er müde war.'
(2) ' Obwohl er müde war, ging er immer fort.'

*Step* 5.—Recapitulate.

*Subject   French Narration.*

Group : Languages.    Class III.    Average age : 13.
Time : 30 minutes.

## OBJECTS.

1. To give the children more facility in understanding
   French when they hear it spoken, and also in
   expressing themselves in it.
2. To teach them some new words and expressions.
3. To improve their pronunciation.
4. To strengthen the habit of attention.
5. To introduce a new branch of the study of French
   and thus increase their interest in it.
6. To have the following passage narrated by the children.

## LESSON.

*Passage chosen :* LE CORBEAU.

"Auguste étant de retour à Rome, après la bataille
d'Actium, un artisan lui présenta un corbeau auquel il
avait appris à dire ces mots : Je te salue, César vainqueur !
Auguste charmé, acheta cet oiseau pour six mille écus.   Un
perroquet fit à Auguste le même compliment et fut acheté
fort cher.   Une pie vint ensuite ; Auguste l'acheta encore.
Enfin un pauvre cordonnier voulut aussi apprendre à un
corbeau cette salutation ; il eut bien de la peine à y
parvenir, il se désespérait souvent et disait en enrageant :
Je perds mon temps et ma peine.   Enfin il y réussit.   Il
alla aussitôt attendre Auguste sur son passage, et lui présenta
le corbeau, qui répéta fort bien sa leçon : mais Auguste se
contenta de dire : J'ai assez de ces complimenteurs là dans
mon palais.   Alors le corbeau, se ressouvenant de ce qu'il
avait souvent entendu dire à son maître, répéta : J'ai perdu
mon temps et ma peine.   Auguste se mit à rire et acheta
cet oiseau plus cher que tous les autres."

*Step* 1.—Read the passage slowly and distinctly, stopping

frequently to make sure that the children understand. Write the new words and expressions on the board and give their meanings.

*Step* 2.—Let the children repeat the story in English.

*Step* 3.—Read the passage straight through.

*Step* 4.—Let the children read the passage, paying special attention to the pronunciation.

*Step* 5.—Have the passage narrated in French, helping the children when necessary with questions.

Speak as much French as possible throughout, but always make sure that the pupils understand.

### *Subject : Italian Gouin.*

Group : Language.    Class IV.    Average age : 16.
Time : 30 minutes.

#### OBJECTS.

1. To increase the girls' interest in foreign languages.
2. To enlarge their Italian vocabulary.
3. To give the girls more facility in understanding Italian when they hear it spoken, and also power to express themselves in it.

#### LESSON.

*Step* 1.—Tell the children in a few words what the series is about.

*Step* 2.—Explain the verbs in the infinitive, by doing the actions when possible.

*Step* 3.—Let the children say the verbs in the infinitive.

*Step* 4.—Let them write the verbs on the board.

*Step* 5.—Explain, by actions, when possible, the rest of the series.

*Step* 6.—Repeat each sentence several times slowly and carefully.

*Step* 7.—Let the children repeat the sentences.

*Step* 8.—Let them write the series on the board.

| *Verbs.* | *Italian.* |
|---|---|
| Volere esercitarse | Luigia *vuol esercitarsi* sul piano. |
| Aprire | *Apre* il piano. |
| Suonare | *Suona* una scala e degli arpeggi. |
| Studiare | Poi *studia* una Sonata di Beethoven. |
| Volere imparare | Che *vuol imparare* a mente. |

### *English.*

Louise *wishes to practise.*
She *opens* the piano.
She *plays* a scale and some arpeggi.
Then she *studies* a Sonata by Beethoven,
Which she *wants to learn* by heart.

### *Subject: Geography.*

Group : Science.　　Class III.　　Average Age : 13.
Time : 30 minutes.

## SCANDINAVIA—NORWAY IN PARTICULAR.

### OBJECTS.

1. To introduce the children to Scandinavia.
2. To foster interest in foreign countries.
3. To teach the children how to learn the map of a country by means of map questions.
4. To implant mental pictures of the characteristic scenery of Norway in the children's minds.
5. To show, by means of comparison, the great difference in the physical features of the two countries which are included in Scandinavia, although they form only one peninsula.

### LESSON.

*Step* 1.—Let the children learn the map of Scandinavia, Norway in particular, by means of the map questions previously written on the blackboard, writing down their answers.

*Step* 2.—Ask for a general description of Scandinavia.

*Step* 3.—Let the children fill in the blank map on the blackboard.

*Step* 4.—Require the children to give the answers to the questions, and, as they answer, give information, in order that they may become acquainted with each place as it is mentioned, and be able to picture it in their minds.

## MAP QUESTIONS.

### From the *Geographical Readers*, Book IV.

1. What waters bound the Scandinavian peninsula? To what land is it attached? What countries does it include?

#### NOTE.

Describe the government of Scandinavia briefly, showing that, although Sweden and Norway have a common sovereign, each country has an independent parliament, elected in very much the same way as our English Parliament.

2. Through how many degrees of latitude does this peninsula stretch? What other countries of the world lie partly in the same latitude?

3. Describe the coast of Norway. Compare it with that of Sweden. Name the four largest fiords or openings, beginning at the extreme north.

#### NOTE.

Give the idea of the extraordinary way in which the coast is cut up, and the immense number of islands which fringe it. Girls to notice how these islands form an effective break-water to the force of the Atlantic breakers, so that within their boundary the water is as calm and still as a lake.

Describe the rocky, almost perpendicular sides of the fiords, over which the rivers fall in roaring torrents. Mention the fact that many ships of the Spanish Armada were driven as far north as Stadtland, and wrecked around this dangerous headland.

The Sogne is the largest and most important fiord. It is like a long sea channel running into the country for a distance of 100 miles, with branches right and left, over which wonderful torrents fall. The sides are very steep, and the water is very deep at the entrance. At the Sulen Islands, at the mouth of the fiord, Harold Hardrada collected his force for his expedition against England.

4. Name a group of islands north of the Arctic Circle. The most northerly island. The cape on this island. The most northerly cape on the mainland. The most southerly cape.

### NOTE.

The Lofoden Islands are granite rocks, rising from the water in hundreds of peaks, with jagged and fantastic outlines. The cod fisheries of these islands are very important, and employ a great number of people.

Nordkin, which means 'north chin,' is the most northerly point on the mainland of Europe. Incessant storms rage round the island of Mageröe, so that it is extremely difficult for anyone to land there.

Lindesnaes means 'Lime nose.'

5. Name five towns on the west, and three on the south-east coast of Norway.

### NOTE.

Stavanger is the fourth largest city in Norway. Its chief trade is in herrings. It has a very ancient Cathedral.

At Bergen the houses are built on the slopes of the hills which run out into the deep sea. It was formerly the capital, and is now a great fish port.

Trondhjem is the oldest capital. The name means 'home of the throne,' and in the Cathedral the kings of Norway are crowned.

Hammerfest is the most northerly town in Europe. Tourists go there to see the midnight sun. Read Charles H. Wood's description of the midnight sun, from the *Geographical Reader.*

Christiania, the capital of Norway, is not a big town, but has a most beautiful situation. It is at the head of the Christiania Fiord, which is studded with countless grassy and wooded islands. Most of the houses are of wood, painted white, with green blinds. The fiord, which used to be very much frequented by the old Vikings, is blocked by ice for four months of the year.

6. The Scandinavian mountains nearly fill Norway—by what name is the range known in the north, south, and centre? Name three or four of the highest peaks.

### NOTE.

There is no continuous range in the Scandinavian mountains; the whole is a high table-land, which increases in height as we go south, with here and there groups of peaks which appear like huge rocks dotted over the surface. These plateaux are topped with moors or snowfields from which glaciers descend right down into the sea.

7. How does the position of the mountains affect the rivers? Compare the rivers of Norway with those of Sweden.

### NOTE.

Describe how, in Norway, the rivers rush in torrents over their rocky beds, while those in Sweden flow more gently down the gradual slope of the land. Give the threefold reason—great rainfall, small evaporation owing to the coldness of the climate, and small waste owing to the hardness of the rocks—for the great volume of water in the short, quick, Norwegian rivers.

8. Recapitulate with blank map, the girls adding descriptive notes as they answer the map questions.

### *Subject : Astronomy.*

Group : Science.    Class IV.    Age : 16.
Time : 30 minutes.

#### OBJECTS.

1. To interest the pupils in studying the heavens for themselves.
2. To show where the planets may be looked for and how they may be recognised.
3. To help the pupils to apply their theoretical knowledge of the planets to explain the movements they can observe with the naked eye.
4. To exercise the reasoning powers.

#### LESSON.

*Step* 1.—Get the pupils to describe the changes to be seen in the sky at night, and, excluding the apparent motion caused by the earth's rotation, find out whether they have noticed and contrasted the constellations of fixed stars and the planets (wanderers).

Let the pupils tell which of the planets are visible to the naked eye, and ask whether they have noticed when and where are to be seen, at the present date, Jupiter, Saturn, and Mars, which are in Capricornus, Sagittarius, and Leo, respectively.

*Step* 2.—Draw from the pupils, if possible, the marks by which planets can be distinguished from stars —

(*a*) Their steady light.
(*b*) Size (in the case of Venus and Jupiter).
(*c*) Colour (in the case of Mars).

(*d*)  Position (relatively to known constellations).

(*e*)  Motion (noticeable after successive observations).

*Step* 3.—To enlarge on Point (*d*), let the pupils name the planets whose orbits are within that of the earth and those whose orbits are outside ours.  By the help of a diagram (blackboard) of the solar system, get them to infer, from the nearness to the sun of Venus and Mercury, that these planets are never visible at midnight, but only just before sunrise and after sunset.

*Step* 4.—To appreciate Points (*d*) and (*e*), get the pupils to recognise the advantage of knowing the constellations by sight.   Show Philip's Planisphere, and refer to the Zodiac, showing that, besides being the sun's apparent path, this is the region in which to seek the planets.

Let the pupils find the portion of the heavens visible at 6 p.m. to-day, and indicate, both in the heavens and with respect to our landscape, the positions of Jupiter and Saturn.   Also show how Mars may be looked for in the south, too, about 6 o'clock in the morning.

*Step* 5.—To enlarge on Point (*e*), show a diagram of the path of Venus among the constellations in 1868 (Lockyer's *Elementary Lessons in Astronomy*, p. 183), and get the pupils to notice how large a distance she travelled in one month, in order to induce them to make personal observations.   Prepare them to see the planets sometimes move backwards and sometimes remain stationary.   Explain this by letting one of the girls move round the table, while the other watches how, with respect to her background, she appears to move first from left to right, then to remain stationary, then to move from right to left, and again to remain stationary.   The moving girl, observing the other with respect to her background, notices the same phenomena.

Then show the diagram in Lockyer, which illustrates these facts, p. 178, and also another in Reid's *Elements of Astronomy*, p. 137, which shows the apparent motion of one planet viewed from another in motion.

## A PICTURE TALK.

Group : Art.　　Class III.　　Age : 13.　　Time : 25 minutes.

### OBJECTS.

1. To give the girls some idea of composition, based
   on the work of the artist Jean François Millet.
2. To inspire them with a desire to study the works of
   other artists, with a similar object in view.
3. To help them with their original illustrations, by
   giving them ideas, carried out in Millet's work, as
   to simplicity of treatment, breadth of tone, and use
   of lines.

### MATERIALS NEEDED.

See that the girls are provided with paint-boxes, brushes,
water, pencils, rulers, india-rubber, and paper.

Photographs of some of Millet's pictures.

A picture-book by R. Caldecott.

### LESSON.

*Step* 1.—Introduce the subject by talking with the children
about their original illustrations. Tell them how our great
artists have drawn ideas and inspiration from the work of
other artists ; have studied their pictures, copied them, and
tried to get at the spirit of them.

Tell them that to-day we are going to study some of the
pictures of the great French artist, Millet, some of whose
works Mr Yates has drawn for us on the walls of our Millet
Room, considering them to be models of true art.

*Step* 2.—Tell the children a little about the life of Millet
(giving them one or two pictures to look at meanwhile) ;
give only a brief sketch, so that they will feel that he is
not a stranger to them.

Just talk to them a little about his early childhood , how

he worked in the fields; how he had two great books—the Book of Nature and the Bible, from which he drew much inspiration; how later on he went to Paris and studied the pictures of great artists, Michael Angelo among them.

*Step* 3.—Show the pictures to the girls, let them look well at them, and then draw from them their ideas as to the beauty and simplicity of the composition; call attention to the breadth of tone, and the dignity of the lines. Help them, sketching when necessary, to reduce a picture to its most simple form; half-closing their eyes to shut out detail, help them to get an idea of the masses of tone, etc.

*Step* 4.—Let the children reproduce a detail of one of the pictures, working in water-colour with monochrome and making their washes simple and flat, reducing the tones to two or three.

*Step* 5.—Suggest to them to study the works of other artists in a similar way, and show them how the books of R. Caldecott will help them in making their figures look as if they were moving.

### *Subject: Fra Angelico.*

Group: Art. Class IV. Average age: 16½.
Time: 30 minutes.

#### OBJECTS.

1. To show reproductions of some of Fra Angelico's pictures.
2. By means of them, to point out such distinguishing features as will enable my pupils to recognise Fra Angelico's work wherever they may see it.
3. To show in what degree his work holds a place in high art.

#### LESSON.

*Step* 1.—Give a short sketch of the life of Fra Angelico.
*Step* 2.—Allow time for my pupils to look at the pictures

provided, namely, various reproductions of 'Christ in Glory,' 'Saints in Paradise,' 'Angels,' 'Christ as Pilgrim,' 'Annunciation,' 'Crucifixion,' 'Noli me tangere,' 'Descent from the Cross,' 'Transfiguration.'

*Step* 3.—To notice what strikes us most in Fra Angelico's work — the exquisite jewel-like finish; the pure open skies and unpretending clouds; the winding and abundant landscapes; the angels; the touches of white light; the delicacy and grace of form ; the colouring ; the peace.

*Step* 4.—If high art is to be seen 'in the selection of a subject and its treatment, and the expression of the thoughts of the persons represented,' how far does Fra Angelico come up to this standard ?

He unites perfect unison of expression with full exertion of pictorial power. This will be illustrated by further reference to the pictures, and by reading some passages from *Modern Painters.*

*Step* 5.—Allow my pupils time to look again at the pictures, summarising meanwhile by a few questions.

### *Subject : Design.*

Division : Art.    Class IV.    Average age : 16½.
Time :  40 minutes.

#### OBJECTS.

1. To give the girls an idea of how to fill a space decoratively, basing the design on a given plant.
2. To show them that good ornament is taken from nature, but a mere copy of nature to decorate an object is not necessarily ornamental.
3. To give them an appreciation of good ornament and help them to see what is bad.
4. To draw out their originality by letting them make designs for themselves.
5. If possible, to give them a taste for designing by giving them some ideas as to its use.

## LESSON.

*Step* 1.—Ask the girls what is meant by a design.

*Step* 2.—After getting from them as much as possible, explain to them that a design is not a mere copy from nature, although it should be true to nature; make them see this by simply copying a plant in a required space to be designed (let this space be for a book cover). It will look meaningless and uninteresting, and does not fill the space, therefore it will not be ornamental. Then show the girls that a design requires thought and invention in arranging it to ornament the object. In the case of the book cover the flower must be designed to fill the space in some orderly pattern, and should be massed in good proportion. Give a few examples of this by illustrations on the board, and show them a book with a design upon it.

*Step* 3.—Point out to them that the most beautiful designs and those that have had the most thought spent upon them are the most simple. Show examples of this in Greek Ornament—Greek Honeysuckle, Egg and Dart Moulding.

*Step* 4.—Tell the pupils that you wish them to make a design for a linen book cover, 7 in. by 5 in., and if they have not time to finish to go on with it at home; if they like to carry the design out practically, to transfer it to linen and work it.

*Step* 5.—Show the girls the flower from which they are to take their design, and point out its characteristics—the general growth of the plant, the curves which it makes, the form of the flower and leaves, and the way the leaves are joined to the central stem; these characteristics should not be lost sight of, but be made use of in giving character to the design, and treated as simply as possible.

*Step* 6.—Let them begin their designs first of all by construction lines, and then clothe them with flowers and leaves, seeing that the masses are in good proportion. If time permits the design could be tinted in two colours, one for the background representing the linen, and the other for the pattern upon it.

*Step* 7.—Suggest to them different ways in which they can make use of design in making simple patterns for their handi-crafts, such as leather-work, wood-carving, and brass-work.

*Subject : Leather-work (Embossed).*

Group : Handicrafts. Class IV. Age : 16½.
Time : 40 minutes.

### OBJECTS.

1. To cultivate the artistic feeling in the pupils.
2. To train them in neatness and in manual dexterity.
3. To give training to the eye.
4. To introduce them to a new handicraft.
5. To work, as far as possible in the time, the top of a penwiper.

### LESSON.

*Step* 1.—Show the pupils a shaded drawing of the design, also a partly finished penwiper top, with the same design on it. When they have compared the two, they will see that the effect of light and shade is obtained in the leather by raising the light parts and pressing back the dark ones.

*Step* 2.—Let the pupils trace the design on the leather with a pointer. Remove the tracing-paper and accentuate the lines with a pointer. (This is best done with a wheel in a large design.)

*Step* 3.—Damp the leather and with a moulder press the background away from the outline of the design, also the dark parts under the folds at the top of the petals and round the centre. From behind, raise up the light parts with a moulder, and fill the holes thus made with a mixture of sawdust and meal, wet enough to make a kind of rough thick paste. Press away the dark parts again, and make any ornamental lines, etc., while the stuffing is wet, as it soon dries very hard. For this reason a very little must be stuffed at once; in this design, about one petal at a time.

*Step* 4.—Let the pupils punch their background or not as they prefer.

Work on my own half-finished piece of leather to avoid touching the pupils' work.

### *Subject: Cooking.*

Division : Handicrafts.　　Class IV.　　Age : 16½.
Time . 45 minutes.

#### OBJECTS.

1. To teach the children to make little cakes.
2. To show them that cooking must have method in it.
3. To give them opportunity of thinking for themselves why certain things should be done.
4. To show them how they can alter a recipe to make it richer or plainer.
5. To interest them in cooking.

#### LESSON.

*Step* 1.—Show the girls how to manage the stove for cooking.

*Step* 2.—Show them all the utensils to be used, and let them arrange them on the table.

*Step* 3.—Let them write out the recipe from dictation.

*Step* 4.—Let them grease the tins first of all with melted butter. Then let them each weigh out the ingredients on pieces of kitchen paper, and let them work independently of each other, the teacher also doing the same thing, so that the pupils may be able to see how to set to work without having their own work interfered with. During the process ask them *why* certain things should be done—for instance, why baking powder should be used, why the patty-pans should be greased. Tell them that if they wished to make the cakes plainer they could use milk instead of eggs, or if richer, they could add raisins and currants and spice. When the mixture is sufficiently beaten and put into the patty-pans, let the girls put them into the oven.

*Step* 5.—While the buns are cooking (they take about ten minutes), let the children and teacher wash up the things they have been using and put them away.

*Step* 6.—Let the children see for themselves if the cakes are done ; they should be a light brown. Then let them place them on a sieve to cool, and then arrange them on plates for the table.

# Index

Abraham, 4, 139.

*Academy, The,* 81.

Accuracy, 120.

Adams, John Quincy, 178.

Adams, Professor J., 59.

Affinities, further, 194-203 ; for material, 194 ; children have, 208.

Albert Memorial Chapel, 133.

Alertness, 108.

Alison's *History of Europe,* 178.

' Allegoria filosofica della Religione Cattolica,' 155.

Alleys, blind, 243.

Ambidexterity, 244.

Amiens, the Bible of, 132.

Animals, intimacy with, 80.

Angelico, Fra, 57.

Angelo, Michael, 152, 155.

Anxiety, note of transition stage, 26.

Apostles' Creed, The, 146.

Appendices, 248-359.

' Apperception masses,' 245.

Appliances, 230.

Appreciation, Æsthetic, 77.

Arena Chapel, Padua, 132.

Aristotle, 154.

Armada, Spanish, 231.

Armenia, 26.

Arnold, Dr, 242.

Arnold, Matthew, 131, 220.

Art, 234, 238.

Attention, 120.

Aurelius, Marcus, 86.

Austen, Jane, 243.

Authority, and docility in home and school, 1-24 ; dethronement of, 6 ; not inherent but deputed, 7 ; and docility fundamental prin-

ciples, 9 ; what is,? 10 ; vested in the office, 11 ; distinguished from autocracy, 15 ; behaviour of, 17 ; response of docility to, 19 ; avoids cause of offence, 22 ; is alert, 22 ; who gave thee this,? 23 ; basis of moral teaching, 126 ; limitations of, 127 ; in religious education, 137 ; how, works, 139.

Autocracy, of elder generation of parents, 2 ; distinguished from authority, 15 ; behaviour of, 16.

Basedow, 91, 97.

Behistun Rock, 82.

*Benedicite,* 134.

Benson, H. C., 221.

Bible, the, of Amiens, 132 ; habit of reading the, 142 ; the great storehouse of moral impressions, 175, 235.

Biography, the value of, 133.

Biology, utility of, 157.

Bloch, M., 230.

Board of Education, 247.

Books, first-hand, 162 ; school, how they make for education, 164 ; that sustain life of thought, 168 ; school, of publishers, 168 ; how to select school, 177 ; marks of fit school, 178 ; how to use school, 178 ; intelligent reading of school, 180 ; other ways of using school, 180 ; Ruskin's delight in, 196 ; Wordsworth's delight in, 197 ; every child should have *own living* books, 214 ; children

*⁎* As frequent mention has been made of the *Parents' National Educational Union* and its various agencies, it may be well to add that information about these may be had from the Secretary. The " *Questions for the Use of Readers* " are inserted with a view to the P.N.E.U. READING COURSE. Persons who wish to become "Qualified Members" of the Union by undertaking this course should communicate with the Secretary, 26 Victoria Street, London, S.W.

PRINTED BY NEILL AND CO., LTD., EDINBURGH.